Miss Ruby's
American Cooking

Miss Ruby's
American Cooking

From Border to Border
& Coast to Coast,
the Best Recipes from
America's Regional Kitchens

★

Ruth Adams Bronz

ILLUSTRATIONS BY BETH KROMMES

1817

HARPER & ROW, PUBLISHERS, NEW YORK
GRAND RAPIDS, PHILADELPHIA, ST. LOUIS, SAN FRANCISCO, LONDON,
SINGAPORE, SYDNEY, TOKYO, TORONTO

To the memory of my grandmother,
Lucy Elouise Tucker Adams,

and of my mother,
Lucy Julia Harrison Adams,

and to my sister,
Lucy Elouise Adams Cooper:

three generations of Texas cooks.

Recipes in the chapter entitled "The Midwest: David Blackburn's Ohio" are used by permission of David Blackburn. Copyright © 1989 by David Blackburn.

Recipe for Lace Cookies reprinted by permission of Henry Holt and Company, Inc., from *Favorite Meals from Williamsburg: A Menu Cookbook,* compiled by Charlotte Turgeon. Copyright © 1982 by The Colonial Williamsburg Foundation.

Recipes for Travis House Oysters, Clam and Chicken Bisque, Crabmeat Ravigote, and Smithfield Ham and Batter Cakes with Creamed Crab reprinted by permission of Henry Holt and Company, Inc., from *The Williamsburg Cookbook: Traditional and Contemporary Recipes,* compiled and adapted by Letha Booth and the Staff of Colonial Williamsburg. Copyright © 1971, 1975 by The Colonial Williamsburg Foundation.

Recipes for Yellow Velvet, Cranberry Bean Soup, Herb Soup, Codfish Croquettes and Honeyed Apple Rings with Milk Gravy, Cidered Beef Stew with Herb Dumplings and Ohio Lemon Pie reprinted by permission of Macmillan Publishing Company from *The Best of Shaker Cooking, Revised and Expanded,* edited by Amy Bess Williams Miller and Persis Wellington Fuller. Copyright © 1985 by Amy Bess Miller.

Recipes for Bollitos la Florida and Bolichi reprinted by permission of The Junior League of Tampa from *The Gasparilla Cookbook,* compiled by The Junior League of Tampa. Copyright © 1961 by The Junior League of Tampa, Inc., P.O. Box 10223, Tampa, FL. 33679.

Recipes for Fig Pudding, Hampton Frozen Pudding, Kossuth Cakes, Cold Veal and Ham Pie, Sirloin Steak Jubilee, Snapper Turtle Soup and Green Beans with Summer Herbs and Fresh Tomatoes are reprinted by permission of the Hammond-Harwood House Association, Annapolis, MD., from *Maryland's Way.*

Recipes for Black Bottom Pie and Tangerine Sherbet reprinted by permission of Charles Scribner's Sons, an imprint of Macmillan Publishing Company, from *Cross Creek Cookery* by Marjorie Kinnan Rawlings. Copyright © 1942 by Marjorie Kinnan Rawlings; copyright renewed © 1970 by Norton Baskin.

Recipes for *Dressing for Grapefruit Salad, Angel Food Charlotte Russe Cake, Hugenot Torte,* and *Benne Seed Wafers* reprinted by permission of The Junior League of Charleston from *Charleston Receipts,* collected by The Junior League of Charleston. Copyright © 1950 by The Junior League of Charleston, Inc., 51 Folly Road, Charleston, S.C. 29407.

FIRST EDITION

DESIGNED BY JOEL AVIROM

Library of Congress Cataloging-in-Publication Data
Bronz, Ruth Adams.
  Miss Ruby's American Cooking.
  Includes index.
  1. Cookery, American.   2. Miss Ruby's Café (New York, N.Y.)
I. Title.
TX715.B8491345   1989   641.5973   88-45887
ISBN 0-06-016080-2

89 90 91 92 93 DT/RRD 10 9 8 7 6 5 4 3 2 1

ACKNOWLEDGMENTS

This is the kind of book that's never written alone: I owe an immense debt to every cook in every region of America who's ever touched spoon to pan or knife to onion; I'm enormously grateful to the authors of the countless regional cookbooks I've pored over since I was in my teens, and to the cooks who've shared their ideas and their recipes with me by phone, in laundromats, in airplanes, in restaurants, in theatres at intermission, and anywhere else cooks talk. And above all, I owe a lifelong debt to the cooks who've been willing to come along with me in the adventure of translating American cooking into restaurant terms, cooks who've had to take chances with their careers to work with me, cooks who often had no idea what I was talking about at first, but who forged right on and often gave me the best ideas and the best execution of ideas that I could imagine. So, to Suzy Curtin and Sara Burke and Pam Cullen of Berkshire County, Massachusetts; to all the cooks past and present of Miss Ruby's Café in New York; and to Kathy Casey of Seattle and Fern Greenberg of the James Beard Foundation: Thank you.

Charles Kahlstrom has worked for Miss Ruby's since we opened in New York. A gifted cook whose soups and stews have helped to make our reputation, he also understands that great dictum of Woody Allen's: Ninety-five percent of life is just showing up. Bless you, Charles.

It's never easy to live with someone who is writing a book; and to live with someone who is writing a book and running a restaurant is doubly difficult: Michael Dorsey, I love you.

Ruth Adams Bronz
May 1989

CONTENTS

I started Miss Ruby's Café out of a passionate desire to cook, serve, promote, and teach American cooking. I discovered, among other things, that I had to define American cooking as I went along: It's not precisely regional—because whole populations of immigrants have had their effect—and it includes a mess of influences neither regional nor ethnic but religious, utopian, and commercial. In fact, one of the reasons that those persistent culinary codifiers, the French, fail to find an American traditional cookery (on the rare occasions when they look for one) is that it is too diverse to be seen as a national phenomenon—just as Americans themselves, with their diversity of class, religious, and ethnic origins, hardly seem nationally defined to Europeans. But the truth is, Americans and their cookery are immediately recognizable, at least to each other, in part *because* of their diversity.

Of course, if I had limited the menus at Miss Ruby's to what most *restaurants* identify as American food, I would have served steak, fried fish, hamburgers, and—perhaps—barbecue . . . and little else. The great range of American cooking isn't much seen in restaurants, even now, though regional cuisines are turning up in theme restaurants, some of which have only the dimmest relationship to the food of the region in question. But the food of America is available to American restaurants in old and new cookbooks and in the home kitchens of Americans all over the country.

All we have to do is cook the dishes. My experience is that Americans love to eat their own food, even though they're surprised to find it outside their own dining rooms.

I often feel like a culinary patriot—insisting on the virtues of the native over the foreign. But, where food is concerned, "my country right or wrong" just won't do; whatever it is has to be *both* American and good tasting. Fortunately, none of the reasons that American cooking has been neglected has much to do with its tasting second rate. What we have in this country is a whole lot of really great-tasting food: baked beans and boiled dinners from New England; ducks and oysters and mussels from New York's Long Island; jambalayas and gumbos and creoles from Louisiana; pork with green chiles, *tacos al carbón,* and *fajitas* from the Southwest; meat loaf, stuffed pork chops, and succotash from the Midwest. All we have to do is cook it. Ah, bliss.

American cooking is not technically complicated; most of its dishes fall easily into the range of what the French call "bourgeois cuisine"—hearty, simple food that has no pretensions to anything but tasting good. Many bourgeois dishes in France are *pots-aux-feu*—many ingredients slow-cooked together in a single vessel, sometimes served separately (as the vegetables, broth, and meat are in a *daube*), sometimes together (as in a *boeuf Bourguignon*). Americans use some of the same simple cooking techniques —stewing, roasting, baking, poaching—but we use the plate instead of the pot as our unit. The combinations, though, are just as satisfying: ham with tomatoes and potato salad; steak with stuffed baked potatoes and sliced tomatoes and onions; green chiles with pork and tortillas; chicken-fried steak with greens, black-eyed peas, and mashed potatoes. My grandmother treated the whole buffet table as a grand unit: She composed a great array of vegetables, relishes, sauces, and breads around two or three simple meat (ham, turkey, fried chicken) or fish (poached salmon, crab imperial, or boiled shrimp) dishes, trusting that her composition was so strong no diner would be able to come up with anything but a good combination of flavors. I use her method in making menus: If the sense of region is strong, and my choices happy, any combination of dishes within a menu will be good—and most will be stronger in combination than alone. Of course, some restaurant practices cramp the style of American cooking. I'd like a big salad on the table for every southwestern and southern menu to eat straight through the meal. That's hardly practical so I content myself with putting out two salads and hoping they'll be ordered lavishly.

So, from region to region we compose dishes into plates, and plates into tables—that's what is common to our cookery. All over the country, too, we use ingredients that are either unique to us, such as corn and molasses, or are uniquely used, such as tomatoes, avocados, and baking powder. One of the reasons I wanted to explore traditional American cooking—as opposed to that new cookery that makes use of American ingredients to exercise largely French, largely *haute cuisine* techniques—is because American traditional cooking is so little recognized outside home kitchens. Its use of unique American ingredients and unique treatments of more common ingredients has never been recognized. In fact, some ingredients have tended to disappear from larger view: Corn was thought of, until recently, as a regional ingredient used exclusively in the South. Corn bread, corn pudding, spoon bread, and grits were identified with the South from Texas to Maryland, as if johnnycake, corn chowder, succotash, tortillas, corn on the cob, the Shakers' yellow velvet, and corn-and-tomato pudding didn't exist or weren't corn. Peanuts are just beginning to gain culinary stature, and the wonderfully smooth, butter-based Midwestern tomato sauce, so different from the Italian, is still invisible, except in its inferior school cafeteria form. Miss Ruby's exists, in part, to present these ingredients and recipes in a form that will make them part of a recognized, accepted body of cooking—because, no matter how diverse we are in our approaches, chili is still chili, corn is corn, baking powder was *never* accepted by the French, and the lima bean is all ours. Ohio, Texas, Vermont, or California—they all contribute to a diverse but recognizable body of culinary works. And Miss Ruby's Café cooks it all in order to show it all for what it is.

Marianne Moore says that Americans are different from people of other nationalities in their "accessibility to experience." We are exposed to a bewildering variety of experiences: I was born to a Texas-Louisiana family with strong influences from southern black cooking and the upwardly mobile cuisine of my small-town mother. My reaction to those influences was typically American: I embraced every one of them and was enthusiastic about all of them, sometimes combining recipes across cultures, at other times setting up menus as pure examples of the parent influences (oyster and artichoke soup, jambalaya, and bourbon-pecan pie). Paul Prudhomme, born in Opelousas, Louisiana, and trained for hotels, likes to make highly successful border raids; his jalapeño-cheddar chicken, for example, shows the unmistakable mark of Tex-Mex *chili con queso.* That's another American tradition—marrying influences in a single dish.

Miss Ruby's Café has embraced such marriages and remains, as far as I can manage, open to all the influences of American traditional cooking while preparing menus that are solidly recognizable by region or ethnicity. Even the difficulties of this approach have been interesting: I've never made a dish that wasn't questioned in its authenticity at the moment it was being accepted ("That tastes *just* like home, but my mama always added garlic and cut down on the tomatoes a little"). Craig Claiborne once called chili the American national dish and then gave four radically different recipes for it, acknowledging that the simplest—for Texas Red—was probably the original but otherwise making no judgments among them. Now *that's* the American way. And that's Miss Ruby's way, too. We've tried to be as inclusive as American cooking—and will be in this book, border to border and coast to coast.

Miss Ruby's
American Cooking

MARYLAND

Maryland is far enough north that it is hard to think of it as southern; the raunchy roughness of Baltimore almost convinces visitors that this is New Jersey with a slight southern accent. Not true. The Englishness of the South is found in the Maryland countryside, and the greatest of all regional American cookbooks (with the possible exception of *Charleston Receipts*) is *Maryland's Way,* a beautiful combination of photographs, menus—from clubs, government events, old families, and historical occasions—and an encyclopedic spread of recipes from colonial times to the near present. We cook from *Maryland's Way* routinely, as well as from a much less distinguished but charming compendium put together as a campaign document by a Maryland governor's wife. Chesapeake Bay is a great national treasure, a huge repository of crabs, rockfish, shrimp, and every other kind of great seafood, but the rolling richness of the inland counties is more characteristic.

Mrs. Keidel's Crab Cakes

Of all the crab recipes native to Chesapeake Bay, we like this one best, mainly because it doesn't distract from the basic and wonderful taste of lump crabmeat.

1 pound lump crabmeat
Juice of 1 lemon
½ teaspoon cayenne pepper
½ medium onion, grated
1 slice white bread, trimmed and soaked
   in milk
1½ cups Basic Homemade Mayonnaise
   (recipe follows)
2 cups all-purpose flour
Salt and pepper
1 cup (2 sticks) unsalted butter

Pick over the crabmeat and discard any cartilage or shells. Toss the crabmeat with the lemon juice, cayenne, and onion. Work the soaked bread into the mixture lightly and quickly. Stir in the mayonnaise. Season the flour with salt and pepper to taste. Form the crab mixture into 2-ounce cakes and flatten them slightly. Dip the cakes in the seasoned flour to coat. Melt the butter over medium heat. When the butter is frothy, add the cakes. As the bottoms brown, turn the cakes and cook until both sides are light gold.

Serve with lemon wedges and tartar sauce (recipe follows).

Makes 8 crab cakes

Tartar Sauce

1 cup Basic Homemade Mayonnaise
1 teaspoon Dijon mustard
1 teaspoon minced cornichons
1 teaspoon chopped fresh chervil
1 teaspoon chopped fresh parsley
1 teaspoon chopped fresh chives
2 teaspoons chopped green olives
1 teaspoon chopped capers
1 teaspoon grated onion
Dash of cayenne pepper
Tarragon vinegar

Stir together all the ingredients except the vinegar. When well combined, add the vinegar slowly until the sourness is to your taste.

Makes 1½ cups

Basic Homemade Mayonnaise

2 large egg yolks
1 teaspoon dry mustard
1 teaspoon salt
Dash of Tabasco
1½ cups olive oil
Juice of ½ lemon

Have all ingredients at room temperature. Beat the egg yolks until thick and sticky; add mustard, salt, and Tabasco. Beating constantly, add the olive oil a drop at a time, increasing the volume of oil as the sauce thickens. When all the oil has been absorbed and the mayonnaise is thick and cream-colored, add the lemon juice.

VARIATIONS: To make Lemony Mayonnaise, make Basic Mayonnaise as directed above, using the juice of 1 whole lemon. To make Curry Mayonnaise, stir 1 tablespoon mild curry powder into 1 cup of Basic Mayonnaise. To make Tarragon Mayonnaise, add 2 teaspoons chopped fresh tarragon to 1 cup Basic Mayonnaise.

Makes 2 cups

Green Beans with Summer Herbs and Fresh Tomatoes

Americans usually eat vegetables on the same plate with the main course—and in fact I think of American food as a series of plates composed of a starch, a meat, and a vegetable: chicken-fried steak with greens and mashed potatoes and gravy; salmon croquettes with crisp home fries and green peas; ham with mashed sweet potatoes and black-eyed peas. But every now and then, especially when summer produce is at its height, I succumb to a greedy urge to cook a vegetable dish, like this one from Anne Arundel, and serve it alone and wonderful.

2 pounds young green beans
¼ cup (½ stick) unsalted butter
1 teaspoon chopped fresh summer savory
2 teaspoons chopped fresh parsley
2 teaspoons chopped fresh basil
Salt and pepper
3 large ripe tomatoes, peeled and
    chopped

Garnish
Whole basil leaves
Chopped fresh parsley

Remove stem ends from the beans, leaving the curly blossom ends intact. Bring 1 gallon salted water to a rapid boil, then add the beans all at once. When the water returns to a boil, strain the beans and plunge them into ice water to stop the cooking and set the color.

Melt the butter over medium heat, then sauté the herbs 2 minutes. Season with salt and pepper to taste. Add the tomatoes, stir to blend, and cook just long enough to blend and heat the tomatoes through. Add the beans and cook, stirring and tossing until just blended and bubbling. Serve the beans at once, and top with more basil and parsley.

Makes 8 servings

Cold Veal and Ham Pie

I once catered a reception for a former Episcopal bishop of Maryland. He was stocky, red faced, bully voiced, and charming. It didn't surprise me at all that he had blessed the hounds at a local hunt as part of his official duties. Maryland is probably closer to its English origins than any state in the union, and it shows—especially in its food.

Veal Stock
1 veal knuckle and shin bone, cracked
2 medium onions
2 carrots
2 cups dry white wine
1 teaspoon salt
6 whole black peppercorns
1 bay leaf
Bouquet garni of fresh thyme, parsley, marjoram, and savory

Put all the ingredients in a large kettle and add water just to cover. Bring the water to a boil, then reduce the heat to a bare simmer and cook, skimming foam from the surface as necessary, 8 hours. Strain the stock, skim the fat, and reduce by half.

Pie Filling
2 pounds lean veal shoulder
3 cups Veal Stock
1 tablespoon unflavored gelatin
1 tablespoon cold, dry white wine
¼ pound cooked Maryland ham (water added)
2 hard-boiled eggs
Butter Pastry (recipe follows)
Sprinkle of nutmeg
Salt and pepper to taste
3 tablespoons dry mustard
2 tablespoons cider vinegar

Garnish
Cornichons
Pickled onions

Preheat oven to 375° F.

Trim the veal of any fat, then cut it into small slices. Simmer the veal in the stock until just tender, about 30 minutes. Strain, and reserve the stock. Soften the gelatin in the wine, then dissolve in the hot stock. Slice the ham into slivers and the eggs into thin rounds.

Line a deep 8-inch pie plate with half the pie pastry. Layer half the veal, ham, and eggs (in that order) on top of the crust, sprinkling on nutmeg, salt, and pepper to taste as you go. Repeat with the remaining ingredients. Fill the pie to the top with the warm stock. Cover with the remaining pastry and make vents to let steam escape. Bake 30 to 40 minutes, or until crust is nicely browned.

Cool, then refrigerate until ready to serve. Cut the pie into wedges, and serve with dry mustard moistened with cider vinegar. Garnish with cornichons and pickled onions.

Makes 10 servings

Butter Pastry

2 cups sifted all-purpose flour
¼ teaspoon salt
¾ cup (1½ sticks) very cold unsalted butter
Ice water to mix (about 2 tablespoons)

Sift the flour and salt into a bowl. With two dinner knives, a pastry cutter, or your fingers, very quickly and lightly cut the butter into flour. When the mixture is the texture of fine oatmeal, stir in the ice water with a fork. Blend just until the dry mixture absorbs the water and lightly holds together. If there are crumbs around the ball of dough, add a smidgen more water. Without handling further, wrap the dough loosely in a square of plastic wrap and chill for 1 hour or more. Divide the dough into 2 equal parts, and quickly and firmly roll each out on a floured board to a thickness of ¼ inch. Use as needed.

Makes 1 10-inch double-crust pie pastry

SOUPS

Crab Soup with Sherry

This soup is an addiction; I have to charge an arm and a leg for it because of the high concentration of ruinously expensive crabmeat, and even so, customers order it in multiple bowls. And they're right: It's beyond price.

1 small onion, minced
2 small celery stalks, minced
1 tablespoon unsalted butter
1½ teaspoons all-purpose flour
1 cup Chicken Stock (see page 28)
1 quart half-and-half
Juice of ½ lemon
1 tablespoon fresh parsley, chopped fine
½ teaspoon ground nutmeg
¼ teaspoon cayenne (ground red) pepper
Salt and pepper to taste
8 ounces lump crabmeat, picked over
¼ cup amontillado

Garnish
Fine-chopped fresh parsley
Paprika

Sauté the onion and celery in butter until the onion is transparent. Sprinkle the flour over the mixture and stir in. Cook over low heat, without browning, 5 minutes.

Whisk in chicken stock and half-and-half. Add all the seasonings, and simmer 10 minutes or until the soup is well blended and very slightly thickened. Add the crabmeat, and simmer until just heated through.

Just before serving, stir in the sherry. Garnish with parsley and paprika.

Makes 8 servings

Snapper Turtle Soup

This Maryland classic may have become an anachronism by the time we're in print; every time we've tried to get turtle meat in the last couple of years, we've been told that the current source, the Everglades of Florida, has dried up and cemented the turtles in. It would be a shame if there were no more turtles to provide this lovely stuff.

2 stalks celery, with leaves
1 medium carrot
1 large onion
2 bay leaves
1 garlic clove
Bouquet garni of thyme and parsley
Salt and pepper to taste
3 cups Veal Stock (see page 6)
3 cups Chicken Stock (see page 28)
2 cups turtle meat, cut into small pieces
¼ cup (½ stick) unsalted butter
2 tablespoons all-purpose flour
½ cup dry sherry

Garnish
2 or 3 hard-boiled eggs

Simmer the celery, carrot, onion, bay leaves, garlic, bouquet garni, salt, and pepper in the veal and chicken stocks until reduced to 4 cups.

Meanwhile, brown the turtle meat in butter, then blend in the flour and cook gently, without browning, 5 minutes. Add the stock and vegetables and simmer until meat is tender.

To serve, ladle the soup into bowls and top each serving with a tablespoon of sherry. Garnish with sliced hard-boiled eggs.

Makes 8 servings

SALADS

Iced Cucumbers

This is a near-perfect example of the goodness of Maryland cooking: its English heritage, its purity of line, and its simplicity—ignored at one's peril. Follow this recipe (add nothing, especially not oil), and the experience of pure refreshment will be almost shocking.

4 large young unpeeled Kirby cucumbers
Salt
4 tablespoons chilled white vinegar
½ teaspoon cayenne pepper

Bury the cucumbers in ice lightly laced with salt until they are very cold.

At the last moment before serving, peel the cucumbers, leaving a touch of green, and slice them into very thin rounds. Toss the slices with vinegar, cayenne, and 1 teaspoon salt, and serve immediately.

Makes 8 servings

Cold Maryland Fantasy

This cold first course makes use of some terrific Maryland raw materials. With hot rolls and a watercresss salad, it's a lovely lunch.

4 slices Maryland ham
4 slices smoked turkey, from the frame (do not use a roll)
4 medium ripe peaches, sliced
1 cup Basic Homemade Mayonnaise (see page 4), mixed with 2 tablespoons Dijon mustard
4 lime wedges
4 large salad bowl lettuce leaves, for bedding

Arrange the ham, turkey, and sliced peaches with a dollop of mayonnaise and the lime wedges on top of the lettuce.

Serve with Cheese Straws (recipe follows).

Makes 4 servings

Cheese Straws

Butter Pastry (see page 7), for single-crust pie
2 teaspoons cayenne pepper
½ teaspoon each salt and pepper
1 cup grated sharp cheddar cheese

Preheat the oven to 400° F.

Roll the pastry into a square ⅛-inch thick, then sprinkle with half the cayenne and pastry in half, then roll out again. Sprinkle with the remaining spices and cheese, then fold again and roll out once more.

Cut the pastry into 2-inch strips, then twist the strips to resemble old-fashioned candy canes. Bake 12 to 15 minutes, or until golden brown. Cool and serve.

Makes 20 to 25 straws

MAIN COURSES

Blue Crabs on Newspapers

This is another Maryland feast that requires only a washtubful of crabs and a big table covered with newspapers. It is perhaps presumptuous to call this a recipe—but since it tastes so good and satisfies so completely, it must be included. Don't make the mistake of trying to eat anything *with* the crabs—have an ear or six of corn on the cob first, or a baked stuffed potato, or some good garlic bread, then a big mixed vegetable salad afterward, to save all your energy for crab picking in between.

All crabs should be alive and kicking before being placed in the steamer. Discard any dead crabs since you can not be sure how long they've been dead, and their meat begins to deteriorate immediately.

Plan to serve at least six large hard-shell blue crabs per person. Prepare two tablespoons of the following for each serving.

Crab Boil
4 parts paprika
2 parts cayenne pepper
1 part crushed bay leaves
1 part dried oregano
1 part mustard seed
1 part celery seed
¼ part whole allspice

Boil water in the bottom half of a steamer large enough to hold the crabs. In the top half of the steamer, layer the crabs and Crab Boil. Set the steamer basket over the boiling water and cover tightly. Steam until the blue of the crabs has turned red, about 5 to 7 minutes.

Turn crabs onto a large table covered with at least two layers of newspapers. Pick and eat the crabs and wash them down with a good cold lager.

Soft-Shell Crabs in Lemon-Parsley-Caper Sauce

Compared to the rule of simplicity in the preceding recipe, this is a model of sophistication, requiring two steps, some delicate sautéing, and a side dish or two to complete the meal. Be sure, by the way, that all your crabs are alive and waving their claws before you begin. They begin to deteriorate within minutes of expiring.

8 soft-shell crabs
2 cups all-purpose flour
Salt and pepper to taste
½ cup (1 stick) unsalted butter
4 tablespoons chopped fresh parsley
2 tablespoons capers, drained
Juice of 1 lemon
White wine

Remove the eyes, belly flap, and filaments under the points from each crab. Dredge the crabs in flour, salt, and pepper.

Melt the butter in a large frying pan over medium heat, then turn up the heat until the butter foams. Slip the crabs into the pan just before the butter browns. Cook the crabs 4 to 5 minutes on each side, or until browned and firm. Remove the pan from the heat, lift out the crabs with a slotted spatula, and arrange them on a heated platter.

Toss the parsley, capers, and lemon juice in the pan with the remaining butter. Return the pan to the heat and deglaze with enough white wine to bring up all the good bits in the pan.

Pour the sauce over the crabs and serve at once with Onion Rice Pilaf (recipe follows) or boiled Parslied New Potatoes.

Makes 4 servings

Onion Rice Pilaf

True pilafs are made by sautéing rice with other ingredients and adding water to moisten and finish cooking the rice. I often make my rice, then add raw vegetables and melted butter for a brighter, fresher effect. Tabasco is lovely with crab.

2¼ cups water
½ teaspoon salt
2 cups converted rice
¼ cup (½ stick) unsalted butter
1 cup fine-diced onion
1 teaspoon Tabasco

Boil the water with the salt and add the rice. Stir well, allow water to return to a full boil, and turn down the heat to medium. Cook the rice, uncovered, until the water is almost absorbed, about 17 minutes. Turn the heat down to low, cover, and steam the rice until fluffy, about 3 minutes. Meanwhile, melt the butter and toss the onions in it. Add the Tabasco, but do not cook. Toss the rice with the onion mixture and serve at once.

Makes 8 servings

Sirloin Steak Jubilee

This dish, not often encountered in the South, calls for another powerfully simple rule. Don't try this on anything but a charcoal grill or a ceramic-tiled restaurant broiler—the broiler of a domestic stove is just not hot enough.

1 3-pound prime sirloin steak, 2 to 3
  inches thick
Dijon mustard
Kosher salt
Unsalted butter

Prepare the grill.

Spread the steak with a thick coating of mustard, covering both surfaces completely. Pour salt over both surfaces of the steak to coat the mustard layer completely.

Grill the steak 3 inches above very hot coals, allowing 10 to 12 minutes per side for rare meat and turning frequently as the meat catches fire (an essential part of the process).

Remove the steak from the fire, dress with a large pat of butter on each side, and carve in ½-inch-thick slices.

Serve with herbed and buttered French bread, baked potatoes, and sliced tomatoes and onions.

Makes 6 to 8 servings

Maryland Fried Chicken

Maryland's fried chicken is the most innocent of dishes. The chicken is not soaked, just cut up and dredged and fried quickly, and it is served with the simplest of gravies. The lard used in the earliest recipes is really a good idea—try it instead of vegetable shortening. Please take the suggestion of a cast-iron skillet seriously; there is no proper substitute for its weight and the evenness with which it heats.

2 2½-pound frying chickens, cut at
    every joint, seasoned with salt and
    pepper
4 cups all-purpose flour
3 cups lard

Gravy
¼ cup (½ stick) unsalted butter
¼ cup all-purpose flour
2 cups milk
Salt and pepper

Dredge the seasoned chicken in the flour, placing each finished piece on a rack. Melt the lard in a large cast-iron skillet over medium heat until almost smoking hot.

Place the chicken in the skillet, leaving plenty of room between each piece (the fat should boil up around the pieces). Fry the chicken until golden brown, then turn the pieces. When each side is brown, turn the heat down and cook the chicken until done, about 7 minutes.

Remove the chicken from the skillet and pour off the lard. Melt the butter in the skillet until it froths. Add the flour and stir briskly to loosen the browned bits from the bottom of the pan, until the flour is just browned. Add the milk, and whisk until the mixture thickens slightly. Season the gravy with salt and pepper to taste and pour over the chicken.

We serve Maryland Fried Chicken with Mashed Potatoes (see page 151), Fried Cornmeal Mush (see page 70), and long-cooked broad beans or broiled tomatoes. (Fried Cornmeal Mush, also called Polenta, is eaten all over the South. The Italians are the only Europeans to use corn at all, and only as polenta. Italians who were not raised on polenta tend to react as other Europeans do, calling corn *fodder*.)

Makes 6 to 8 servings

DESSERTS

Kossuth Cakes

General Kossuth was one of a series of impoverished patriots from embattled countries who visited the newly minted United States to seek aid for their own revolutionary efforts. Kossuth was from Hungary, and perhaps his country wasn't familiar enough for Marylanders to open their pocketbooks: Baltimore came up with only twenty-five dollars. But a pastry cook of the era managed a neat tribute in the form of these colorfully iced cakes.

1 cup (2 sticks) unsalted butter, softened
1 cup sugar
2 large eggs, beaten, at room
  temperature
1¾ cups flour
2½ teaspoons baking powder
½ teaspoon salt
½ cup milk, at room temperature
½ teaspoon vanilla extract
Sweetened whipped cream

Preheat the oven to 350° F.

Cream the butter and sugar until the sugar dissolves. Add the eggs. Sift together the dry ingredients, and fold in alternately with the milk. Add the vanilla and mix well.

Fill muffin pans lined with cupcake papers with batter until about ¾ full. Bake in the oven until a toothpick or straw comes out clean, about 15 minutes. Cool the cakes on racks.

When the cakes are completely cooled, peel the paper away from the top halves of the cakes. Split each cake crosswise about halfway down from the top, and fill with sweetened whipped cream.

Ice the tops and sides of the cakes to cover the cream. Use Chocolate, White, and Strawberry icings (recipes follow), and cover ⅓ of the cakes with each.

To serve, arrange the cakes alternately on a large platter lined with a doily.

Makes 12 cakes

Chocolate Icing

2½ 1-ounce squares unsweetened chocolate
¼ cup (½ stick) unsalted butter
½ pound (1½ cups) confectioners' sugar
2 large egg yolks
¼ teaspoon salt
1 teaspoon vanilla extract

Melt the chocolate and butter together over low heat. Add the sugar and 1 tablespoon hot water. When just soft enough to spread, beat in the egg yolks and add the salt and vanilla. The icing will be soft.

Makes 1½ cups

Strawberry Icing

12 ripe strawberries, washed and stemmed
½ teaspoon lemon juice
½ pound (1½ cups) confectioners' sugar

Place the berries in the bowl of a food processor and process very briefly, just until berries are roughly puréed. Add the lemon juice, then stir in the sugar until stiff enough to spread but still soft enough to run over the edge of the cakes and down the sides.

Makes 2 cups

White Icing

⅓ cup (⅔ stick) unsalted butter
½ pound (1½ cups) confectioners' sugar
1 teaspoon vanilla extract
¼ teaspoon salt

Soften the butter and work into sugar with a wooden spoon. Add the vanilla and salt. If the icing is too stiff, add 1 tablespoon hot water as you blend.

Makes 2 cups

Hampton Frozen Pudding

From the Hampton Society for the Preservation of Maryland Antiquities we have this variation on frozen fruit with cream, a favorite all over the South. The macaroons make this resemble a frozen ambrosia.

1 quart heavy cream
⅔ cup confectioners' sugar
1 tablespoon light rum
3 tablespoons cream sherry
1⅓ cups canned pitted dark cherries,
  drained and juice reserved
1 dozen coconut macaroons, broken into
  small pieces

Whip the cream until soft peaks form, stirring in sugar a little at a time. Fold in the liquors, then the cherries and 2 tablespoons of the reserved juice, then the macaroon pieces.

Pour the mixture into a 2-quart mold lightly coated with oil and freeze. To unmold, invert on a plate and lay a hot, wet dish towel over the mold to loosen; serve in generous slices.

Makes 10 servings

Fig Pudding

This dessert is as old in tone as any recipe I've found in this country. It feels almost medieval—a reminder of how conservative Maryland really is. I'm a bit surprised Maryland agreed to join the colonies in the Revolution.

1 cup suet, chopped fine
1 pound dried figs, chopped fine and
    sprinkled with 1 cup brandy
1 cup packed dark brown sugar
2 cups light bread crumbs
½ teaspoon ground cinnamon
½ teaspoon ground nutmeg
½ teaspoon salt
1 teaspoon baking soda
1 cup sour milk *
3 large eggs, beaten

* To sour milk: Add a few drops of vinegar and let
    stand for an hour.

Lightly toss together the suet and figs. Add the brown sugar, bread crumbs, cinnamon, nutmeg, and salt. Stir the soda into the sour milk and add to the eggs. Stir the liquid mixture into the dry ingredients and blend.

Fill 2 1-pound pudding tins or coffee cans ⅔ full with the mixture, cover tightly (in the case of the coffee cans, cover with aluminum foil tied securely with a string), and steam on a rack over boiling water 3 hours.

Serve with Hard Sauce (recipe follows).

Makes 8 servings

Hard Sauce

½ cup (1 stick) unsalted butter
½ cup packed dark brown sugar
½ cup confectioners' sugar
2 tablespoons bourbon whiskey

Cream the butter, adding the sugars gradually, until the brown sugar grains disap-

pear and the mixture is fluffy. Continue beating while adding the whiskey.

Serve at once. Or pack the mixture into a decorative mold and chill. When cold, unmold and dust the Hard Sauce with cinnamon before serving.

Makes 1 cup

Whiskey Apple Pie

This is an almost-too-sophisticated apple pie that gets away with it. It's a perfect example of the American capacity for developing variations on a theme.

2 cups peeled sour green apples, cooked
    lightly in ¼ cup water until soft
1 cup brown sugar
¼ cup (½ stick) unsalted butter
3 large eggs , separated
4 ounces bourbon whiskey, plus
    additional if desired
1 cup heavy cream
¼ teaspoon ground nutmeg
Butter Pastry (see page 7)
Whipped cream

Preheat the oven to 425° F.

Beat the hot apples with the sugar and butter, cool the mixture slightly and beat the egg yolks. Stir the yolks, whiskey, cream, and nutmeg into the apples. Beat the egg whites to soft peaks, and fold into the apple mixture with a bit more whiskey.

Line a pie plate with butter pastry and pour the filling into the pie pastry and bake 8 to 10 minutes to set the crust. Reduce the heat to 325° F. and bake 30 minutes longer, or until the filling is just set.

Cool the pie, and cover the top with whipped cream just before serving.

Makes 8 servings

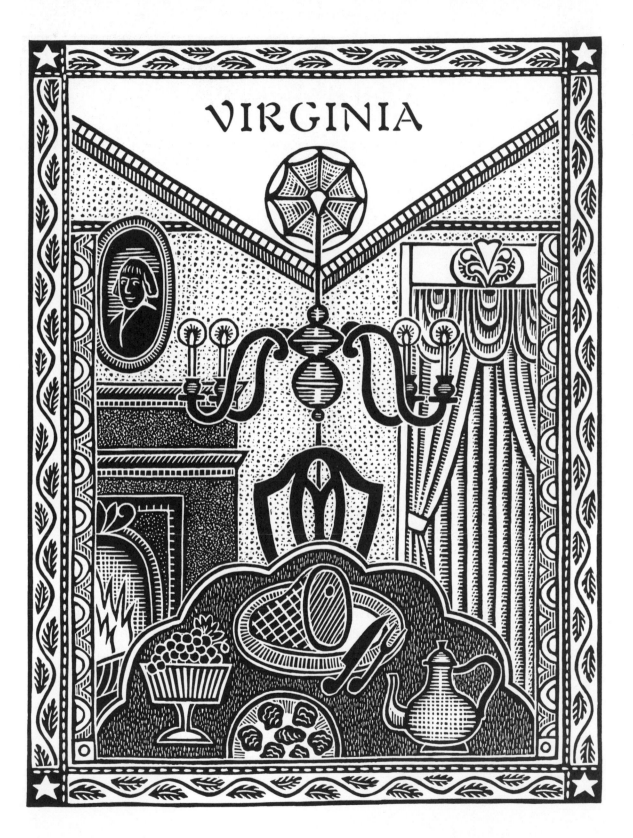

Virginia is not only the cradle of presidents, it's the home of that invaluable eccentric (and only incidentally president), Thomas Jefferson, who contributed more to American cookery than any other single individual. Whether Jefferson had an insatiably curious palate or was just insatiably curious is hard to tell. He imported new foods (including broccoli) to grow in his gardens and was certainly the first president, if not the first citizen of any kind, to serve pasta in America. The diary entry of a congressman who dined with Jefferson on the memorable occasion of his first pasta dinner and described the new dish is a sight to behold. Jefferson also imported European cooks to Virginia and insisted upon training his local cooks in the odd ways he had learned abroad. There's not a lot of evidence that any of this was done in aid of the pure pleasures of the table. For all we know, Jefferson was simply indulging his odd determination to fit everything that he encountered in his reading and travels into his bucolic Virginia life—the same determination that led him to advertise abroad for a gardener who could play the clarinet. Given what we owe him, I hope Jefferson enjoyed the taste of broccoli, pasta, and everything else he dragged home to Virginia.

Jefferson was no lonely adventurer in a culinary backwater, though, as Karen Hess's beautifully edited *The Virginia Housewife* makes clear. Her book is another that is still easy to cook from—

partly because of her scrupulous notes on food and the period, and partly because the original recipes are so appealing.

Colonial Williamsburg, that odd early version of the theme park, has preserved in its restaurants a number of good southern dishes, including spoon bread and corn-batter cakes—which would justify the overclean and overcostumed streets of that little village if anything could. We make wide use of the Williamsburg cookbooks, for years the only restaurant collections that had any savor of southern home cooking. It's possible even now to get a taste of the genteel South at the Williamsburg Inn. Better get there fast, though; someone is going to start calling those batter cakes "corn crêpes" and filling them with morels any minute, and then where will we be?

SMALL PLATES

Smithfield Ham or Ham Spread Biscuits

This is classic southern-gathering food: No funeral, christening, or family party is ever complete without a tray of ham biscuits passed with drinks. They are equally good with bourbon and branch water or with hot coffee or tea.

The Biscuits

2 cups all-purpose flour
1 teaspoon salt
1½ tablespoons baking powder
¼ cup shortening
¾ to 1 cup milk
Mustard (optional)

Preheat the oven to 425° F.

Sift together the flour, salt, and baking powder. Rub in the shortening until the mixture is the texture of rough cornmeal. Stir in the milk just until a firm dough forms. Do not work the dough.

Tip the dough onto a floured board and sprinkle with more flour. Pat or roll the dough to a thickness of ½ inch, then cut biscuits with a 2-inch cutter and place them close together in a shallow pan. Bake 12 to 14 minutes, or until golden brown.

For ham biscuits: Split and butter the hot biscuits and tuck a sliver of Smithfield Ham (see pages 30–31 for basic Smithfield preparation) between the halves. Pass with mustard.

Makes 18 biscuits

Ham Spread

1 cup Smithfield ham pieces
1 cup water-processed smoked ham pieces
½ cup Basic Homemade Mayonnaise (see page 4)
2 teaspoons dry mustard
Pepper to taste

With the fine blade of a food grinder or using the steel blade of a food processor, grind 1 cup of Smithfield ham and 1 cup of smoked ham pieces very fine. Stir the mayonnaise and mustard into the ham, and season with pepper.

Split and butter the biscuits and put ham spread thickly between halves.

VARIATION: Add ¼ cup sweet pickle relish or fine-chopped sour dill pickles to the Ham Spread.

Makes 2½ cups

Crabmeat Ravigote

All over the South, crab is king, and no fish can compete with it. No oyster, no matter how succulent, can stand up to the southern dedication to the sweet, delicate meat of the blue crab.

1 pound lump crabmeat
1 tablespoon tarragon vinegar
1 teaspoon chopped fresh tarragon
Juice of 1 lemon
¼ cup drained minced pimientos
¼ cup minced celery
2 tablespoons minced scallions
1 tablespoon minced cornichons
½ to 1 cup Basic Homemade
   Mayonnaise (see page 4)
Salt and pepper to taste
Dash of Tabasco
4 cleaned crab shells, lettuce leaves, and
   avocado or tomato halves, for serving

Garnish
4 hard-boiled egg yolks, pressed through
   a sieve
Capers, drained
Pimientos

Pick over the crabmeat and discard cartilage and shells. Toss the crabmeat with the vinegar, tarragon, and lemon juice, and let stand for 10 minutes.

Lift the crabmeat from the marinade with 2 forks, leaving most of the liquid behind. In another bowl, mix the pimientos, celery, scallions, cornichons, mayonnaise, salt, pepper, and Tabasco and mix with crabmeat.

Mound the crabmeat in crab shells, avocado or tomato halves, or on lettuce leaves. Sprinkle with the yolks and garnish with capers and more pimiento.

Makes 4 servings

Travis House Oysters

Oysters are celebration food all over the South, as they seem to have been in the days when they were so cheap they were practically poor man's food. On the half shell, fried, scalloped, in pies, with ham, with fowl, or as dressing, oysters make everything more festive. Travis House Oysters are from one of the many restaurants long operated in Colonial Williamsburg, the Rockefellers' Valentine to squirearchical Virginia. The recipe was developed by Mrs. Lena Richards, a cook at Travis House in the forties and fifties.

½ cup (1 stick) unsalted butter
½ cup all-purpose flour
2 teaspoons paprika
½ teaspoon salt
¼ teaspoon pepper
⅛ teaspoon cayenne pepper
½ garlic clove, minced
1 cup white mushrooms, sliced
1 medium onion, chopped fine
½ medium green bell pepper, chopped
   fine
1 quart shucked oysters
1 teaspoon lemon juice
2 teaspoons Worcestershire sauce
¼ cup saltine cracker crumbs

Preheat the oven to 400° F.

Melt the butter in a large skillet over medium heat. Remove the skillet from the heat, whisk in the flour, and stir until smooth.

Return the skillet to the heat and cook, stirring constantly, 7 to 10 minutes, or until the mixture is light brown. Add the paprika, salt, pepper, cayenne, garlic, mushrooms, onion, and bell pepper.

Cook 3 to 5 minutes more, continuing to stir. Add the oysters and their liquid, the lemon juice, and the Worcestershire sauce. Stir well to combine.

Pour the oyster mixture into a buttered 2-quart casserole, sprinkle with cracker crumbs, and bake 15 minutes, or until the crumbs begin to brown.

Makes 8 servings

S O U P S

Corn and Shrimp Soup

2 tablespoons (¼ stick) unsalted butter
1 onion, minced
2 celery stalks, minced
2 tablespoons all-purpose flour
1 teaspoon salt
½ teaspoon pepper
1 pound shrimp, peeled and chopped
2 cups corn kernels, cut from the cob
2 cups Shrimp Stock (recipe follows)
2 cups heavy cream
1 tablespoon Worcestershire sauce
½ teaspoon Tabasco

Garnish
Fresh parsley, chopped
Red bell pepper, chopped

In a large stockpot over medium heat, melt the butter and sauté the onion and celery until soft. Stir in the flour, salt, and pepper and mix until smooth. Cook 5 minutes, stirring constantly. Do not brown.

Stir in the shrimp and corn and blend well. Add the Shrimp Stock, heavy cream, Worcestershire sauce, and Tabasco, and stir together.

Simmer until shrimp are just done. Serve at once, garnished with chopped parsley and red pepper.

Makes 8 servings

Shrimp Stock

1 gallon shrimp shells
½ bunch celery, chopped coarse
1 large onion, chopped coarse
2 bay leaves
½ bunch fresh parsley
Handful crushed black peppercorns
½ teaspoon crushed red pepper
1 cup canned tomatoes with their juice, or
    1 large fresh tomato, peeled and chopped
Pinch saffron

Bring all the ingredients to a boil in a large stockpot with water to cover. Boil 45 to 60 minutes, skimming foam from the surface as necessary. Strain and use the liquid as a base for sauces or soups.

Makes 3 quarts

Clam and Chicken Bisque

½ small onion, minced
3 celery stalks, minced
1 bay leaf
2 tablespoons chopped fresh parsley
2 cups dry white wine
2 pounds littleneck clams, scrubbed and
    soaked
2 cups Chicken Stock (recipe follows)
2 tablespoons (¼ stick) unsalted butter
3 tablespoons all-purpose flour
1 cup poached chicken, chopped fine
1 cup heavy cream
Salt and cayenne pepper to taste

Garnish
¼ cup heavy cream
Paprika
Minced fresh parsley

Combine the onion, celery, bay leaf, and parsley with the white wine in a large saucepan with a tight-fitting lid. Add the clams, cover, and bring the liquid to a fast boil. Steam until the clams open. Lift the clams from the broth, let cool, and strain broth into another saucepan.

Add the Chicken Stock to the broth and bring to a boil, then reduce the heat to simmer. Discard the clamshells and chop the clams fine.

Melt the butter over medium heat until it froths. Add the flour and whisk 5 minutes. Add the hot chicken-clam broth, whisking as you go. Add the chicken, clams, heavy cream, salt, and cayenne and simmer over low heat 20 minutes, being careful not to boil.

Whip the cream to the soft-peak stage. Garnish each serving of soup with a dollop of cream and sprinkle with paprika and parsley.

Makes 8 servings

Chicken Stock

1 6-pound chicken, with gizzard and neck,
    cut into 4 pieces
2 large carrots, chopped coarse
½ bunch celery, chopped coarse
1 large onion, chopped coarse
2 bay leaves
½ bunch fresh parsley
Handful cracked black peppercorns
2 whole cloves
Bouquet garni of thyme, tarragon, and
    marjoram

Put all the ingredients in a 4-gallon stockpot, and cover with 2 inches water. Bring the water to a boil over high heat, then turn down heat to low at once and simmer, without boiling, 8 to 10 hours, skimming as the fat surfaces. Strain the stock, refrigerate, and skim the fat. Reduce, if you like, to ½ or ⅔ of volume. Store in the refrigerator for up to 1 week, or in the freezer for up to 3 months.

Makes 2 gallons

SALADS

Salmagundi

We're still doing versions of Salmagundi under different names—California Cobb salad and chef's salad are just two. These are always a mixture of vegetables and meats, arranged in a pattern for display and tossed together for eating.

Romaine lettuce, sliced crosswise very
*   fine*
2 poached chicken breasts, chopped fine
10 drained and lightly rinsed anchovies,
*   chopped fine*
4 hard-boiled eggs, chopped fine
1 bunch fresh parsley, chopped fine
1½ cups fine-chopped smoke-cured ham
1½ cups fine-chopped celery hearts
½ cup drained capers
½ cup fine-chopped scallions

Spread the chiffonade of Romaine lettuce over a large platter. Arrange the remaining ingredients, except the capers and scallions, in broad strips on top of the lettuce. Sprinkle the capers and scallions over the top of the salad. Dress with the Virginia Housewife's Salad Dressing (recipe follows).

Present the salad on its platter, then toss in a bowl with the dressing.

Makes 6 servings

The Virginia Housewife's Salad Dressing
2 hard-boiled egg yolks
1 tablespoon ice water
3 tablespoons olive oil
1 teaspoon salt
½ teaspoon confectioners' sugar
1 teaspoon dry mustard
2 tablespoons tarragon vinegar

Mash the egg yolks with the ice water until a fine paste forms. Stir in the olive oil and seasonings, then beat in the vinegar.

MAIN COURSES

Smithfield Ham

Smithfield Ham is one of the glories of regional cooking in America; it is also consistently misunderstood outside the South. My customers call it *oversalted, tough,* and *stringy* until they've tasted it cooked as it should be and served properly accompanied.

First of all, Smithfield Ham *is* salty: The Smithfield curing process uses salt as well as smoke, the chief flavors of the slowly aged pork. Second, Smithfield Ham does tend to be tough because the slow curing compacts the meat and dries it. Never mind. When we get through with it, it is a heady and concentrated treat, as all Southerners know it to be.

To prepare a Smithfield Ham: Scrub the pepper and mold from the ham and soak it in water for 18 hours, changing the water every 6 hours or so. Lower the ham into a large pot of simmering water and cook 2 to 3 hours below the boil. Cool the ham in the cooking water, then peel the skin off carefully, leaving the fat intact. (Reserve the skin to cook with beans or greens.)

Preheat the oven to 275° or 300° F.

Place the ham fat side up in a large roasting pan and bake on a rack until the fat is half rendered and the ham is tender, about 3 hours. Reserve the browned fat from the pan for other uses. If you plan to serve the ham as a main course, score the fat at this point and treat it in one of several ways.

The most traditional Virginia service is to pack the top of the deeply scored ham with the following:

½ cup (1 stick) unsalted butter
2 cups bread crumbs
1 teaspoon pepper
½ teaspoon whole cloves
3 tablespoons dark brown sugar
Dry sherry

Melt the butter and toss with the bread crumbs and pepper. Add the cloves and brown sugar and toss again. Pack the dry glaze mixture onto the scored ham. Drizzle dry sherry over the top.

Bake the ham just long enough to brown the bread crumbs, about 20 minutes.

The most important thing to remember about serving Smithfield Ham is that basic slicing rules are not just a good idea but mandatory; any other method will emphasize toughness, saltiness, and all the other undesirable qualities. Slice—or shave—the meat roughly perpendicular to the bone, as thin as possible. (My grandmother claimed you should be able to read a newsaper through a proper slice of Smithfield Ham.) In the restaurant, we cheat by boning the ham and using an electric slicer; at home, you may want to use an electric knife. A super-sharp thin slicer and a steady hand are the preferred tools.

VARIATION: A wonderful variation is to stuff the boned ham with lightly cooked, peppered, but unsalted greens, tie it, and treat as above.

Allow 6 to 8 ounces per person

Smithfield Ham and Batter Cakes with Creamed Crab

Most Virginians—and most Southerners, for that matter—don't think of Smithfield Ham as a main-course meat. It is the starting point for dozens of dishes, like this one and the two that follow, in which it is a flavoring and textural element.

Batter Cakes
2½ cups milk
2 cups water
1 cup cornmeal
1 cup (2 sticks) unsalted butter, melted
2¾ cups all-purpose flour
2½ teaspoons baking powder
1 teaspoon salt
4 large eggs

Combine the milk and water in a medium saucepan and bring almost to a boil over high heat. Sprinkle in the cornmeal a handful at a time, whisking until smooth. Cool the cornmeal mixture almost to room temperature, then add the remaining ingredients and beat again until well combined.

Ladle the batter by 3-ounce portions onto a lightly greased cast-iron griddle or broad skillet. Allow the cakes to set well—light bubbles will appear and break on the surface—before turning. The cakes will be very delicate and tender, so lift them from the griddle carefully. You should have about 20 cakes. Hold on platter in a warm oven until all cakes are done; serve at once.

(continued)

Creamed Crab

1 pound lump crabmeat
1 scant cup minced onion
2 tablespoons (¼ stick) unsalted butter
1 cup heavy cream
2 dashes of Tabasco
1 scant dash Worcestershire sauce
Salt and pepper to taste

Pick over the crabmeat to remove shells and cartilage and toss lightly in a medium bowl. Sauté the onion in the butter over medium heat until transparent. Add the cream and cook until thick and bubbly and reduced by half.

Add the crabmeat and toss very lightly (do not stir; or crab chunks will break up) until just heated through. Add the seasonings and blend gently.

To assemble the dish: Heat 2 or 3 paper-thin slices baked Smithfield Ham per serving in chicken stock or white wine. Place the slices on 2 cakes placed on a hot plate. Top the ham with the Creamed Crab.

Serve with lightly sautéed sorrel.

Makes 10 2-cake servings

Sautéed Chicken Breasts on Smithfield Ham with Spoonbread and Dried Fruit Chutney

4 whole boneless chicken breasts
2 cups fine saltine cracker crumbs
Salt and pepper to taste
Ground nutmeg to taste
½ cup (1 stick) unsalted butter
8 thin slices Smithfield Ham (see page 30)
4 mandarin oranges, halved and filled with Dried Fruit Chutney (recipe follows)

Skin, trim, and split the chicken breasts. Toss the cracker crumbs, salt, pepper, and nutmeg together. Dredge the chicken breasts in the crumbs. Melt the butter in a large skillet over high heat and let foam. When the foam subsides, place the breasts skin side down in the pan. Brown the breasts, turn, and cook 2 minutes, then lower the heat to medium and cook until the breasts are just done, about 5 minutes more, turning again if necessary.

Place 2 slices ham on each plate and top with 2 chicken breast halves. Add a scoop of spoon bread and drizzle a little butter over the chicken. Arrange mandarin orange halves filled with Dried Fruit Chutney on plates and serve.

Serves 4

Whole-Kernel Corn Spoon Bread

2 cups water
2 cups milk
1½ cups cornmeal
1½ teaspoons salt
3 tablespoons unsalted butter
1 cup fresh corn kernels
6 large eggs
1 tablespoon baking powder

Preheat oven to 350° F.

Combine the water and milk and heat to scalding. Whisk in the cornmeal a scant handful at a time, then add the salt and butter and stir briskly until the mixture thickens, about 5 minutes. Remove from the heat and stir in the corn kernels. Beat the eggs with the baking powder until very light and fluffy, then stir into the cornmeal mixture and mix well.

Pour the batter into a buttered 2-quart baking dish and bake 45 to 50 minutes, or until just set in the center. Serve at once.

Makes 8 servings

Dried Fruit Chutney

½ pound dried peaches
½ pound dried apricots
½ pound dried apples
½ pound dried pitted prunes
2 cups fine-diced onion
1 cup cider vinegar
Boiling water to cover
2 mandarin oranges, cut in quarters and
  seeded
Pulp from 4 mandarin oranges
2 cinnamon sticks, 15 cloves, 1 whole
  allspice, cracked, tied in cheesecloth
½ pound brown sugar

Garnish
4 mandarin oranges, halved

In a one-gallon nonreactive saucepan, combine all the dried fruit, the onions, the vinegar, and cover with boiling water. Stir in the orange quarters and the orange pulp. Add the spice bouquet and bring to a boil over high heat. Lower to a simmer and cook, stirring, until the fruit begins to fall apart and darken in color, about two hours. Stir in the brown sugar, adding water if necessary to prevent sticking, and cook for another hour. Correct sugar and vinegar to taste, remove spice bag and orange quarters (squeeze them out), and cool. Store in the refrigerator for up to four weeks.

Halve the 4 mandarin oranges, cutting them in a decorative zig-zag pattern. Pile the chutney on top of each half.

Makes 3 quarts

Smithfield Ham, Spoon Bread, and Welsh Rabbit with Spiced Apple Rings

1 recipe Whole-Kernel Corn Spoon
   Bread (see page 33)
8 thin slices Smithfield Ham (see
   page 30)
1 recipe Welsh Rabbit (recipe follows)
1 recipe Spiced Apple Rings (recipe
   follows)

For each plate, place spoon bread on 2 slices ham. Top with Welsh Rabbit and decorate the plate with three or four Spiced Apple Rings.

Makes 4 servings

Welsh Rabbit

1 tablespoon unsalted butter
2 teaspoons all-purpose flour
½ pound sharp cheddar cheese, grated
½ cup plus ¼ cup beer
¼ teaspoon cayenne (ground red) pepper
1 tablespoon dry mustard
2 teaspoons Worcestershire sauce
½ teaspoon salt
1 large egg yolk

Melt the butter in a large saucepan over medium heat until it foams. Add the flour and stir over low heat 5 minutes. Do not allow the roux to brown. Stir in the cheese and ½ cup beer. Warm over very low heat until the cheese melts. Stir the seasonings into the ¼ cup beer, then add the mixture to the cheese, stirring to combine. Beat the egg yolk well and stir, off the heat, into the cheese mixture. Return the mixture to lowest heat just long enough to thicken slightly, stirring constantly.

Serve over toast (Welsh Rabbit), poached eggs and toast (Golden Buck), toast and broiled tomatoes (Tomato Buck), or with ham, spoon bread, and apples as described above.

Makes 2 cups

Spiced Apple Rings

2 cups sugar
1 cup water
4 whole cloves
1 cinnamon stick
1 teaspoon vanilla extract, or 1 vanilla bean
4 firm-fleshed tart red apples, such as
   Jonathan, Rome, or Ida Red
1 lemon
2 tablespoons (¼ stick) unsalted butter

Combine the sugar, water, spices, and vanilla in a large saucepan, and bring to a boil. Simmer the liquid until reduced by half, then strain and set aside. Meanwhile, core the apples and cut them into ½-inch-thick rings. Squeeze the lemon over the apples and toss to coat. Melt the butter in a large heavy skillet over medium heat and sauté the apple rings. Drizzle the syrup over the apples, and turn. Let stand briefly. Serve while still warm.

Makes 8 servings

Crabmeat-Stuffed Red Snapper with Champagne Beurre Blanc

My favorite landlady in New York, Eudice Segal, was a Virginian given to the old southern habit of talking to herself in the presence of others. In fact, she often sang to herself in the presence of others, and always when cooking. "A little pepper on his tail will make the fishy sweet," she sang, when cooking fish. Her little song illustrates an ancient principle of southern cooking: Opposites are complementary. Sweet/sour, hot/sweet, salt/sour, oily/astringent are pairs the South loves because the combinations so often turn out to be more intense than their parts. Often, the simple expedient is what achieves this best—like the heavy peppering of fish to bring out its white-sweet flavor.

1 6-pound snapper
2 pounds lump crabmeat
½ cup minced green pepper
½ cup minced pimiento
1 cup minced scallions
1 cup minced celery
2 tablespoons (¼ stick) unsalted butter, melted
1 tablespoon Worcestershire sauce
1 teaspoon Tabasco
1 teaspoon fresh thyme
2 slices white bread, without crusts
1 cup milk
½ cup (1 stick) unsalted butter
1 cup brut champagne
Salt and pepper to taste

Preheat oven to 400° F.

Bone the snapper, leaving the head and tail intact. Pick over crabmeat for filament, and toss with vegetables, butter, and seasonings. Soak bread in milk, squeeze out the excess, and crumble the soggy bread into crabmeat mixture. Stuff the snapper with the crab mixture and place in a shallow baking pan. Moisten with champagne, dot with butter, add salt and pepper to taste and bake for about 30 minutes.

Makes 6 servings

Champagne Beurre Blanc

1 bottle brut champagne
2 cups minced scallions, white portion only
Strong dash of Tabasco
1 teaspoon salt
1½ pounds (6 sticks) unsalted butter

Cut the butter into 1-ounce pieces and keep chilled. Boil the champagne fiercely over a high flame, with the scallions and seasonings, until the pan is very nearly dry. Whisk butter into the hot, damp scallions, still over a high flame. When all the butter is absorbed, remove the pan from the heat, let cool briefly, and strain into a sauce boat. Serve at once.

Makes 3 cups

Smothered Chicken

This legendary recipe for chicken is so simple that it is hard to believe how good it is. The dish is really a lightly browned fricassee, cooked gently until the meat, still moist and tender, is ready to fall from the bone. In the Carolinas, Smothered Chicken would be eaten with rice; in the midwest, with mashed potatoes. On a Virginia menu, it would be a shame not to eat Smothered Chicken with the tender cornmeal delicacy, spoon bread.

2 3-pound broiling chickens, cut up as
    for frying
2 cups all-purpose flour, heavily salted
    and peppered, for dredging
¼ cup oil or chicken fat plus ¼ cup
    (½ stick) unsalted butter, melted
    together
1½ cups chopped onions
2 cups Chicken Stock (see page 28)
1 cup heavy cream
1 bay leaf
½ teaspoon dried thyme
2 small celery hearts, sliced

Preheat the oven to 375° F.

Dredge the chicken in the flour mixture. Lightly brown the chicken pieces in the oil and butter over medium heat. Transfer the chicken, as pieces are browned, to a large casserole with a tight-fitting lid.

When all the chicken is browned, add the onions to the pan and stir from the bottom to loosen any bits of flour and chicken on the bottom. Sauté the onions until transparent, then add the stock, cream, bay leaf, thyme, and celery hearts to the pan. Simmer briefly, then pour the sauce over the chicken. Cover tightly with aluminum foil, then with the casserole lid. Bake 1 hour, or until the chicken is tender and almost falling off the bone.

Serve with Whole-Kernel Corn Spoon Bread (see page 33).

Makes 4 to 6 servings

DESSERTS

Vanilla Custard Ice Cream

When my mother was at William and Mary, she had a beau named Charles Chandler—called Charlie Chan—who used to come see her at the dormitory and take her for long walks. She remembers with special fondness his asking her to "go down to the apothecary, Julia, for a saucer of cream." The ice cream would surely have been a custard-based vanilla accompanied by little crisp cookies; or perhaps a fruit cream—the same frozen custard laced with fresh fruit.

10 large egg yolks
1 cup sugar
1 quart half-and-half
1 vanilla bean, split
¼ teaspoon sugar

Beat the egg yolks and 1 cup sugar together until they are thick and lemon yellow.

In an enamel or stainless steel saucepan, scald the half-and-half with the vanilla bean. Gradually pour the hot half-and-half into the egg mixture, stirring constantly. Return the custard to the heat and cook over very low heat, stirring constantly, until thickened, about 3 minutes. Let stand until the custard is cool. Remove vanilla bean.

Freeze the custard in an ice-cream maker according to the manufacturer's directions until firm. Serve with Lace Cookies (recipe follows) or Sugar Wafers (recipe follows).

Makes 1½ quarts

Lace Cookies

½ cup (1 stick) unsalted butter
⅓ cup sugar
⅓ cup brown sugar
1 large egg
2 teaspoons vanilla extract
¼ cup all-purpose flour
½ teaspoon baking powder
⅛ teaspoon salt
1 cup rolled oats (not instant)
⅓ cup pecans, chopped fine

Preheat the oven to 325° F.

Cream the butter and sugars until you can't feel the sugar grains and the mixture is light and fluffy. Beat in the egg and the vanilla. Sift together the flour, baking powder, and salt and add to the sugar mixture. Blend well. Stir in the oats and the pecans.

Drop the dough by half-teaspoonfuls 3 inches apart onto a foil-covered baking sheet (heed these instructions or you'll have a sheet of run-together cookies). Bake 10 minutes. Cookies will be flat and brown at the edges.

Cool 1 or 2 minutes and peel the cookies from the foil. Cool the cookies on racks, and store them in layers separated by waxed paper or plastic wrap.

Makes 1 dozen cookies

Sugar Wafers

½ cup (1 stick) unsalted butter, softened
1 cup sugar
1 large egg
1 teaspoon vanilla extract
1 tablespoon heavy cream
2 cups sifted all-purpose flour
1½ teaspoons baking powder
¼ teaspoon salt
Sugar

Cream the butter and sugar until you can't feel the sugar grains. Add the egg, vanilla, dry ingredients and add to the mixture. Blend well, stir into a ball, wrap in plastic, and refrigerate at least 3 hours or overnight.

Preheat the oven to 375° F. Roll out the dough to a thickness of ¼ inch, cut out shapes with a cookie cutter, and sprinkle with sugar. Place the cookies 3 inches apart on a greased cookie sheet and bake 15 minutes, or until lightly browned.

Makes 2 dozen wafers

Fresh Raspberry Trifle

Butter Sponge Cake

4 large egg yolks
½ cup sugar
1 teaspoon vanilla extract
1 cup less 2 tablespoons sifted cake flour
4 large egg whites
¼ cup (½ stick) unsalted butter, melted

Preheat the oven to 350° F.

In a warm bowl, beat the egg yolks and sugar until light and fluffy. Beat in the vanilla. Using a spatula, fold in the flour in 3 portions. Beat the egg whites until stiff and fold into the batter. Fold in the cooled melted butter.

Pour the batter into a buttered and floured 9-inch round cake pan to a depth of ¾ inch. Bake 25 to 35 minutes, or until a straw inserted in the center comes out clean. Turn out the cake onto a rack to cool. Split to make 2 layers.

Crème Anglaise

1 quart half-and-half
½ cup sugar
⅛ teaspoon salt
1 vanilla bean, split
12 large egg yolks

Scald the half-and-half in a large saucepan over high heat with the sugar, salt, and vanilla bean. Beat the egg yolks until light and thick. Slowly pour the half-and-half mixture into the yolks, beating constantly. Return the mixture to low heat, whisking constantly, until the custard thickens slightly. Let the custard cool. Remove the vanilla bean.

Raspberry Purée

1½ pints fresh raspberries
1 cup sugar

Purée ½ pint raspberries with ⅔ cup of the sugar and strain to remove seeds. In a separate bowl, toss 1 pint raspberries with remaining ⅓ cup sugar.

Assembly of Trifle

2 layers Butter Sponge Cake
1 cup white wine mixed with 4 ounces
    Chambord liqueur
1 quart Crème Anglaise
1 pint sweetened whipped cream
    flavored with ½ teaspoon grated
    lemon zest
Raspberry Purée
1 pint sugared raspberries

Line a shallow glass bowl with one cake layer. Sprinkle with half the wine and Chambord. Pour on half the Crème Anglaise. Top with half the whipped cream. Top the cream with half the Raspberry Purée and half the raspberries. Repeat. Let stand 2 hours before serving.

Makes 6 servings

Floating Island

6 large egg whites
1 cup sugar
3 cups milk
1 vanilla bean, split
⅔ cup sugar
6 large egg yolks

Beat the egg whites to soft peaks, then add 1 cup sugar gradually and continue beating until they are stiff. In a small deep frying pan, bring the milk to a boil with the vanilla bean. Turn the heat down to a simmer and, using a wet dessert spoon, slip puffs of the beaten egg whites into the simmering milk. Poach for 2 minutes on 1 side, then turn and poach for 2 minutes on the other side. Lift out the puffs with a slotted spoon and drain on brown paper. Remove the vanilla bean.

Beat ⅔ cup sugar and the egg yolks together until fluffy and lemon yellow. Beat in the hot milk, then return the mixture to very low heat to simmer until the mixture thickens slightly, about 4 minutes.

Cool the custard, then pour it into a shallow glass bowl. Drop the meringue islands into the custard, turning the meringues to coat them.

Makes 8 servings

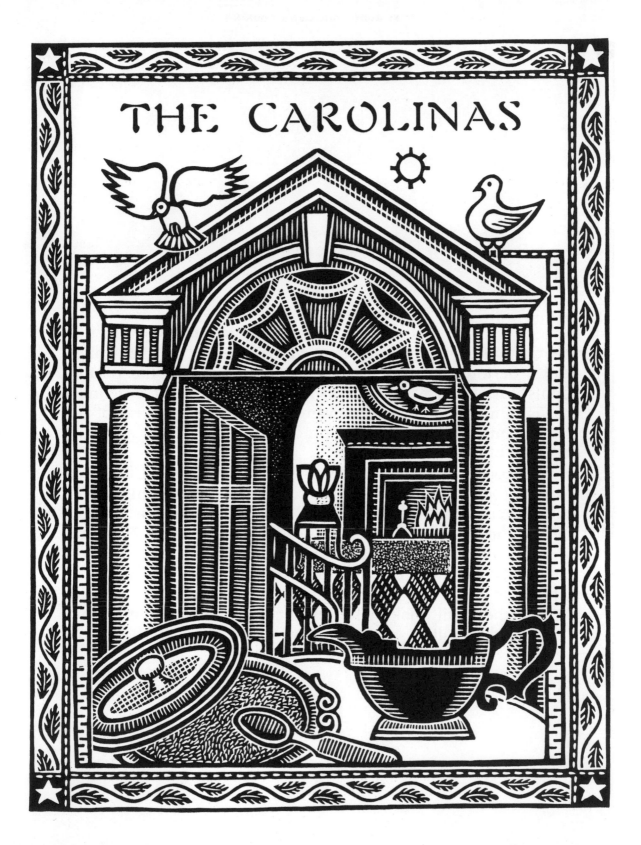

THE CAROLINAS

I have said for a long time that the Carolinas are the best-kept culinary secret in the United States. Serious barbecue from North Carolina and the creamy sophistication of Charleston cuisine combine to create a richness that is unmatched anywhere, even in the culinary context of the South. Some of the great young professionals are there, too, like Bill Neal of Crook's Corner.

The wonderful *Charleston Receipts* and its successor, *Charleston Receipts Too,* are models of regional cookbooks, combining historical with current recipe trends. And the invaluable survival guide, *The Carolina Housewife*—almost as easy to cook from as a contemporary cookbook—preserves dishes with a direct colonial provenance. My Carolina customers are the only ones who not only talk to me about the food they grew up with but promise to get their mothers, still cooking seriously, to call and talk to me about it. I hope they will.

Venison Pâté

1 pound crimini mushrooms, chopped
    fine
1 medium onion, chopped fine
½ cup (1 stick) unsalted butter
2 pounds lean venison plus 1 pound fat
    salt pork, ground together fine
1 large egg
1 cup bread crumbs
1 teaspoon each salt and pepper
½ teaspoon cayenne pepper
½ teaspoon ground nutmeg
1 tablespoon fresh thyme, chopped fine
Aspic (recipe follows)

Preheat the oven to 375° F.

Sauté the mushrooms and onions in a large skillet with the butter until soft but not brown. Cool slightly. Stir together the mushroom mixture and all the other ingredients, mixing well.

Pack into a loaf pan and bake, weighted, about 75 minutes, or until well done throughout. (The best way to weight the pâté is to fold a piece of aluminum foil to fit the top, then set a brick on top of the foil.) Cool the pâté in the pan. Meanwhile, make the aspic.

Aspic

1½ tablespoons unflavored gelatin
½ cup cold Madeira
1½ cups Veal Stock (see page 6), boiling

Soak the gelatin in the Madeira 5 minutes to soften, then dissolve in the boiling stock. Chill the gelatin mixture until it begins to thicken.

Garnish

1 carrot, cooked and sliced in rounds
1 hard-boiled egg, sliced
Fresh tarragon leaves
Pickled onions
Cornichons

To finish the pâté, place the carrot, egg, and tarragon leaves in a decorative pattern in the bottom of a clean, oiled loaf pan and spoon the thickened stock carefully over the design. Place the cooled pâté on top of the thickened stock and chill until the stock is set, about 1½ hours.

To turn out the pâté, run a knife around the edge of the loaf and invert

(continued)

the pan on a plate; drape a hot dish towel over the pan and shake lightly to unmold.

Serve the pâté in slices with pickled onions and cornichons.

Makes 12 servings

Ham and Chutney Toast with Cheddar Cheese

1 cup ground Smithfield Ham (see
  pages 30–31)
1 cup homemade Mango Chutney (recipe
  follows), chopped fine
½ cup heavy cream
8 pieces toast, cut into rounds
1 cup grated cheddar cheese

Stir the ham, chutney, and heavy cream together and spread thickly on toast rounds. Sprinkle the topping with cheddar cheese and heat in 400° F. oven until cheese is melted. Serve at once.

Makes 8 servings

Mango Chutney

6 ripe mangoes, cut in large slices
2 limes, cut in thin quarter rounds
2 lemons, cut in thin quarter rounds
1 large onion, chopped fine
1½ cups brown sugar
1 cup cider vinegar
2 teaspoons cayenne pepper
1 teaspoon ground cinnamon
⅛ teaspoon ground cloves
2 teaspoons ground allspice
Dash of salt

Place all ingredients in a stainless steel or enamel saucepan, and simmer very slowly about 1 hour, or until quite thick.

Store the chutney in jars or a stoneware crock. Keep refrigerated up to 6 weeks.

Makes 2 to 3 cups

Rice Croquettes with Onion and Sweet Pepper Sauce

½ cup White Sauce (recipe follows)
2 large eggs, separated
1 teaspoon salt
¼ cup grated cheddar cheese
¼ teaspoon cayenne pepper
¼ teaspoon ground nutmeg
2 cups soft-cooked, hot rice
2 cups fine bread crumbs

Onion and Sweet Pepper Sauce (recipe follows)

In a large mixing bowl, add the white sauce, well-beaten egg yolks, salt, cheese, and spices to the rice. Blend well. Cool the mixture, then mold into balls, cylinders, or cones. Dip the croquettes in beaten egg white and roll in bread crumbs. Fry in deep fat. Serve hot as a first course with Onion and Sweet Pepper Sauce, or alone as an accompaniment to duck or game.

Makes 8 servings

White Sauce

An American white sauce is a French béchamel; properly, they should be made in exactly the same way. White sauce has fallen into disuse in a lot of modern cooking, but it is supremely useful in holding and binding flavors and distributing the flavor of butter throughout a dish without oiliness.

2 tablespoons (¼ stick) unsalted butter
2 tablespoons all-purpose flour
1½ cups milk
½ teaspoon salt
¼ teaspoon ground white pepper or Tabasco

Melt the butter in a heavy saucepan and whisk in the flour. Continue whisking over medium heat for a full 5 minutes (do not let the flour brown). (This is the crucial period in making a béchamel; if milk is added before the flour is fully cooked, the sauce will taste floury.) Remove the roux from the heat and allow to cool slightly.

Scald the milk in a heavy saucepan over high heat, and add it to the flour all at once. Whisk to mix, scraping the corners of the pan with a wooden spoon to make sure all the roux is incorporated into the milk. Return to the heat at once, lowering the heat and continuing to whisk for about 10 minutes, or until the sauce is fully thickened and the flavors are set. Season with the salt and white pepper or Tabasco.

Makes about 2 cups

Onion and Sweet Pepper Sauce

2 tablespoons vegetable oil
2 tablespoons (¼ stick) unsalted butter
2 large Bermuda onions, minced
1 large red bell pepper, diced fine
1 teaspoon salt
1 teaspoon ground white pepper
½ teaspoon crushed red pepper
1 cup dry white wine
1 cup water
1 tablespoon cornstarch, dissolved in
   1 tablespoon water

Heat the oil and butter in a large skillet over medium heat. Sauté the onions and red bell pepper until very soft. Add the salt, white pepper, and crushed red pepper and cook until almost pasty. Add the wine and water and cook 5 minutes more. Add the cornstarch and cook just until thickened.

Makes about 2½ cups

SOUPS

She-Crab Soup

Precooked crabmeat makes perfectly good crab soup; but for she-crab soup it's necessary to buy only female crabs and to boil and pick them, retaining both the meat and the roe to use in the soup. This is a pain in the neck, but worth it if you value the special richness of crab eggs.

2 tablespoons unsalted butter
1 small onion, grated
3 celery stalks, minced
1 tablespoon all-purpose flour
Salt and white pepper to taste
¼ teaspoon ground mace
½ teaspoon dried thyme
½ teaspoon Worcestershire sauce
½ teaspoon Tabasco
Lemon juice
2 cups heavy cream
2 cups milk
2 cups total white she-crab meat and roe
½ cup sherry

Garnish
Paprika
Chopped fresh parsley

Melt the butter in a large skillet over medium heat and sauté the onion and celery until soft. Sprinkle the flour over the vegetables, stir, and cook 5 minutes. Add all the spices, Worcestershire sauce, Tabasco, and a splash of lemon juice and simmer briefly. Add the cream and milk and heat almost to scalding, stirring constantly. Add the crabmeat and roe and stir. Heat just long enough to warm through. Add the sherry and serve at once, garnished with paprika and chopped parsley.

Makes 8 servings

White Chicken Soup

This is another Southern recipe that feels quite ancient. It is smooth, deeply flavorful, and very simple—a wonderful supper with hot toast and fried green or red tomatoes.

1 5-pound chicken
1 large carrot
3 celery stalks
1 large onion
Bouquet garni of parsley, thyme, and
    tarragon
½ teaspoon mace
2 bay leaves
8 to 10 whole black peppercorns
2 curls lemon zest
32 asparagus stalks
½ cup peeled blanched almonds
½ teaspoon almond extract
3 slices bread, trimmed
1 quart heavy cream
1 pint milk
Salt to taste
Ground white pepper to taste

Quarter the chicken and place it in a 10-quart pot with the aromatic vegetables, bouquet garni, and the other seasonings. Add 5 quarts water and bring to a boil. Lower the heat and simmer until the chicken is very tender, about 4 hours.

Take the chicken pieces from the stock. Remove chicken from bones and discard bones and skin. Strain and skim the stock, then measure out 1½ quarts of the stock into a large saucepan and bring to a boil. Cut the tips from the asparagus. Drop the stalks into the boiling stock and simmer until reduced to 1 quart.

Remove the asparagus stalks from the stock, then strain and boil the stock again. Blanch the asparagus tips in the boiling stock 2 minutes. Remove the asparagus tips and set aside.

Process the almonds and almond extract in a blender or food processor fitted with a metal blade until reduced to a paste. Mince cooled chicken and toss with the almond paste.

Break the bread into small pieces and moisten with ½ cup asparagus stock and ½ cup heavy cream. Mash the bread into a paste, then mix together in a large pot with the chicken and almond paste, 1½ pints heavy cream, 1½ pints asparagus stock, and 1 quart chicken stock. Heat until thick. Add milk to thin the soup as desired and season with salt and white pepper. Garnish with blanched asparagus tips.

Makes 8 servings

SALADS

Frozen Tomato Sherbet

This is perfect Southern-lady food: light, rich in flavor, just right for the long summer months that threaten to kill appetites entirely. The South Carolinian touch, now found all over the South, is the curry powder, brought back in quantity by Charleston sea captains whose palates were as adventurous as their lives.

*8 large tomatoes, scalded, peeled, and
   chopped
1 tablespoon minced fresh basil
1½ teaspoons salt
½ teaspoon pepper
1 small onion, grated
½ cup Lemony Mayonnaise (see page 4)
2 tablespoons minced fresh parsley
1 teaspoon Tabasco
2 teaspoons mild curry powder*

In the bowl of a food processor fitted with a metal blade, chop the tomatoes into a very rough purée. Add the basil, salt, pepper, and onion. Chill in ice trays or freeze in an ice-cream maker until slushy but not frozen.

Mix the mayonnaise, parsley, Tabasco, and curry powder thoroughly.

Serve the sherbet in chilled glass dishes and top with the mayonnaise mixture.

VARIATION: Serve the sherbet garnished with 4 peeled and lightly boiled and chilled shrimp per serving arranged on top of the mayonnaise mixture.

Makes 8 servings

Pink Grapefruit and Bermuda Onions with Charleston Dressing

This is a genuinely peculiar dressing that tastes wonderful with any citrus salad, especially one sparked by onion.

Charleston Dressing
½ cup pickled pearl onions
1 cup pecans
½ cup fresh parsley sprigs
1 cup chopped hard-boiled egg
1 cup soy oil
½ cup ketchup
Salt and pepper

In the bowl of a food processor fitted with a metal blade, process the onions and pecans together until finely minced. Mince the parsley and egg together. Stir the parsley and egg into the onion mixture along with the remaining ingredients.

Citrus Salad
2 pink grapefruits knife-peeled and cut in supremes (sections separated from membrane)
½ Bermuda onion, cut into thin rings
6 oakleaf lettuce leaves

Bed the grapefruit and onion on the lettuce. Top with Charleston Dressing.

Makes 4 servings

MAIN COURSES

Carolina Pilau

Rice dishes are the backbone of Carolina cooking. It isn't the phrase *potatoes and gravy* that activates salivary glands in the Carolinas, it's *rice and gravy*. Often rice means pilau (pronounced *perloo*), a combination of meat, vegetables, or seafood and rice that can serve as an accompaniment to other dishes or stand alone as a staple. This version, with its combination of smoked pork and chicken, is southern, simple, and satisfying. Serve either with all the chicken on the plate, accompanied by a salad for supper, or with the chicken fished out, as a side dish for other chicken dishes, pork, or game.

¾ pound bacon, sliced and chopped
2 cups uncooked rice
4 cups boiling Chicken Stock (see
    page 28)
1 3-pound broiler chicken, cut up for
    frying
4 celery stalks, cut into large diagonal
    slices
1 medium onion, cut into large chunks
1 large carrot, cut into thick rounds
1 bay leaf
Salt and pepper
2 tablespoons chopped fresh parsley

Fry the bacon in a large skillet over very low heat just until it reaches the crisp stage. Remove the bacon from the skillet, crumble, and set aside. Pour off all but 2 tablespoons of the bacon fat, then add the rice and stir from the bottom, cooking slowly until the rice is slightly browned.

Add the boiling stock, stir vigorously, and bring to a full boil. Add chicken, vegetables, bay leaf, salt, and pepper, lower the heat and simmer, covered, 25 to 30 minutes, or until the rice, chicken, and vegetables are done and the stock is absorbed.

Sprinkle with parsley and the reserved crisp bacon before serving.

Makes 8 to 10 servings

Roast Squab with Rice Pilau

Long after hunting became the suburbanite's once-a-year outing in the Northeast, southerners continued to hunt almost daily. Small game, especially, has been a staple of the southern table. And now that many butchers are stocking game from professional farms, these recipes are in use again.

Salt and pepper
8 squabs
6 slices bacon
3 celery stalks, chopped
1 onion, chopped
2 cups uncooked rice
4 cups Chicken Stock (see page 28)
4 large eggs
Unsalted butter
Mustard pickle juice (from a bottle of
    mustard pickles, or a cup of dill
    pickle juice mixed with 1 tablespoon
    Dijon mustard)

Garnish
½ bunch watercress

Salt and pepper the squabs inside and out. Dice the bacon and cook in a large skillet over low heat until crisp. Remove the bacon and reserve, then pour off all but 2 tablespoons fat. Add the celery and onion to the pan and sauté until soft. Cook the rice in chicken stock until tender, then add the celery and onion mixture.

Beat the eggs well and quickly stir them into the hot rice to cook. Season well with salt and pepper.

Preheat the oven to 450° F.

Stuff the squabs with some of the rice mixture, rub them with butter, and arrange in a baking pan. Roast 25 minutes, basting with mustard pickle juice. (Squab is just pink at the bone when done.)

Place the remaining rice in a shallow baking pan and heat, topped with butter, in a 350° F oven 15 minutes. Serve the squabs on a bed of pilau and garnish with watercress.

Makes 4 servings

Veal Shoulder with Baby Vegetables and Toasted Pecans

Salt and pepper
1 3-pound veal shoulder
3 slices bacon
1 each large carrot, turnip, onion, celery
 root, chopped coarse
1 bay leaf
1 sprig fresh thyme
½ bunch parsley
3 cups or more boiling Veal Stock
 (see page 6)
8 tiny turnips, with 2 inches greens
8 tiny carrots, with 2 inches greens
8 tiny redskin potatoes, unpeeled
8 tiny round onions
⅓ pound pecans, toasted with butter and
 salt and cayenne pepper (see
 page 102)

Salt and pepper and tie the veal shoulder, then place it in a large Dutch oven. Blanch the bacon in boiling water 5 minutes, then place it across the veal. Add the carrot, turnip, onion, celery root, bay leaf, thyme, and parsley to the Dutch oven, and completely cover veal shoulder with stock. Cover the pot and cook over low heat (or, if desired, in a 375° F oven) until tender, about 2 hours.

When the veal is done, lift it out of the pot and set aside. Strain and skim the stock, then bring it to a boil on top of the stove. Drop the tiny turnips, carrots, and potatoes into the boiling stock, and cook 5 minutes. Add the tiny onions and cook 2 minutes longer. Remove the vegetables from the stock.

Slice the veal and place it on a large platter. Arrange the baby vegetables around the veal and drizzle with hot stock. Serve at once, sprinkled with the spiced pecans.

A wonderful spring accompaniment is asparagus with Hollandaise Sauce (recipe follows).

Makes 8 servings

Hollandaise Sauce

I make restaurant hollandaise: That is, once the butter is melted and hot, I never let the sauce touch a flame again. If the butter cools while I'm beating it into the yolks, I reheat it.

3 large egg yolks, at room temperature
½ cup (1 stick) unsalted butter
Salt
Dash of Tabasco
Juice of ½ lemon, at room temperature

Warm a heavy 2-quart mixing bowl with hot water. (If you do not have a heavy bowl, dampen a dishtowel, shape it into a ring, and set the lighter bowl in the ring to secure it.) Beat the egg yolks until lemony and thick.

Meanwhile, melt the butter over a medium heat until frothy. Remove the butter from the heat at once and begin whisking it into the yolks very slowly but steadily so that the butter does not cool. If the sauce does not begin to thicken, reheat the remaining butter and continue. When all the butter is incorporated, add the salt, Tabasco, and lemon juice.

Makes about 1 cup

Pink Beans with Ham

1 pound dried pink beans
2 ham hocks
1 bay leaf
1 medium onion, chopped
Salt to taste
1 teaspoon pepper

Soak the beans overnight in a large stockpot with water to cover. Drain.

Add the ham hocks, cover with water to 2 inches above the bean line, and bring to a boil over high heat. Lower the heat and simmer about 2 hours, or until a bean removed from the pot splits when blown on. If necessary, add water as beans cook.

Halfway through the cooking time, add the bay leaf, onion, salt, and pepper. When beans are done, remove ham hocks, cool, pick off the meat and return it to beans. Check the seasoning before serving.

Serve with Sweet and Sour Coleslaw (see page 157) and Potato Salad (see page 158).

Makes 6 servings

North Carolina Pork Barbecue

This is a classic contribution of country cooking to high living. North Carolina barbecue is remarkably simple, but amazingly it isn't often cooked outside its home state. But then, this variety of barbecue in America isn't yet taken seriously. That's part of what we're up to at Miss Ruby's.

You'll need a kettle barbecue grill with a tight lid, 20 pounds of lump charcoal, and wood chips for flavor.

2 quarts cider vinegar
2 quarts water
1 cup Tabasco
1 cup sugar
2 pork shoulders, boned, about 3 pounds
  each

Heat together the vinegar, water, Tabasco, and sugar until the sugar dissolves. Pour the liquid over the pork shoulders to cover and marinate overnight.

Allowing a full 8 hours for cooking, fire the charcoal, and wait until the flames die down and the coals are gray. Be sure the grill rack is as far from the coals as the grill allows. Place the pork shoulders fat side down on the grill. As they begin to brown, turn the pork shoulders every 20 minutes or so. Feed the fire with charcoal, keeping the temperature steady and as low as possible. Dip the pork shoulders in marinade from time to time to keep them moist. Keep the grill lid closed between turnings. In the last hour of cooking, damp wood chips, preferably hickory, can be thrown on the coals to flavor the meat. When the meat is ready to serve, it should be dark brown on the outside, and moist and melting on the inside.

Slice the pork thin, or slice and chop, and serve with Pouring Sauce (recipe follows).

Pouring Sauce

1 cup cider vinegar
½ cup Dijon mustard
½ cup Worcestershire sauce
¼ cup Tabasco
½ cup vegetable oil
1 teaspoon each salt and pepper
1 lemon, sliced
1 medium onion, chopped coarse
½ teaspoon celery seed

Combine the ingredients in a large saucepan and bring to a boil over high heat. Continue boiling until well blended and reduced by ¼. Strain the sauce and store, refrigerated, in a glass container; it will keep for at least 6 weeks.

Makes 12 servings

DESSERTS

Sweet Potato Pone

There are ten or eleven rules for this dessert in *Charleston Receipts,* the justly celebrated book on Carolina cooking. Pone is richer than sweet potato pie, and more various: Ingredients from versions I've read include citron, rosewater, pumpkin pie spices, candied ginger, raisins, oranges, and in the most recent—a recipe that I've found as far west as Texas—coconut. The one here defers to tradition far enough to leave out the coconut.

¾ *cup (1½ sticks) unsalted butter*
¾ *cup packed dark brown sugar*
2 cups grated uncooked sweet potato
2 tablespoons sweet sherry
¼ *teaspoon ground nutmeg*
¼ *teaspoon ground cinnamon*
1 teaspoon ground ginger
2 tablespoons chopped candied ginger
1 cup molasses
2 cups milk
2 tablespoons orange marmalade

Preheat the oven to 325° F. Butter a 2-quart casserole dish.

Cream the butter and brown sugar together in a large mixing bowl until smooth, then add the sweet potato, flavorings, molasses, and milk. Blend well, and stir in the marmalade.

Turn the mixture into the prepared casserole and bake about 1½ hours, or until the sweet potato is completely tender, to the point of dissolving, and the pone is sticky and moist.

Slice and serve with Orange-Flavored Whipped Cream (recipe follows).

Orange-Flavored Whipped Cream
1 cup heavy cream
2 tablespoons sugar
1 teaspoon grated orange zest

Whip the cream in a chilled medium mixing bowl. When soft peaks form, gradually beat in the sugar, then stir in the orange zest.

Makes 8 servings

Angel Food Charlotte Russe

Every traditional Carolina culinary repertoire contains charlotte russe—and angel food cake is the perfect foil for the creamy richness of the charlotte.

1 cup sifted cake flour
1½ cups sugar
¼ teaspoon salt
1¼ cups egg whites (from about 6 large eggs)
1¼ teaspoons cream of tartar
1 teaspoon vanilla extract
¼ teaspoon almond extract

Preheat the oven to 375° F.

Sift the flour 4 times with ½ cup sugar. Sift the remaining cup of sugar separately and set aside.

In a large mixing bowl, combine the salt and egg whites and beat until foamy. Add the cream of tartar, and continue beating until the egg whites hold peaks. Add the sifted sugar to the whites a few tablespoons at a time, beating after each addition. Fold in the vanilla and almond extracts. Fold in the flour and sugar mixture ½ cup at a time.

Pour the batter into a greased and sugared angel food cake pan and bake 35 minutes. Turn the pan upside down and allow the cake to cool on a rack 1 hour before removing from the pan.

Filling

1 ounce unflavored gelatin
¼ cup cool water
¾ cup sherry
1 cup heavy cream
½ cup confectioners' sugar

In a large mixing bowl, dissolve the gelatin in the water. Heat the sherry to the boiling point in a small saucepan, then stir into the softened gelatin and let cool.

In another bowl, whip the cream until soft peaks form, then beat in the sugar, and fold the cream into the gelatin mixture. Let cool in the refrigerator until thickened but not fully congealed.

Using a serrated knife and a gentle sawing motion, cut the cooled cake into 2 layers. Fill the center and spread the bottom layer with filling. Top with the second layer and fill the center with the remaining filling. Cover and chill overnight.

(continued)

Seven-Minute Icing
4 large egg whites
1 cup sugar
1 tablespoon light corn syrup
⅛ teaspoon cream of tartar

Place all the ingredients in the top of a double boiler and heat, stirring occasionally, until very hot. Pour the mixture into the large bowl of an electric mixer and beat at high speed 10 minutes, or until the icing peaks. Ice the filled layers of the cake when cold.

This charlotte is wonderful when served with 3 cups sugared sliced strawberries.

Makes 8 to 10 servings

Huguenot Torte

The Huguenots were driven out of France for Protestantism, and a good many of them ended up in Maryland and the Carolinas. One bunch crossed the country and fetched up in Louisiana, where they converted back to Catholicism and became my immediate ancestors, the Calvets. (It is really hard to stay a French Protestant in southern Louisiana.) Whatever its sacramental origins, this cake is very good.

4 large eggs
3 cups sugar
½ cup all-purpose flour
5 teaspoons baking powder
½ teaspoon salt
2 cups peeled, chopped tart apples
2 cups chopped pecans
2 teaspoons vanilla extract

Garnish
2 cups chopped pecans, toasted,
    buttered, and salted (see page 139,
    for directions on roasting)
Sweetened whipped cream

Preheat the oven to 325° F.

Beat the eggs in a large mixing bowl with an electric mixer or rotary beater until very frothy and lemon colored. Add the other ingredients in the order given. Pour the batter into 2 buttered and floured 8- by 12-inch baking pans. Bake in the oven until brown and crusty, about 45 minutes.

Scoop the torte out of the pan with a pancake turner or a big metal spoon, pile it on plates, and cover with the toasted pecans and the whipped cream.

Makes 8 to 10 servings

Fig Ice Cream and Benne Seed Wafers

Find me a southerner and I will show you a fig lover. Each of my grandmothers had fig trees, and each loved her figs in a characteristic way. My Franklin, Louisiana, grandmother stood under hers in the early morning and ate the fruit from the lower branches "to save them from the birds." My Wharton, Texas, grandmother mounted a tall ladder every spring and picked bushels of figs, which she then preserved and transferred to shelves in the basement. The preserves would be doled out through the year at big family dinners.

Fig Ice Cream

4 large eggs
1 cup milk
1 quart heavy cream
6 cups fresh figs, very ripe
1 cup sugar
1 tablespoon lemon juice
1 teaspoon vanilla extract

In a medium saucepan, beat the eggs together vigorously and well. In another small saucepan, scald the milk, then slowly beat it into the eggs. Cook the egg mixture over very low heat until slightly thick. Set aside to cool. In a large mixing bowl, whip the cream until frothy. Add the cooled egg mixture.

Peel and mash the figs, and purée them in the bowl of a food processor fitted with a metal blade. Add sugar, lemon juice, and vanilla.

Fold together the cream and fig mixtures and freeze until firm in an ice-cream maker according to the manufacturer's instructions. Serve with Benne Seed Wafers (recipe follows).

Makes ½ gallon

Benne Seed Wafers

Bennes are sesame seeds. Carolinians got them from West Africa and believe in them as a good-luck food. They certainly taste good enough to be good luck.

¾ cup (1½ sticks) unsalted butter
2 cups packed dark brown sugar
1 large egg, beaten
1 teaspoon vanilla extract
1 cup all-purpose flour
¼ teaspoon salt
½ teaspoon baking powder
¾ cup toasted benne seeds

Preheat oven to 350° F.

In a large mixing bowl, cream together the butter and the sugar, then add the beaten egg and vanilla extract. Sift the flour with the baking powder and salt, then blend into the butter mixture. Stir in the benne seeds.

Drop by half teaspoonfuls or squeeze from a pastry tube onto greased cookie sheets. Bake about 10 minutes, or until light brown. Cool 2 or 3 minutes before removing the cookies from the pan.

Makes 4 dozen

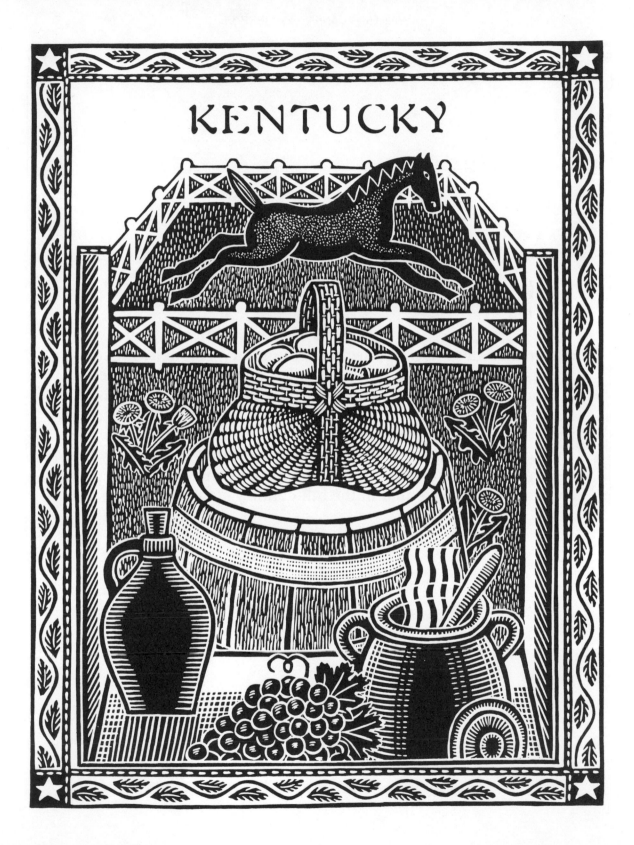

KENTUCKY

There is a genteel Kentucky tradition that gave rise to a legion of honorary colonels, bluegrass brunches before Derby Day, and miles and miles of white fences in horse country. The Kentucky I identify with, though, is the hunters' country, the land Daniel Boone settled and moved on from at regular intervals throughout his life. Appalachian poverty augmented by Appalachian ingenuity has produced a cookery that depends on an aggressive way with wild raw materials. American charcuterie was invented in the hill-country states.

SMALL PLATES

Country Corn

This dish will go anywhere: We serve it as a first course with pickled green tomatoes on the side or as a brunch or lunch dish with hot biscuits. Country Corn depends entirely on its ingredients: good smoky bacon, fresh eggs, and corn as young and fresh from the stalk as possible. Don't even think of using canned or frozen corn.

3 slices double-smoked bacon, diced
1 medium onion, diced fine
4 ears fresh corn
Salt and pepper to taste
3 large eggs, beaten

Garnish
Minced fresh scallions
Minced fresh parsley

Place the bacon in a large skillet over medium heat and fry gently until a good deal of fat is rendered. Add the onion to the skillet and cook until transparent.

Cut the corn kernels from the cobs, scraping the milk into a large mixing bowl with the kernels. When the bacon is almost crisp, add the corn kernels and their milk to the bacon and stir. Add the salt (easy—the bacon is salty) and pepper to the eggs and stir them into the corn mixture, continuing to stir until eggs are done but still soft.

Serve on warm plates with hot toast and sprinkle with scallions and parsley.

Makes 4 servings

Sausage Tarts

Pastry with Vegetable Shortening (see
    page 80)
6 balls uncooked Sausage Meat (recipe
    follows)
1 cup fine-chopped onion
1 cup grated cheddar cheese

Preheat the oven to 400° F.

Roll out the pastry dough ⅛-inch
thick and cut into 6-inch rounds. Line
6 4-inch tart shells with the pastry and
bake until very pale brown, about 12
minutes.

Break up the sausage in a hot cast-iron
skillet and sauté over medium heat
until the fat begins to render. Add the
onion and cook until the sausage is
light brown and the onion transparent.

Divide the meat mixture among the
tart shells and top each with cheese.
Bake until the cheese is melted and the
tarts are golden brown. Serve at once
as a first course, or 2 at a time with a
salad for lunch.

Makes 6 tarts

Sausage Meat

It's possible to stuff this mixture into cas-
ings, but I am fonder of the rough-and-
ready method of just patting the sausage
into plump rounds and dropping them on
a hot griddle.

5 pounds lean ground pork
2 tablespoons salt
3 tablespoons packed dark brown sugar
3 tablespoons fresh sage
2 tablespoons fresh thyme
2 teaspoons pepper
2 teaspoons crushed red pepper
1 teaspoon ground allspice

Mix together all the ingredients well, and
form the mixture into 3-ounce balls. Drop
the sausage balls onto a dry griddle over
high heat and mash with a pancake turner.

Turn the heat down to medium and cook
until brown. Turn the sausage and continue cooking until brown on the other
side and done through, about 5 minutes.

For long-term storage: Put sausage balls
on freezer paper in convenient quantities
(I make packages of a dozen) about 2
inches apart. Top with freezer paper 2
inches larger than the bottom piece. Tuck
the edges under and wrap in freezer foil.
Freeze until needed.

Or: Pack partly cooked sausages in a wide-
mouthed crock, and pour hot pork fat
over them. Put plate over mouth of crock
and invert so the fat seals the top. The
sausage will keep up to 2 weeks in the refrigerator.

Makes 25 balls

Stuffed Eggs

This is an intense version of the picnic classic, wonderful as a first course with pickles and pimientos.

12 hard-boiled eggs
1 tablespoon unsalted butter
2 tablespoons fine-chopped cooked
    country ham
1 tablespoon fine-chopped onion
1 tablespoon fine-chopped fresh parsley
1 tablespoon brown or grainy mustard
Salt and pepper to taste
Paprika

Peel the eggs and halve them. Remove the yolks and mash with remaining ingredients, except paprika, mixing well. Fill the egg whites with the yolk mixture and sprinkle with paprika.

Makes 24

Fried Green Tomatoes

This is an American classic, typical of the way we use tomatoes—typical, in fact, of a use we make of tomatoes that no one else does: We don't scorn green tomatoes, and we're right not to; they have a citrusy sharp firmness not at all like the ripe tomato. Pickled, cooked into mince for pies, or simply fried like this, they are one of our glories.

4 large fresh green tomatoes
2 cups cornmeal
Salt and pepper to taste
Smidgen dark brown sugar
1 cup bacon drippings

Garnish
8 fresh cherry tomatoes, halved

Cut the green tomatoes into thick slices. Mix the cornmeal, salt and pepper, and brown sugar. Dredge the tomatoes in the cornmeal mixture. Heat the bacon drippings in a large cast-iron skillet over medium heat and fry the tomato slices, turning as necessary, until golden brown on both sides. Serve at once, garnished with ripe cherry tomato halves.

Makes 6 to 8 servings

Fried Okra

Okra, brought here by slaves or slave traders, is part of our African-American heritage. The vegetable is a major (though not invariable) ingredient of gumbo, which gets its name from a West African word for okra. Okra is loved in the South and resisted strongly elsewhere—mainly because of its reputation as slimy. A good hard frying in hot oil or a quick blanch, as below, usually solves that problem, freeing us to enjoy the subtle flavor and pleasant crunch of yet another vegetable that Europe ignores and we have mastered.

4 cups small tender whole fresh okra
   pods
2 large eggs, beaten
½ cup half-and-half
2 cups fine cracker crumbs
Salt and pepper to taste
2 cups all-purpose flour
6 cups soy oil

Bring 4 quarts water to a boil in a large stockpot over high heat. Blanch the okra in the boiling water 30 seconds, then drain and rinse with ice water.

Lightly beat the eggs with the half-and-half and season the cracker crumbs with salt and pepper. Dip the okra in the flour, then in the egg mixture, then into the cracker crumbs.

Heat the soy oil in a large skillet over high heat, and fry the okra until golden brown. Serve the Fried Okra with a rich tomato sauce as a first course or alone, as an hors d'oeuvre, with drinks.

Makes 8 servings

SOUPS

Vegetable Soup

This is a very old-fashioned and satisfying soup; I think the abundance of root vegetables and the absence of meat make it very innocent.

2 cups split yellow peas
1 tablespoon celery seed
2 large carrots, cut into rounds
1 small cauliflower, separated into small flowerets
4 parsnips, cut into rounds
2 potatoes, diced fine
3 salsify roots, cut into rounds
2 turnips, diced fine
2 tablespoons (¼ stick) unsalted butter
Juice of 1 lemon
Salt and cayenne pepper to taste

Soak the peas overnight in water to cover. Drain the peas, then add 4 quarts water and stir in the celery seeds. Bring to a boil over high heat and cook until peas are soft and virtually dissolved, about 2 hours, stirring often and adding water as needed.

Add all the vegetables at once and simmer until tender. Finish with the butter and lemon juice, plus salt and cayenne to taste.

Makes 12 servings

Tomato-Corn Soup

My tendency would be to repeat this soup for every southern state, but its simplicity seems to place it in hill country. This version makes it a very light cream soup; many others are just unadulterated combinations of corn and tomatoes.

2 cups heavy cream
2 cups fresh tomatoes, peeled, chopped,
   and lightly stewed
1½ cups fresh corn kernels, with their
   milk
2 tablespoons (¼ stick) unsalted butter
Salt and pepper to taste

Garnish
Chopped fresh parsley

Scald the cream in a large saucepan over high heat. In another saucepan, bring the tomatoes and corn to a boil, then add the hot cream slowly, stirring constantly to prevent curdling. Add butter, salt and pepper, and garnish with parsley.

Makes 8 servings

SALADS

Hot Dandelion Greens

6 cups young tender dandelion greens.
1 teaspoon salt
6 slices double-smoked bacon
2 large eggs
½ cup cider vinegar

Soak the dandelion leaves in cold water overnight. Rinse the greens and toss with the salt. Set aside.

Fry the bacon in a large heavy skillet over high heat. When bacon is crisp, remove from the pan and turn off the heat.

Beat the eggs with the vinegar. Pour the hot bacon grease over the dandelion greens and toss together. Quickly add eggs and vinegar. Chop the reserved bacon and garnish the greens with it.

Makes 8 servings

Soft Lettuce with Egg Dressing

1 head Boston lettuce

Egg Dressing
3 large hard-boiled egg yolks
1 teaspoon Dijon mustard
Salt to taste
3 tablespoons (¼ stick) unsalted butter, melted
2 tablespoons cider vinegar

Garnish
1 large hard-boiled egg, sliced

Separate the leaves of one head of Boston lettuce; wash and dry.

Mash the egg yolks with the mustard and salt. Add the melted butter and mix to a paste. Pour in the vinegar gradually, mixing well.

Pour the Egg Dressing over the lettuce and garnish with hard-boiled egg slices.

Makes 2 to 4 servings

MAIN COURSES

Cornmeal Mush

There is no more American ingredient than corn—and, to the extent that the American kitchen remains unrecognized for its most original contributions to the world kitchen, there is no more anonymous ingredient. The name of this dish doesn't help, of course—but it is beloved all over the South, especially in the hill states, where it is eaten without cheese at breakfast, cold with leftover meat or cold gravy at noon, and sautéed in butter or bacon grease with hot meat at dinner.

1 teaspoon salt
2 cups yellow or white stone-ground
  cornmeal
2 tablespoons (¼ stick) unsalted butter
Pepper

Bring 4 quarts water to a boil in a large saucepan over high heat, add the salt, then sprinkle the cornmeal onto the surface of the water by the scant handful, whisking briskly as you go. Don't allow the water to settle until you've whisked in all the cornmeal; keep the mixture moving until it has thickened enough to prevent the cornmeal from settling to the bottom of the pan.

Turn the heat to low, cover the pan, and simmer until the meal is tender,

about 12 minutes. Beat in the butter, add more salt and pepper if you like, and serve at once.

AS BREAKFAST, serve the mush in bowls with more butter melted on top, warm cream for pouring, and sugar or molasses or honey.

AS A SIDE DISH, serve the mush plain or stir in chopped fresh parsley, scallions, grated cheddar cheese, or a combination.

FOR FRIED CORNMEAL MUSH, pour the hot mush into a buttered cookie sheet. When cooled and set, slice the cake into rectangles (or squares or triangles) and sauté in butter until lightly brown on both sides. Serve the slices plain with meat; as a main course with cheese or tomato sauce and a salad or vegetable; or as a bed for grilled or sautéed rabbit or quail or squab.

Makes 4 servings as a main course, or 8 as a side dish

Grilled Quail on Fried Cornmeal Mush Squares with Wild Grape Conserve

A fine hallooing song called "The Hunters of Kentucky" communicates a good deal of the adventure and uncertainty that made the first American frontier the only place Daniel Boone wanted to live. (When cabins and traders and farmers arrived, he moved on.) Hunting and game eating are still a large part of the culture of the state.

Allow 3 quail for each person. Snip up the backbone of each bird with poultry shears; do not cut the breast. Drizzle the birds with a mixture of 3 parts warm bacon grease to 1 of cider vinegar. Set aside to marinate while you prepare the grill.

When the flames have subsided and the coals are gray, place the quail bone side down on the grill about 3 inches above the coals. Cook 5 minutes, then turn and cook 3 minutes. Check doneness by piercing the flesh of the thigh (the meat should be just barely pink at the bone). Salt and pepper the quail as they come off the grill.

Serve the quail on sautéed Fried Cornmeal Mush squares (see page 70) with Wild Grape Conserve (recipe follows) and a salad of wilted mustard and dandelion greens.

Wild Grape Conserve

Wild grapes were a source of natural sweetness for the earliest settlers. Later they became a favorite free raw material for the preserve, conserve, and jelly recipes that run all the way across the country in countless regional variations. This one is especially good with Grilled Quail.

2½ pounds Concord grapes
½ cup raspberry, currant, or other fruit
    vinegar
½ pound sugar
3 lemons, sliced thin
3 cinnamon sticks
5 whole cloves
2 whole allspice berries, cracked

Wash, stem, crush, and skin the grapes. Reserve the skins. Put the crushed grapes in a large stainless steel or enamel pot and cook over medium heat until the seeds loosen from the pulp.

Press the cooked pulp through a sieve and discard the seeds. Add the skins, vinegar, sugar, and lemons to the pulp. Tie the cinnamon sticks, cloves, and allspice loosely in cheesecloth and add to the pulp mixture. Cook over low heat until thick, about 1½ hours. The conserve may be canned by the boiling-water method (see below) or kept in jars in the refrigerator for up to 4 weeks.

Serve Wild Grape Conserve with game, smoked meats, and fresh pork.

Makes 1½ gallons

A Note on Canning and Preserving

Unless you have a windfall of gallons and gallons of some ingredient or are short on refrigerator space, you shouldn't worry about the sort of preserving that requires sterilization and water-bath canning. At the restaurant, we take old and new recipes for relishes, pickles, preserves, chutneys, and the like, making them in small amounts and keeping them in the refrigerator until they're used up. I haven't given detailed instructions for pantry preserving because I've had very little experience of

it: If you'd like to do it, using the recipes here or others, I'd recommend two wonderful books: *Fancy Pantry,* by Helen Witty (Workman, 1986), and *Putting Food By,* by Ruth Hertzberg et al. (Stephen Greene Press, 1988).

All the pickle and preserve recipes given here are in small enough amounts that you can refrigerate them conveniently until they're used up; I've given outside times for keeping.

Pan-Fried Catfish with Hush Puppies

Hush puppies, according to the time-honored story, were so named because the morsels were tossed out the backdoor to hush the dogs excited by the smell of frying fish. In their original version, hush puppies were simply the cornmeal used for dredging the fish mixed with a little water and fried in the same oil. Most contemporary recipes are a bit more complex and a lot lighter—more palatable to humans.

The best catfish I've ever had was in western Kentucky and it belied the assumption made nowadays that only farm-raised catfish taste really sweet. The ones I had were from the great man-made TVA lakes near Paducah, and they were better by a country mile than the farm-raised fillets on the same restaurant menu. Of course, any wild catfish is just as good—or as muddy-tasting—as the bottom it fed from, and certainly the gently bred ones from Mississippi have the virtue of consistency, so much so that catfish is at last coming into its own as a great freshwater fish.

4 6- to-8-ounce catfish fillets
1 cup fine yellow cornmeal
1 teaspoon each salt and pepper
¼ cup bacon fat
¾ cup vegetable oil
1 medium onion, chopped fine
1 cup all-purpose flour
1 tablespoon baking powder
1½ cups milk

Garnish
Lemon slices

Rinse the fillets and shake dry. Combine the cornmeal, salt, and pepper on a platter. Combine the bacon fat and the oil in a large skillet and heat until almost smoking. Quickly dredge the fish in the cornmeal mixture and carefully lay in the pan, being careful not to crowd.

While the fish browns, transfer the remaining cornmeal mixture to a small bowl and add the onion, flour, baking powder, and milk. Stir until just mixed and somewhat thicker than a batter, but a bit thinner than a dough.

Turn the fish and add the hush-puppy mixture, a tablespoon at a time, to the pan—one for each fillet. Turn the hush puppies as they brown, lowering the heat just slightly to allow the hush puppies and fish to cook through. When the fish and hush puppies are done, transfer them to a hot platter, and garnish with lemon slices.

Serve with sliced tomatoes and onions on a bed of field greens and Hot Potato Salad (recipe follows).

Makes 4 servings

Hot Potato Salad

One of the loveliest culinary moments in film history is about potato salad. In Jean Renoir's *Rules of the Game* one of the servants of a Jewish baron is indulging in a little belowstairs anti-Semitism when the chef interrupts. The baron had, the very last week, come to the kitchen to tell him that some fool of an underchef had failed to toss the hot potatoes with white wine for salad, and the salad had suffered for it. *That,* said the chef, was proof enough to him that the baron was a true Frenchman, whatever else he was. So in honor of Renoir and a solid standard of citizenship, I always soak the warm potatoes in white wine.

1 pound small red potatoes
1 cup dry white wine
1 tablespoon Dijon mustard
2 tablespoons tarragon vinegar
½ cup virgin olive oil
Salt and pepper to taste
1 tablespoon fine-chopped cornichons
1 tablespoon chopped fresh parsley
1 tablespoon minced red onion

Bring a large pot of water to a boil, and cook the potatoes in their jackets just until tender. Cut the potatoes in quarters and toss at once with the white wine (any delay and the baron's stricture will apply).

While the potatoes marinate in the wine, put the mustard and vinegar in a warm bowl and whisk in the olive oil a little at a time to form an emulsion. Season with salt and pepper.

Strain the potatoes (there should be very little wine unabsorbed) and toss with the vinaigrette, cornichons, parsley, and onion. Serve the salad warm or at room temperature.

Makes 4 servings

Burgoo

Burgoo is a small-game stew, simpler than Brunswick stew, whose home place seems to have been North Carolina. Hearty, spicy burgoo is easy to make, though the simmering takes a while. Originally, it was made with squirrel—home-hunted or store-bought. However, squirrel is almost unheard of in butcher shops, and, in any case, if you live in a large urban area you may be accused of stalking in the park. Here I've substituted rabbit, which is available at most Italian butchers or from major frozen-meat outlets.

2 cups all-purpose flour
1 tablespoon salt
1 tablespoon plus ¼ teaspoon pepper
1 3-pound frying chicken, cut up and
    excess fat reserved
1 2-pound rabbit, cut at every joint
½ cup vegetable oil
2 large onions, chopped coarse
2 cups Chicken Stock (see page 28)
1 27-ounce can tomatoes
2 bay leaves
¼ cup Worcestershire sauce
¼ cup tarragon vinegar
½ teaspoon cayenne pepper
1 tablespoon Tabasco
2 pounds potatoes, peeled and diced
2 pounds fresh tomatoes, peeled and
    diced
6 carrots, sliced
½ head cabbage, chopped coarse
12 small white onions, peeled
2 cups fresh corn kernels

Garnish
Chopped fresh parsley

Season the flour with salt and 1 tablespoon pepper, then dredge the chicken and rabbit in the mixture. Heat the vegetable oil and chicken fat in a large skillet over medium heat. When the chicken fat is rendered, brown the chicken pieces and set aside. Brown the rabbit pieces, then add the onions and stir until they are lightly browned. Add the stock, tomatoes, and all the seasonings. Cover and simmer for 1 hour. Add the chicken and simmer 45 minutes longer.

Test the rabbit and chicken for doneness. Add the potatoes, fresh tomatoes, carrots, cabbage, whole onions, and corn and cook gently until the potatoes and carrots are done, adding more chicken stock if necessary. The stew should be quite juicy, with the meats not quite falling off the bone.

Serve the Burgoo in large soup bowls with generous sprinklings of parsley.

Makes 8 servings

Sausage-Stuffed Roast Chicken

2 cups ½-inch dry bread cubes
1 cup Sausage Meat (see page 64)
½ cup chopped celery
½ cup chopped onion
2 cups Chicken Stock (see page 28),
    divided in half
1 garlic clove, chopped
Salt and pepper to taste
1 6-pound roasting chicken
¼ cup all-purpose flour
1 cup milk

Preheat the oven to 425° F.

Crumble the bread into a mixing bowl. Sauté the sausage meat in a small skillet over medium heat until browned, then add to the bread crumbs along with the celery, onions, and 1 cup stock. Add the garlic, salt, and pepper, and adjust the seasonings to taste.

Remove any excess fat from the cavity of the chicken and set aside. Stuff the bread and sausage mixture into the cavity of the chicken and truss. Salt and pepper the chicken and set on a rack in a roasting pan. Top with the chicken fat. Bake 1¼ hours, or until the fat from the pierced thigh runs yellow. Lift the chicken and rack from the roasting pan and pour off all but ¼ cup fat. Set the pan over medium heat on top of the stove and stir up chicken bits from the bottom. Stir in the flour, blending well, and continue to stir until flour is lightly golden. Add the milk and remaining 1 cup stock and blend well. Continue cooking until the gravy thickens slightly. You can strain the gravy, but we like it with the chicken bits. Serve the chicken and stuffing topped with gravy.

Makes 4 servings

DESSERTS

Dried Apple Stack Cake

1 pound dried apples
1 cup packed dark brown sugar
1½ teaspoons ground cinnamon
¼ teaspoon ground cloves
½ teaspoon ground allspice
3 tablespoons unsalted butter
½ cup shortening
½ cup granulated sugar
1 large egg, well beaten
⅓ cup molasses
½ cup buttermilk
3½ cups all-purpose flour
½ teaspoon baking soda
½ teaspoon salt
1 teaspoon ground ginger
1 teaspoon vanilla extract
Confectioners' sugar

Put the dried apples in a large saucepan and cover with water. Cook the apples over low heat until just soft enough to mash, adding water as necessary to keep very moist. Mash the apples (they should retain a slightly rough texture) with the brown sugar, cinnamon, cloves, allspice, and butter. Cool to room temperature.

Preheat the oven to 350° F.

Cream the shortening and granulated sugar. Add the beaten egg, molasses, and buttermilk and mix well. Sift the flour, baking soda, salt, and ginger together into a large bowl. Make a well in the dry ingredients and add the creamed mixture, stirring until well blended. Add the vanilla and stir well. Divide the dough into 7 parts and roll out each part into an 8 inch circle ½ inch thick. Bake the layers on cookie sheets lined with pastry paper for 10 to 12 minutes, until lightly browned and done through.

Cool on racks and stack the layers, spreading cooked apples between them and smoothing the apples around the sides. Sprinkle the top of the stacked cake with confectioners' sugar and let stand overnight so that the apples soak into the cake.

Makes 8 to 10 servings

Sara Burke's Race-Day Pie

My first restaurant was in Berkshire County, Massachusetts. I acquired the premises from a lady who had sold antique clothes and soup and the occasional piece of pie. The piemaker arrived on the day I signed the lease, a two-year-old clinging to her skirt, to announce that she came with the territory. I agreed, bemused, and soon discovered that she was everything a pastry cook ought to be: consistent, rich-minded, and free with sweetness. One of our customers, convinced that honey was the healthy move in desserts, once asked Sara what she sweetened her pies with. Sara answered firmly, "Lots and lots of white sugar." Ah, freedom. Ah, truth.

Crust

2 cups sifted all-purpose flour
1 teaspoon salt
⅔ cup shortening
⅓ cup ice water

In a large mixing bowl sift the flour and salt together. Cut or rub in the shortening very quickly, until the mixture resembles cornmeal. Add the ice water and toss the pastry together with a fork, stirring to the center until the pastry forms a ball. (Do not work the pastry; it will fall together.) Divide the pastry into 2 parts, form each into a ball, wrap in plastic, and chill at least 1 hour.

Roll 1 ball to a thickness of ⅛ inch and line a 10-inch pie plate with it. (Wrap tightly and freeze the other ball for later use.)

Preheat the oven to 375° F.

Filling

¼ cup (½ stick) unsalted butter
1 cup sugar
¾ cup light corn syrup
½ teaspoon salt
3 large eggs
1 cup semisweet chocolate bits
1½ cups broken walnuts
1 teaspoon vanilla extract
1 tablespoon bourbon

Cream the butter and sugar together gradually in a large mixing bowl and beat until blended. Add the corn syrup and salt and mix well. Add the eggs, 1 at a time, beating well after each addition. Stir in the chocolate bits, walnuts, vanilla, and bourbon. Pour the filling into the pie shell and bake 40 to 50 minutes.

Makes 8 servings

Prune Cake with Buttermilk Icing

This unlikely sounding combination is actually a natural: It combines the dark, rich sweetness of prunes with the light pungency of buttermilk. One of the sadder losses in modern American cooking is buttermilk; it makes a great mixing element for breads, it is a good cream-soup base, and its acidity is a nice foil for the deep sweetness of dried fruit.

Cake
1½ cups sugar
1 cup vegetable oil
3 large eggs, beaten
2 cups all-purpose flour
1 teaspoon baking soda
1 teaspoon ground cinnamon
1 teaspoon ground nutmeg
1 teaspoon ground allspice
½ teaspoon salt
1 cup buttermilk
1 cup broken walnuts
1½ cups cooked chopped pitted prunes
1 teaspoon vanilla extract

Preheat the oven to 300° F.

In a medium bowl, blend the sugar and the oil. Add the eggs and beat well. In a large mixing bowl, sift the dry ingredients together 3 times, and add the egg mixture and buttermilk alternately, beating well after each addition. Add the nuts, prunes, and vanilla, and stir well to distribute evenly through the batter.

Pour the batter into a buttered and floured Bundt pan and bake 1 hour. When the cake is done, turn it out onto a rack and glaze with Buttermilk Icing while the cake is still warm.

Buttermilk Icing
1 cup sugar
½ cup buttermilk
2 teaspoons vanilla extract
⅓ cup (⅔ stick) unsalted butter

Combine all the ingredients in a saucepan and boil 1 minute without beating.

Blue-Ribbon Peach Pie with Berries

The twist in this variation on an American classic is the peach preserves, which double the peach flavor and enhance the sweetness—a deeply southern idea.

Pastry with Vegetable Shortening
5 cups sliced peeled fresh peaches (about
   8 or 9 peaches)
Juice of 1 lemon
¼ cup peach preserves
¾ cup packed dark brown sugar
¼ cup all-purpose flour
¼ teaspoon ground cinnamon
2 cups raspberries or blueberries
2 tablespoons (¼ stick) unsalted butter
Milk
Granulated sugar

Prepare the pie crust. Preheat the oven to 400° F.

In a large bowl, mix the peaches, lemon juice, and jam. Fold in the brown sugar, flour, and cinnamon. Turn half the fruit into the prepared pie pastry. Sprinkle with the berries, cover with the remaining half of the peach mixture, and dot with butter. Cover the pie with the top crust, seal and flute the edges, and cut slits in the top. Brush the crust with milk and sprinkle with granulated sugar.

Bake 45 to 60 minutes, or until the crust is brown and juice is bubbling through the slits.

Makes 8 servings

Pastry with Vegetable Shortening

2 cups all-purpose flour
1 teaspoon salt
1⅓ cups shortening
Ice water to mix (about ⅔ cup)

Sift the flour and salt together in a bowl. Cut in shortening with a pastry cutter or 2 knives. Or very quickly work together with your hands. Stir in enough ice water to mix and absorb the flour. Do not handle. Wrap the dough in plastic wrap and chill 1 hour or more. Divide the dough into 2 equal parts and roll out on a floured surface to a thickness of about ¼ inch.

Makes 1 10-inch double-crust pie pastry

Honey Cake

Many cakes use honey as a flavoring, but this one uses it as its only source of sweetness, marking it as a descendant of early frontier treats, devised when settlers had no access to sugar.

½ cup (1 stick) unsalted butter
1½ cups honey
3 large eggs, separated
5 cups cake flour
2 teaspoons ground cinnamon
½ teaspoon salt
1½ teaspoons baking soda
2 tablespoons water
¼ cup confectioners' sugar

Preheat the oven to 350° F.

In a large mixing bowl, cream the butter and slowly add the honey until thoroughly blended. Continue beating, add the egg yolks, and beat in thoroughly. Sift together the flour, cinnamon, and salt into the egg mixture. Dissolve the baking soda in the water and add to the batter. In a separate large bowl, beat the egg whites to stiff peaks and fold into the batter.

Pour the batter into a greased and floured 9- by 12-inch baking pan and bake about 30 minutes, or until the cake springs back when pressed. Sprinkle with confectioners' sugar while warm and serve plain, or spread with Honey-Nugget Icing (recipe follows).

Honey-Nugget Icing

1 apple, peeled, cored, and grated fine
¾ cup fine-chopped hickory nuts
1 cup honey

Fold the apple and nuts into the honey and spread the icing on the cake. Serve the cake in squares, or roll up jelly-roll fashion while still warm and serve like a jelly roll.

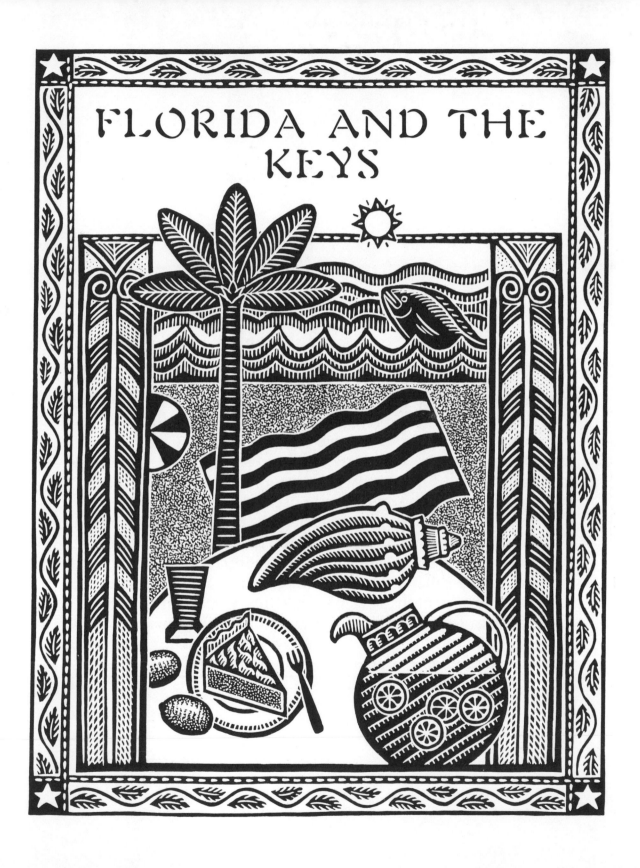

FLORIDA AND THE KEYS

I went to Florida expecting the worst: condominiums and geriatrics and not much fun. What I found was the northern end of the Caribbean island chain. The restaurants aren't up to much yet (with the exception of the incomparable, and incomparably old-fashioned, Joe's Stone Crab), but the raw materials are superb, and the mix of Cuban, Puerto Rican, and northern-expatriate cooking is wonderful. Sooner or later, all this will find its way into restaurants, and we won't have to wait to be asked to someone's house to enjoy it.

There is an almost piratical quality to southern Florida and the Keys, and a settled, southern air to the northern part of the state that makes it clear you're adjacent to Georgia—north and south Florida are two different states. The real culinary excitement is in the south because of the raw materials that aren't found anywhere else and because of the bustling crush of cultures marrying one another. The intensity of blue sky and sea, green palms, and white sand are exactly those of the Caribbean to the south, and the spicy food is designed to cope with the sullen heat that is never far off, especially in the brutal summers.

SMALL PLATES

Conch Salad

A whole school of thought believes conch is seafood-flavored rubber invented by a mean-spirited sailor. In chowders and fritters and salads, though, conch works beautifully, much as it does in scungilli.

1 pound uncooked conch, chopped fine
1 medium onion, minced
Juice of 4 limes
1 green bell pepper, minced
2 celery stalks, minced
1 cucumber, diced fine
1 garlic clove, minced
2 teaspoons Worcestershire sauce
1 tablespoon chopped fresh parsley
4 ripe tomatoes, chopped
½ teaspoon dried oregano
½ cup olive oil
Grated zest of 2 limes
2 tablespoons Tabasco
Dash of curry powder
Lettuce leaves

Combine conch, onion, and lime juice, and refrigerate at least 8 hours.

When conch has finished marinating, toss it, marinade and all, with remaining ingredients, except lettuce, and let stand 2 to 3 hours longer before serving.

When ready to serve, make a bed of lettuce leaves on a large platter or shallow bowl, then pile the Conch Salad on top. The salad is also good served in an avocado or cold poached mirliton boat with mayonnaise, or with crackers as an appetizer.

Makes 6 servings

Bollitos la Florida

This is northern Florida food, from the *Gasparilla Cookbook,* and unusual in American cooking because the beans are ground before they are cooked, so the dish has some of the texture and flavor of falafel, the Middle Eastern fried chick-pea patties.

1 pound dry black-eyed peas
2 garlic cloves
1 teaspoon salt
Soy oil for deep frying

Soak the peas overnight in water to cover. Slip the skins from the peas by rubbing them between your hands. Discard the skins, then wash and drain the peas.

In a food mill or processor fitted with a metal blade, grind the peas and garlic almost to a paste. Work in the salt, and beat until the paste has a thick cake-batter consistency. Chill 2 hours.

Heat the oil to 350° F in a large skillet. Drop the chilled paste by the tea-spoonful into the oil and cook until brown. Serve hot with Spicy Tomato Sauce or Cheese Sauce (recipes follow) for dipping.

Makes 8 servings

Spicy Tomato Sauce

½ cup fine-diced celery
½ cup fine-diced green bell pepper
½ cup fine-diced onion
2 tablespoons olive oil
2 large garlic cloves, minced
½ teaspoon dried oregano
1 teaspoon dried basil
1 teaspoon dried thyme
½ teaspoon grated lemon zest
1 teaspoon Tabasco
Salt and pepper to taste
2 cups peeled fresh tomatoes, or canned
   tomatoes, drained and chopped
Red wine

In a large skillet over medium heat, sauté the celery and green bell pepper in the olive oil until the onion is limp. Add the garlic, herbs, and lemon zest. Stir briefly and add the Tabasco, salt, and pepper. Add the tomatoes and simmer about 30 minutes, thinning with red wine if the sauce is too thick. To serve, pour the sauce over the bollitos. Or pour sauce onto serving plates and arrange bollitos on top.

Makes 2½ cups

Cheese Sauce

2 cups White Sauce (see page 45)
⅔ cup grated sharp cheddar cheese
1 teaspoon dry mustard
1 teaspoon Tabasco
1 teaspoon Worcestershire sauce
Salt and pepper to taste
½ cup chopped scallions or minced pickled
   jalapeños

In a medium saucepan, heat the White Sauce and stir in the cheddar cheese. Stir constantly over low heat until the cheese melts. Add the mustard and the other seasonings. When ready to serve, add the scallions or jalapeños and stir in. Pour the sauce over the bollitos. Or pour sauce onto serving plates and arrange bollitos on top.

Makes 2 cups

S O U P S

Verzada (Green Soup)

Verzada, a very rich and deep version of bean soup with sausage and greens, works especially well as a first course before cold fish.

½ cup dried Great Northern beans
2 quarts water
1 ham shank bone
1 ham hock
1 pound beef short ribs
1 bay leaf
1 teaspoon salt
2 unpeeled red potatoes, diced
1 bunch collard greens, chopped
1 tablespoon bacon grease
½ large onion, chopped
½ green bell pepper, chopped
½ pound morzilla (blood sausage), cut into 3 pieces

Soak the beans overnight in water to cover. In a heavy 6-quart pot, combine the water, ham shank bone, ham hock, short ribs, bay leaf, and salt. Bring to a boil, then lower the heat and simmer 1 hour, skimming foam as necessary. Drain and rinse the beans, then add to the pot and cook until tender, about 1 hour longer. Add the potatoes and collard greens. In a large skillet over medium heat, melt the bacon fat and sauté the onion, pepper, and sausage until the onion and pepper are soft.

Add the sausage mixture to the soup base and cook, uncovered, 10 minutes. When the potatoes are done and collard greens are tender, the soup is ready to serve.

Makes 3 quarts

Grouper Soup

Grouper, firm with large flakes, has the proper texture for soup. The corn and tomatoes give this dish a lightness that works very well in hot weather.

¼ cup olive oil
2 medium yellow onions, chopped
4 garlic cloves, minced
2 celery stalks, chopped
1 green bell pepper, chopped
4 large ripe tomatoes, peeled and
    chopped
2 quarts Fish Stock (recipe follows)
2 tablespoons chopped fresh parsley
4 bay leaves
1 tablespoon dried basil
1 teaspoon dried oregano
1 curl orange zest
Salt and pepper
Tabasco
Corn kernels, freshly cut from 4 cobs
4 unpeeled medium potatoes, diced
4 pounds grouper, skinned, boned, and
    cubed

In a large stockpot, heat the olive oil over medium heat and sauté the onion, garlic, celery, pepper, and tomatoes. Add the rest of the ingredients except the corn, potatoes, and fish. Simmer 1 hour. Add the corn, potatoes, and fish, and simmer 30 minutes, or until the potatoes are tender.

Remove the bay leaves and orange zest. Serve the soup with a drizzle of olive oil in each bowl, accompanied by Garlic Toast (recipe follows).

Makes 3½ quarts

Fish Stock

Remember that fish stock, unlike other stocks, can be boiled (it is made with white fish and has no oil to spoil the stock), but be careful not to overcook it: Fish stocks begin to taste musty and tired if cooked more than an hour.

2 pounds heads and bones of white fish, such
*   as flounder, tilefish, bass, or snapper*
1 large onion, chopped coarse
½ bunch celery, with leaves, chopped coarse
2 bay leaves
½ bunch fresh parsley
1 cup canned tomatoes and their juice or
*   1 large fresh tomato*
1 sprig tarragon
Handful cracked black peppercorns
1 curl lemon zest

Combine the ingredients in a large stockpot with water to cover by 2 inches. Bring to a boil over high heat. Lower the heat to medium and boil gently 1 hour. Strain and use at once, refrigerate up to 3 days, or freeze up to 3 months.

Makes 1 gallon

Garlic Toast

Preheat the oven to 400° F.

Slice French bread ½ inch thick and brush the slices with olive oil. Place the slices on a cookie sheet and bake until brown at the edges. Remove the toast from the oven and spread each slice with a mixture of minced garlic, chopped fresh parsley, and oregano. Return to oven 3 minutes.

SALADS

Sunshine State Salad

Floridians believe they invented the orange, and it's all right with me if they persist in this illusion as long as they go on growing them. Here, nutmeg and sour cream smooth the orange's acid edge and make it very suave.

4 oranges, peeled and sectioned
1 tablespoon Cointreau (orange-flavored
    liqueur)
Juice of 1 lemon
½ cup sour cream
Dash of ground nutmeg
Lettuce leaves

In a large mixing bowl, toss the oranges with the Cointreau and lemon juice. Marinate the fruit 2 hours, refrigerated. Mix the sour cream with the nutmeg.

Serve the orange slices on lettuce leaves with a dollop of sour cream on each serving.

Makes 4 servings

Shipboard Salad

This salad—called *picnic salad* in the interior of the country—is made to travel. It's crunchy, rich, and a testament to the usefulness of much-maligned iceberg lettuce, which is ideal when you want crunch, moisture, and a long shelf life.

1 large head iceberg lettuce, cut into chunks
1 large cucumber, peeled, seeded, and shredded
3 celery stalks, shredded
1 package frozen peas, thawed and drained
1 onion, cut into quarters and sliced very thin
1½ cups Lemony Mayonnaise (see page 4)
⅓ cup grated Parmesan cheese
8 slices bacon, fried crisp and crumbled
20 cherry tomatoes, halved
2 tablespoons chopped fresh parsley

In a 2-quart glass bowl or plastic container with a tight lid, layer the lettuce and the other vegetables, except the tomatoes, in the order given. Spread the mayonnaise on top of the vegetables, and sprinkle the Parmesan cheese and bacon on top. Pave the top of the salad with the tomatoes, cut side up. Sprinkle with parsley and cover tightly.

Chill the salad at least 2 hours, or overnight. When ready to serve, toss all the ingredients in the bowl or container until well mixed. Serve on small plates.

Makes 8 servings

MAIN COURSES

Bolichi

This Cuban pot roast owes its rich flavor to the chorizo sausage it's stuffed with.

4 pounds beef eye-of-round
1 chorizo, about 4 ounces, chopped
1 6-ounce slice smoked ham, chopped
1 large garlic clove, minced
1 medium onion, chopped
½ large green bell pepper, chopped
Salt and pepper
1 tablespoon paprika
3 tablespoons bacon grease
1 cup hot water
½ pound suet, sliced
1 bay leaf
4 whole cloves
4 large Maine potatoes, peeled and
  sliced

Preheat the oven to 325° F.

Cut a lengthwise slit in the side of the beef and form a pocket using your fingers. Mix the sausage, ham, garlic, onion, and bell pepper and stuff the beef. Use a skewer to close the pocket. Salt and pepper the roast all over and sprinkle with paprika.

In a large skillet, brown the roast in the bacon fat, turning often until the meat is a dark mahogany color. Add the hot water, scraping the bottom of the pan well.

Place the meat in a large roasting pan, cover with the suet, and add the bay leaf and cloves. Cover the roast and bake about 3 hours. Baste and turn every 40 minutes or so to ensure even cooking. In the last 30 minutes, add the sliced potatoes and cook until both potatoes and roast are tender.

Makes 8 servings

Pompano en Papillote

½ cup fine-chopped shallots

2 tablespoons (¼ stick) unsalted butter, plus additional

2 tablespoons heavy cream

1 cup Fish Stock (see page 102)

½ cup white vermouth

½ teaspoon lemon juice

Salt and pepper to taste

¼ teaspoon cayenne pepper

1 cup peeled uncooked shrimp, chopped fine

½ cup lump crabmeat, picked over

4 large sheets parchment, or 4 medium brown paper bags

4 8-ounce pompano fillets, skinned and boned

In a small saucepan over medium heat, sauté the shallots in the butter until transparent. Add the cream and reduce until thick and bubbly. Add the fish stock, vermouth, lemon juice, salt, pepper, and cayenne. Remove the sauce from the heat and stir in the shrimp and crabmeat.

Preheat the oven to 350° F.

Cut each sheet of parchment paper in half and into a 10-inch circle. Butter each circle (or butter the insides of the paper bags well). Place each fillet on a parchment circle or in a paper bag and top with sauce. Place a second parchment circle on top of each fillet and crimp the edges with small turns (or fold over the openings of the paper bags) to seal completely.

Place the packets on an oiled cookie sheet and bake 40 minutes, if using paper bags. If using parchment, bake 30 minutes, then increase the heat to 450° F until the parchment puffs up and turns light brown, about 10 minutes more. Cut open the packets at the table with a sharp knife.

Makes 4 servings

Creamed Smoked Turkey with Wild Rice Pilaf

A dish from northern Florida happily based on cream sauce, like many from the southern states.

3 tablespoons unsalted butter, melted
3 tablespoons all-purpose flour
1 cup chopped mushrooms
½ cup chopped celery
⅓ cup chopped pimiento
2 cups diced smoked turkey
2 cups scalded milk
1 teaspoon Worcestershire sauce
Heavy dash of Tabasco
Salt and pepper to taste

In a large skillet over medium-low heat, stir the flour into hot melted butter and cook slowly 5 minutes. Add the vegetables and cook until the celery is beginning to soften. Add the turkey and stir briefly, then add the scalded milk and cook just until the sauce is thickened. Add the seasonings and stir to blend.

Serve over hot Wild Rice Pilaf (recipe follows).

Makes 4 to 6 servings

Wild Rice Pilaf

This is not a true pilaf but cooked rice mixed with raw vegetables. The crisp surprise of the carrot and celery has made customers ask me what exotic things I put into it.

2½ cups water
1 teaspoon salt
3 slices gingerroot
2 cups wild rice
¼ cup (½ stick) unsalted butter
1 teaspoon Tabasco
1 large carrot, diced fine
2 celery ribs, diced fine
1 onion, diced fine

In a large saucepan over high heat, boil the water with the salt and gingerroot. Rinse the wild rice, then add to saucepan and stir. Reduce the heat to medium. Simmer until the wild rice begins to swell and split, about 30 minutes.

Meanwhile, in another saucepan, melt the butter and add the Tabasco. Remove butter from the heat and add the vegetables, but do not cook.

When the rice is done, stir in the vegetables and toss to mix. Remove the gingerroot slices before serving.

Makes 8 to 10 servings

Black Bottom Pie

This and the following recipe are from a wonderful resource for early Florida cooking, *Cross Creek Cookery,* by Marjorie Kinnan Rawlings. When Ms. Rawlings left New York to settle in northern Florida, she embraced the culture—and her cookbook is the most obvious fruit of her long residence and happy immersion in the life of her adopted state.

Crust
14 ginger snaps, crushed fine
5 tablespoons unsalted butter, melted

Preheat the oven to 350° F.

Mix the ginger snap crumbs with the butter and press the mixture evenly into a 9-inch pie tin. Bake 10 minutes to set.

Basic Filling
1 tablespoon unflavored gelatin
4 tablespoons cold water
1¾ cups milk
½ cup sugar
1 tablespoon cornstarch
Pinch of salt
4 large egg yolks, beaten

To make the basic filling, soak the gelatin in the water. In the top half of a double boiler, scald the milk. Mix the sugar with the cornstarch, then add to the milk with the salt. Stir in the egg yolks. Cook, stirring constantly, until the custard thickens and coats the back of a wooden spoon. Stir in the dissolved gelatin. Divide the custard in half.

Chocolate Layer
2 1-ounce squares semisweet chocolate, melted
1 teaspoon vanilla extract

To make the chocolate layer, stir the melted chocolate and vanilla into half the custard. Turn into the cooled crust while hot, pouring carefully so as not to disturb the crust.

Rum-Flavored Layer

4 large egg whites
⅛ teaspoon cream of tartar
½ cup sugar
1 tablespoon dark rum

To make the rum layer, cool the remaining half of the custard. In a large mixing bowl, beat the egg whites until stiff with the cream of tartar, and slowly add the sugar. Fold the whites into the cooled custard and stir in the rum. Carefully spread the rum filling over the chocolate layer.

Place the pie in the refrigerator and chill thoroughly, overnight if desired.

Topping

1 cup heavy cream
2 tablespoons confectioners' sugar
Grated bitter or semisweet chocolate

When ready to serve, whip the cream, slowly adding the confectioners' sugar, until stiff. Pile the cream over the top of the pie and sprinkle with chocolate.

Makes 8 servings

Tangerine Sherbet

Tangerines are as common in Florida as oranges—and their flavor is ravishing. Of this sherbet Marjorie Kinnan Rawlings wrote, "My friends cry for it."

1 cup sugar
1 cup water
Grated rind of 4 tangerines
4 cups tangerine juice (from about 40 tangerines)
Juice of 2 lemons

In a large saucepan boil the sugar and water together 10 minutes. Add the tangerine rind to the hot syrup. Allow the syrup to cool slightly, then add the tangerine and lemon juices. Taste for sweetness and acidity, as tangerines vary, and adjust with more sugar or lemon juice. Chill the syrup thoroughly, strain, and freeze in an ice-cream maker according to manufacturer's instructions.

Makes 1 quart

Key Lime Pie

The original Key Lime Pie recipe used a traditional short crust. When I tried the graham cracker crust, I was an instant convert.

Graham Cracker Crust

5 tablespoons unsalted butter, melted
1½ cups graham cracker crumbs

Preheat the oven to 350° F.

Stir the butter into the graham cracker crumbs, and evenly press the mixture into a 10-inch pie tin. Bake 10 minutes, or until the crust is set. Leave oven setting at 350° F.

Filling

1 8-ounce can sweetened condensed milk
6 large eggs, separated
½ cup Key lime juice
Grated zest of 1 Key lime
1 tablespoon cream of tartar
1 cup sugar

Using a wire whisk or electric beater, whip the milk and egg yolks together in a large mixing bowl until light and creamy. Add the lime juice and zest and beat until thoroughly blended, about 1 minute. Pour the lime mixture into the pie shell.

In another large mixing bowl, beat the egg whites with the cream of tartar, and gradually add the sugar until the whites stand in high, dry peaks. Spread the meringue on top of the pie filling and pull into peaks with a spatula.

Bake just until the meringue is brown, about 15 minutes. Cool the pie and serve with whipped cream flavored with Midori (melon liqueur).

Makes 8 servings

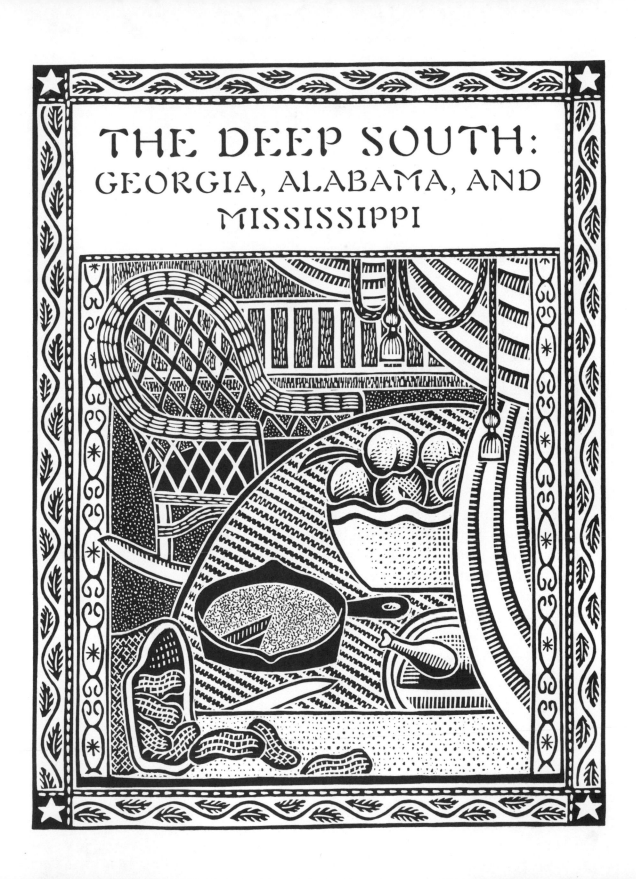

THE DEEP SOUTH:
GEORGIA, ALABAMA, AND MISSISSIPPI

The culinary history of the South is marked, though this is not always acknowledged, by black people cooking for white people. Blacks brought with them from Africa a huge legacy of ingredients and techniques never before seen in the Western world. They obliged their white masters' demands for white food, but with ingenious alterations. From the English tradition, Southerners inherited white sauces, jelled and marinated cold vegetable mélanges, and large pieces of meat—poultry, hams, roasts—but these simple (and often dull) basic ingredients were transformed by black geniuses of the kitchen into a cookery full of spice and vinegar and dark greens and okra and garlic and peanuts and sweet potatoes.

Dreams of integration were realized in the kitchens of the South years and years before social integration could take place, and the southern accent in food—like the southern accent in speech—has always been a happy combination of black and white.

SMALL PLATES

Seafood with Alabama Cocktail Sauce

Southerners like variety at table: Any seafood in this dish would strike a Georgian as dull indeed if used on its own, just as the sauce would seem lacking in depth without the anchovy. In this part of the country, more is more.

2 cups Basic Homemade Mayonnaise
   (see page 4)
1 fine-chopped hard-boiled egg
1 cup ketchup
1 tablespoon Worcestershire sauce
1 tablespoon fresh-grated horseradish
2 teaspoons Tabasco
Juice of 1 lemon
1 anchovy, mashed
1 tablespoon chopped fresh parsley
Pepper to taste
4 cups cooked cleaned shrimp, clams,
   lobster meat, and crawfish tails

Stir together the mayonnaise and egg in a small bowl, and gradually mix in the other ingredients except the seafood.

Arrange the seafood on a platter and serve with the sauce, for dipping.

Makes 8 servings

Cayenne Pecans with Cheese Balls

What we have here is cocktail food, perfect with bourbon and ice on the front porch (the air-conditioned front porch) on a summer day. But this kind of food also satisfies the southern craving for "a little something"—a bite, a taste, just a snack to nibble on in the late morning with lemonade, or in the middle of the afternoon with coffee, or even late at night when you can't sleep but something tells you that you just might be able to choke down a bite or two.

¼ cup (½ stick) unsalted butter
¼ cup soy oil
1 pound pecan halves
1½ teaspoons salt
1 teaspoon cayenne pepper

Preheat the oven to 350° F.

In a large saucepan over medium heat, melt the butter in the oil. Add the pecan halves and toss. Spread the pecans on a cookie sheet in a single layer, and bake until golden brown, about 15 minutes, checking frequently to make sure the pecans do not burn. Toss the nuts with salt and cayenne, then spread on paper towels to absorb any excess oil. Pile the cooled pecans in the middle of a platter and surround with Cheese Balls (recipe follows).

Makes 8 to 12 servings

Cheese Balls

1½ cups fine-grated cheddar cheese
3 large egg whites, beaten until stiff
  but not dry
Fine dry bread crumbs
2 large egg yolks, lightly beaten
3 cups soy oil

Fold the cheese into the egg whites. Drop the mixture by the teaspoonful into the bread crumbs and roll each puff into a ball. (This is a delicate business. Use two dessert spoons.) Dip the balls in the egg yolks and then again into the crumbs.

Heat oil to 375° F in a large skillet. Fry the balls until golden.

Makes 2 dozen

SOUPS

Charles Kahlstrom's Peanut Soup

By now most southerners probably eat a lot of their peanuts just as other Americans do—as peanut butter. But peanut soup is, undoubtedly, a much more elegant way to deal with a goober. Charles Kahlstrom is the invaluable day chef at Miss Ruby's. His soups and stews are legendary.

½ cup (1 stick) unsalted butter
4 tablespoons all-purpose flour
½ cup fine-chopped onion
½ cup fine-chopped celery
1½ cups natural peanut butter
6 cups hot Chicken Stock (see page 28)
1½ teaspoons salt
½ teaspoon pepper
½ teaspoon cayenne pepper
1 cup heavy cream

Garnish
½ cup fine-chopped unsalted roasted
   peanuts
Paprika

Melt the butter in a large heavy saucepan over medium heat and whisk in the flour. Continue whisking 4 or 5 minutes, then stir in the onion and celery and lower the heat. Cook until the onion is soft, taking care not to brown the flour.

Remove the saucepan from the heat, add the peanut butter, and stir in thoroughly. Gradually stir in the chicken stock, salt, pepper, and cayenne. Return to the heat and bring to a boil, stirring, then simmer for 20 minutes.

Strain the peanut mixture and add the cream, stirring thoroughly. Bring the soup briefly to a simmer, then serve sprinkled with peanuts and paprika.

Makes 8 servings

Georgia Peach Soup

This is wonderful stuff—like many southern fruit-based preparations, it is not at all sweet but very peachy.

2 tablespoons (¼ cup) unsalted butter
1 tablespoon minced scallions, green and
    white parts
1 tablespoon fine-chopped celery
1 tablespoon fine-chopped fresh parsley
1 tablespoon all-purpose flour
2 cups Chicken Stock (see page 28)
4 cups thin-sliced peeled peaches
⅛ teaspoon dried thyme
¼ teaspoon ground allspice
¼ teaspoon fresh-ground pepper
2 cups light cream
4 tablespoons peach schnapps

Garnish
½ cup whipped cream
2 tablespoons toasted slivered almonds

Heat the butter in a large heavy saucepan over medium heat and sauté the scallions, celery, and parsley until golden. Sprinkle with flour and cook, stirring, 4 minutes. Add the stock, peaches, thyme, allspice, and pepper. Bring the fruit mixture to a boil and simmer gently 30 minutes.

Purée the soup. Run in a food processor fitted with a metal blade, then strain through a china cap strainer. Add cream and reheat. Stir in schnapps and serve at once. Or chill well and serve with the whipped cream and toasted almonds as garnish.

Makes 8 servings

SALADS

Pickled Black-Eyed Peas

I love black-eyed peas as a side dish, with rice in Hopping John as a main course, and with fine-chopped greens in ham stock as a soup. But they're never exactly refreshing—except in this salad, a good thing to eat standing in front of the refrigerator.

2 cups dried black-eyed peas
4 cups water
1 bay leaf
1 small onion, quartered
2 celery stalks with leaves
2 whole garlic cloves
1 teaspoon salt
½ cup fine-diced celery
½ cup fine-diced onion
½ cup fine-diced pimiento
¼ cup fine-diced California black olives
1 tablespoon small capers, drained
½ cup Mustard-Garlic Vinaigrette
    (recipe follows)
Strong dash of Tabasco
8 lettuce leaves
4 fresh tomatoes, sliced

Soak the peas overnight in water to cover. Rinse the peas, then add the water, bay leaf, quartered onion, celery stalks, garlic, and salt. Cook the peas gently, until very tender but not broken, adding water as necessary if the peas get dry.

Allow the peas to cool slightly, then toss with the diced vegetables, olives, capers, vinaigrette, and Tabasco. Chill and serve on lettuce leaves with tomato slices.

Makes 10 servings

Mustard-Garlic Vinaigrette

⅓ cup cider vinegar
1 garlic clove, minced
2 teaspoons dry mustard
Salt and pepper to taste
1 cup olive oil

Combine vinegar, garlic, mustard, salt, and pepper. Beat in olive oil a few drops at a time to form an emulsion.

Makes 1½ cups

Daisy's Chicken Salad

From a great black cook of Alabama comes this very rich chicken salad. Serve it on a chiffonade of lettuce with tomato slices and you'll have an echo of a BLT that's a special pleasure.

3 cups chopped cooked chicken
1 cup chopped celery
½ cup pecan pieces
½ cup halved green grapes
3 hard-boiled eggs, chopped
Salt and pepper to taste
1½ cups Lemony Mayonnaise
   (see page 4)

Garnish
1 pound bacon, fried crisp and crumbled
10 scallion tops, chopped fine

Toss together all the ingredients lightly but thoroughly. Serve the salad sprinkled with the bacon and scallions.

Makes 6 servings

MAIN COURSES

Braised Short Ribs

A good bit of southern cooking is so simple it's almost simpleminded. A restaurant-trained cook might almost be convinced that it has to be added to, tricked up, or decked out just to make it interesting enough to get on the menu. This is a perfect example. Take my word for it: These ribs don't need a thing but a starch to soak up the gravy and greens to foil their richness.

¼ pound suet
1 cup all-purpose flour
Salt and pepper
3 pounds beef short ribs
4 cups Beef Stock (see page 160)

Garnish
Parsley sprigs

Preheat the oven to 375° F.

Cut the suet into small pieces and render the fat in a large heavy casserole set over medium heat. Lift out the browned suet pieces and reserve.

Stir together the flour, salt, and pepper, dredge the ribs in the mixture, and lay in the hot fat. Cook, uncovered, in the oven about 1 hour, stirring and turning so the ribs brown evenly.

Pour off the excess fat and add the beef stock. Cover tightly and return to the oven. Cook 1½ hours, or until the beef is almost falling from the bones. Return the suet cracklings to the pot.

Serve the ribs on noodles, mashed potatoes, or rice, garnish with parsley, and complete the plate with Collard Greens (see page 152).

Makes 4 servings

Roast Chicken with Corn Bread Dressing

This heart-breakingly good recipe is almost the national dish of the South; the stuffing is an everyday treat with chicken, a holiday specialty with turkey, and a great comfort as leftovers—with chicken bits and stuffing in the icebox, there's never any reason to despair.

1 large (7 to 8 pound) roasting chicken
Salt and pepper to taste
6 cups chopped hot fresh Corn Bread
    (recipe follows)
1 cup fresh corn kernels
½ cup chopped green bell pepper
½ cup chopped pimiento and juice
⅔ cup chopped onion
⅔ cup chopped celery
¼ cup chopped fresh parsley
2 teaspoons chopped fresh thyme, plus
    additional
1 teaspoon chopped fresh sage, plus
    additional
2 garlic cloves, chopped
4 cups Chicken Stock (see page 28)
2 strong dashes of Tabasco
1 teaspoon Worcestershire sauce
¼ cup (½ stick) unsalted butter, melted
3 tablespoons all-purpose flour
1 bay leaf
1 celery stalk
1 cup light cream

Preheat the oven to 400° F.

Remove and reserve the body fat from the chicken and salt and pepper inside and out. In a large bowl, toss the Corn Bread, corn kernels, chopped vegetables, herbs, garlic, salt, and pepper together. Moisten lightly (the dressing should not be gummy) with the stock and stir in the Tabasco and Worcestershire sauce.

Stuff the cavity of the chicken with the bread mixture and truss. Butter a 9-inch square cake pan and pile the remaining stuffing into it. Top with melted butter.

Set the chicken on a rack inside a roasting pan, top with the body fat, and bake 1½ to 2 hours, turning on one side after about 30 minutes and to the other after about 1 hour. When the fat from a pierced thigh runs yellow, remove the chicken from the oven and let stand 30 minutes.

While the chicken is resting, put the pan of stuffing in the oven to warm, and the chicken-roasting pan over medium heat on top of the stove. Stir the juices in the roasting pan from the bottom, tip the pan, then skim off all but 3 tablespoons fat. Add the flour and stir. When the flour is dark and peanut-butter colored, add 3 cups stock and stir briskly from the bottom. Simmer, and while simmering, add the bay leaf, celery stalk, and a sprinkle of thyme and sage. Simmer until the gravy is slightly viscous, or bubbling heavily. Strain the gravy into a saucepan, and add the cream. Stir, then season with salt and pepper. Remove the pan of dressing from the oven after 20 minutes, or when the edges turn crusty and brown.

Carve the chicken. Remove the dressing from the cavity and serve with the gravy. Pass the extra dressing for second helpings.

Makes 4 to 6 servings

Corn Bread

2 cups yellow cornmeal
2 cups all-purpose flour
2 tablespoons baking powder
1 teaspoon salt
2 cups fresh corn kernels
1 cup corn oil
5 large eggs
1 quart milk

Preheat the oven to 400° F.

Sift the cornmeal, flour, baking powder, and salt together in a large mixing bowl, and add the corn. Beat together ½ cup of the oil, the eggs, and the milk. Stir into the dry ingredients, mixing thoroughly.

In a 10-inch round cast-iron pan, heat the remaining oil until almost smoking. Pour in the batter and at once place the pan in the hot oven. Bake 20 to 30 minutes, or until the top is lightly browned and a knife inserted in the center comes out clean. Turn the corn bread out on a board and slice, or cool and use for stuffing.

Makes 8 to 10 servings

DESSERTS

Peach Cobbler

8 large peaches
⅔ cup packed light brown sugar
½ teaspoon almond extract
2 tablespoons (¼ stick) butter, melted
1 cup plus 1 tablespoon all-purpose flour
½ teaspoon salt
6 tablespoons sugar
1 teaspoon ground nutmeg
¼ cup (½ stick) unsalted butter
¼ cup plus 2 tablespoons milk
Heavy cream

Preheat the oven to 375° F.

Peel, stone, and slice the peaches and toss with the brown sugar, almond extract, melted butter, and 1 tablespoon of the flour. Sift together the cup of flour, salt, sugar, and nutmeg, then cut in the butter with a pastry knife or your fingers until it is the consistency of fine cornmeal. Stir in the milk, adding as much as you need to form a soft dough.

Pour the peach mixture into a 6- by 8-inch shallow pan and pat the dough onto the top, to a thickness of about ¾ inch. Bake about 45 minutes, or until golden brown with peach bubbles showing at the edges. Serve warm with heavy cream.

Makes 8 servings

Lane Cake

People all over the country dread the onset of the Christmas holidays because they will almost certainly be given a fruitcake or two and then will have to figure out a way to dispose of it. This is not true in the South, where most people actually like to eat fruitcake and will, in fact, invent recipes that make leavened cakes taste like fruitcake—hence the popularity of Lane Cake.

Cake

3½ cups all-purpose flour
Pinch of salt
2 teaspoons baking powder
1 cup (2 sticks) unsalted butter, softened
2 cups sugar
1 cup milk
1 teaspoon vanilla extract
8 large egg whites, beaten until stiff

Preheat the oven to 375° F.

Sift together the flour, salt, and baking powder 6 times. In a large mixing bowl, cream the butter and sugar together until fluffy. Add the flour mixture and milk to the butter and sugar alternately in small batches, beginning and ending with the flour. Add the vanilla and fold in the egg whites.

Pour the batter into 4 greased and floured 8-inch layer cake pans that have been lined with greased brown paper or parchment. Bake the layers 30 minutes. Let the cake layers cool on racks 10 minutes, then turn out to cool thoroughly.

Filling

8 large egg yolks
1 cup sugar
Pinch of salt
½ cup (1 stick) unsalted butter
1 cup dark raisins, chopped
1½ cups freshly grated coconut
1 cup chopped pecans
1 cup brandy
1 teaspoon vanilla extract

Beat the egg yolks until lemony, then add the sugar and salt, and continue beating until the mixture is cream

colored. In a large saucepan, melt the butter over very low heat, then beat in the egg mixture, alternately on and off the heat, until the mixture thickens. Stir in raisins, coconut, pecans, brandy, and vanilla.

When both filling and cake are cool, spread the filling between the layers of cake. Ice the cake with Seven-Minute Icing (see page 58).

Makes 8 to 10 servings

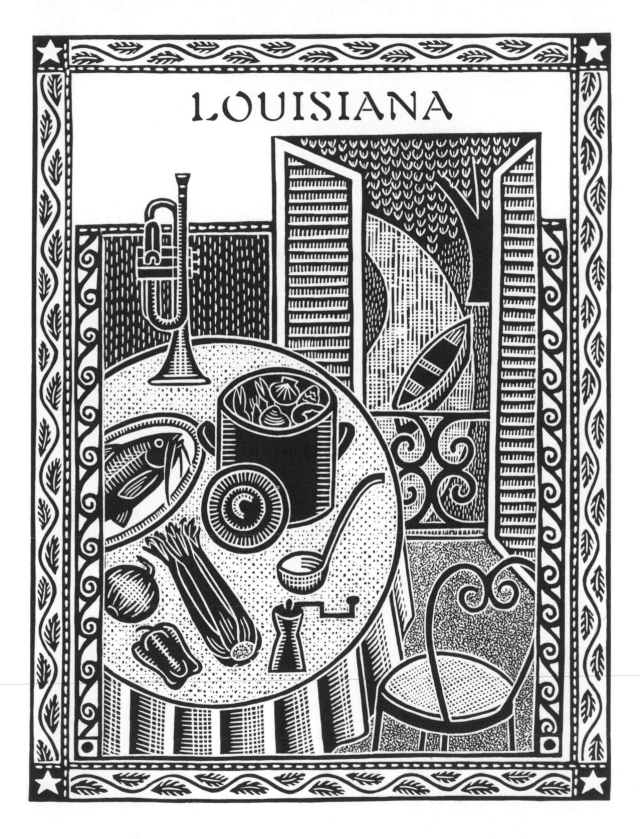

LOUISIANA

My introduction to Louisiana was from across the border in Texas. My grandmother had been raised in Franklin and in Lake Charles, Louisiana, and believed in the innate superiority of all things Louisianan to things Texan. She told me shamelessly that I need never admit that I was born in Texas; I simply could say my people were from Louisiana. She herself went back to Franklin every summer to be photographed under a family-historical oak tree, just to demonstrate her true origins.

The upshot of this propaganda was that I had a romance with Louisiana long before I visited the state. I believed that the bayous weren't swampy; that the Gulf Coast somehow produced better weather around the bend in Plaquemines Parish; and that the food was spicier, broader, and deeper in flavor than anything we had at home.

I was right about the food. At home, my grandmother adapted Creole and Cajun recipes to the milder and less sophisticated tastes of Texans. In Louisiana, I discovered that the spicy hotness of five or six peppers; the complexity of celery, onion, and sweet pepper used as background in practically every sauce; and the powerful flavor of roux cooked light tan to blue-black informed the cooking in completely different ways from those I'd been taught at home.

Texans have no one kitchen: They'll eat anything that tastes good, and their culinary culture is so young that it doesn't subsume, only gathers what it acquires. In Louisiana the willingness to cook and eat anything edible is firmly grounded in a complex but homogeneous cuisine that was set at least 150 years ago—as various in its origins as any cookery in the country but joined and braided together early enough that it's hard now to see its distinct aspects. Surely, though, we can find three or four quite easily: The terminology is French, from the Acadians who moved to Louisiana from Nova Scotia and from the Creoles who arrived from the French Caribbean islands. Many of the ingredients (okra) and some of the techniques (the blackening of roux, the extensive use of greens, the great one-pot stews) are African in origin. The spices and heat, the assumptions that complexity is better than simplicity and that more is definitely more are island based.

The terminology makes clear both the French origins of much Louisiana cooking and just how far from the French source the Creole and Cajun cuisines have come. Sometimes it's as if Louisianans are playing conscious jokes on the classic language of French cuisine. To give you some idea of how this works and a sense of the terms as used in Louisiana, here is a short glossary.

Andouille A spicy, garlicky pork sausage. Its heat differs with the maker; some andouille is a lot like kielbasa, some others have a distinct kick. An ingredient in gumbo, jambalaya, and red beans and rice, andouille is also grilled on its own.

Court Bouillon Pronounced *coobayon*. A spicy, tomato based red sauce with green bell peppers, onions, and celery, flavored with thyme, garlic, Worcestershire sauce, and Tabasco. Sometime used as a base for a soup of the same name. No relation to the classic French poaching liquid.

Étouffée Literally, "stuffed" in French. In Louisiana, refers almost always to a sauce, roux-based, tomato-enriched, and stuffed with good things, as in crawfish etouffée.

Hollandaise The Louisiana version is similar to the French, but it is often tan with Worcestershire sauce, flecked with thyme and basil, and hot with cayenne. Watch out.

The "Holy Trinity" Green peppers, celery, and onions in combination are found in almost every Louisiana sauce, and turn up in other dishes as well. When we make Cajun food at Miss Ruby's, the day begins with chopping gallons of each vegetable.

Rémoulade A sauce of minced peppers, onions, and celery thickened with mashed hard-boiled egg yolks, enriched with oil, and flavored with garlic, paprika, lemon juice, and cayenne. Not mayonnaise based, like the French sauce.

Roux Until the recent wave of nouvelle cooking made simple reductions so popular, many of the great French sauces were thickened and stabilized with roux—flour and butter cooked together until the flour is permeated with the fat and thoroughly cooked. In classic French cooking, meat stocks, milk, or cream are then stirred into the roux to form sauces: béchamel, velouté, suprême. In Louisiana, roux is not so much a thickening agent as a flavoring element—the lighter the roux, the milder the flavor. The darkest blue-black roux has almost no thickening power (the burned flour molecules can't absorb liquid) but is very powerful. Blue-black roux tastes burned but rich and combines with the classic ingredients of gumbo to produce an idiosyncratic but delicious flavor. Louisiana roux are almost never thinned with stocks; water is used because the strong flavors of the roux and other ingredients make stocks almost irrelevant. David Fetherolf, a droll man and a good cook, once said that hearing two Cajuns talk about company coming must be really odd: "Dey'll be heah in a couple hours, Gaston. You boil the water and I'll boin the flour."

Scallions These are everywhere. Scallions are tossed into sauces to augment onions and used for color against white preparations. They are an ever-present garnish, too. Only Szechuan cooking uses more scallions.

Shallots In Louisiana, always a synonym for scallions or green onions. Until recently, none of the fat little brown bulbs known as shallots everywhere else were available.

Tasso A spiced smoked ham mostly used for flavoring. Paul Prudhomme makes tasso that is covered with one of his pepper powders; it's very good, but the more traditional version is smoothly smoked and very pungent.

Thyme Basil, oregano, and many other herbs, too, find their way into Louisiana cooking, but thyme is queen; its flavor dominates.

Vin de Marchand A New Orleans version of the wine-enriched beef sauce, packed with minced tasso, green peppers, celery, onion, garlic, tomato, thyme, basil, and a touch of vinegar. A long way from Paris.

SMALL PLATES

Lucy-Mama's Scalloped Oysters

This may have been the first dish that convinced me food was more than simple nourishment; as my grandmother Lucy Tucker Adams cooked it, the dish was a tribute to the family, to the holidays (scalloped oysters were a mainstay of Christmas Eve), and to the oyster itself. In Texas we took oysters for granted, but Louisianans see them as a staff of life.

1 quart shucked Gulf oysters and their liquid
30 saltine crackers
½ cup (1 stick) unsalted butter
½ cup chopped fresh parsley
¾ cup chopped scallions, white and green parts
½ pint heavy cream
1 tablespoon Worcestershire sauce
2 teaspoons Tabasco
Salt and pepper to taste

Preheat the oven to 425° F. Butter an 8-inch pie plate.

Strain the oysters and reserve the liquid. Crush the saltines into medium crumbs. In a large skillet over medium heat, melt ⅔ of the butter until foamy. Add ⅔ of the saltine crumbs to the melted butter and stir to distribute butter evenly. Add the parsley and scallions and toss together (the mixture should be quite dry and just browning). Add the oyster liquid and cream and simmer, stirring often, until reduced by ¼. Watch carefully. Add the oysters, Worcestershire sauce, Tabasco, salt, and pepper, and stir to mix thoroughly.

Pour the oyster mixture into the prepared pie plate. Sprinkle with remaining saltine crumbs and dot with remaining butter. Bake until bubbly, about 10 minutes.

Makes 8 servings

Grilled Andouille and Shrimp with Creole Barbecue Sauce

I love this recipe because it captures a very basic Louisiana taste—shellfish combined with smoked pork—in a wonderfully simple way. It's almost an introduction to Cajun protein.

¼ cup soy oil
1 tablespoon unsalted butter
1 medium onion, minced fine
3 large garlic cloves, minced fine
2 teaspoons dried thyme
1 teaspoon dried basil
½ teaspoon dried oregano
Pinch of ground cloves
½ teaspoon each salt and pepper
½ teaspoon cayenne pepper
1 tablespoon paprika
¼ cup Worcestershire sauce
1 tablespoon Tabasco
1 tablespoon fresh lemon juice
1 long curl lemon zest
¼ cup crushed-tomato purée
1 pound andouille sausage
1 dozen jumbo shrimp, in the shell

Garnish
*½ cup chopped scallions, green and
 white parts*

In a large skillet over medium heat, heat the soy oil and butter together until the butter melts. Add the onion and garlic and sauté gently until the onion is transparent and soft. Add the herbs and spices, Worcestershire sauce, Tabasco, lemon juice, and zest, and simmer 5 minutes. Stir in the tomato purée and simmer 5 minutes longer. Remove from the heat and cool the mixture to room temperature.

Split the andouille lengthwise. Put the andouille and shrimp in a large, shallow, nonreactive dish and pour the sauce over them. Refrigerate at least 4 hours, or overnight.

Prepare the grill and wait 5 minutes, or until the charcoal is gray. Set the grill rack at the lowest position over the coals, and cook the sausage until slightly blackened and sizzling, about 4 minutes per side. Grill the shrimp 2 minutes on each side, just until pink. Remove the shrimp from the grill immediately.

Cut the sausage into 2-inch pieces. Strain the leftover sauce into a saucepan and heat to boiling. Divide the sausage and shrimp among 4 small plates, sprinkle with scallions, and serve with the sauce on the side.

Makes 4 servings

Catfish Pâté with Crawfish Tails

This is a classic with the delicate and rich filling of crawfish as a twist. I've added a powerful red pepper sauce that you can take or leave; we love it for both color and flavor.

3 tablespoons minced scallions, white
    part only
3 tablespoons unsalted butter
3 tablespoons all-purpose flour
1 cup half-and-half
3 dashes of Peychaud bitters, or 1
    tablespoon Pernod or Ricard liqueur
½ teaspoon salt
½ teaspoon white pepper
½ teaspoon Tabasco
1 pound deep-water catfish fillets
1 tablespoon dry vermouth
1 tablespoon lemon juice
½ teaspoon grated lemon zest
4 large egg whites, beaten to soft peaks
¾ cup peeled crawfish tails
Salt and white pepper to taste

In a small saucepan over medium heat, sauté the scallions in the butter for 1 to 2 minutes, or until wilted. Stir in the flour and cook for 5 minutes, but do not allow the flour to brown. Whisk in the half-and-half, and, continuing to stir, add the bitters, salt, white pepper, and Tabasco. Cook until thick and smooth, then cool the sauce.

Preheat the oven to 350° F. Butter a 1½-quart terrine or loaf pan.

In the bowl of a food processor fitted with a metal blade or in a food mill, purée the fish with vermouth and lemon juice, then add the zest, and salt and white pepper to taste. Fold in the egg whites and cooled sauce in alternate batches, turning with a rubber spatula.

Spoon ⅔ of the fish mixture into the prepared terrine or pan. Make a trench down the center of the fish mixture and fill with the crawfish tails. Spoon the remaining fish mixture over the crawfish. Cover closely with foil. Set the terrine in a larger pan filled with boiling water and bake in the oven 1 hour, or until a knife inserted in the center of the loaf comes out clean.

Serve the pâté hot or cold with a dill or watercress garnish, or with Garlic-Pepper Sauce (recipe follows).

Makes 12 servings

Garlic-Pepper Sauce

3 tablespoons good-quality mild olive oil
2 large red bell peppers, roasted, peeled,
   seeded, and chopped
6 chili pequins
1 small onion, minced
4 large garlic cloves, minced
Salt and pepper
2 tablespoons crushed-tomato purée

In a large saucepan over high heat, warm
the olive oil and add the roasted peppers
and chiles and stir briskly. Add the onion
and garlic, lower the heat to medium, and
simmer until the onion is quite soft and
the garlic is cooked through but not
brown. Add salt and pepper to taste.

Cool the mixture slightly, then purée in
the bowl of a food processor fitted with a
metal blade, adding the tomato purée
gradually. Strain the sauce and adjust the
seasoning to taste. Serve hot or cold.

Makes 2 cups

Crawfish Pie

For the record, I have never, in forty years or so on the Louisiana border and just over the border in Texas, heard the word *crayfish.* It was always *crawfish,* and it referred to both the whole bird, so to speak, and the tails. It may be, of course, that *crawfish* is a mispronunciation of *crayfish,* or at least a local pronunciation, and that there is only one proper spelling. But until I have an authoritative reading, I'll stick to the word of my youth.

This pie is somewhat different from those of my youth, which were all two-crust with the crawfish cooked in the pie shell. Since crawfish tails come precooked these days, it seems to me a shame to cook them again. So we cook the trinity and seasonings together, add the tails, and put them into warm precooked tart shells.

4 tablespoons soy oil
½ cup all-purpose flour
1 cup chopped onions
⅓ cup chopped green bell pepper
⅓ cup chopped celery, with leaves
2 minced garlic cloves
½ cup chopped canned tomatoes, with juice
½ teaspoon each salt and pepper
½ teaspoon cayenne pepper
1 teaspoon Tabasco
1 teaspoon dried thyme
2 bunches scallions, green and white parts diced separately
2 cups Fish Stock (see page 102)
3 cups crawfish tails, thawed
½ cup chopped fresh parsley
6 prebaked 5- by 2-inch tart shells, warmed (see Meat Pie Pastry, page 123)

Garnish
Scallion brushes
Whole boiled crawfish

Heat the oil in a large heavy skillet over medium heat. Stir in the flour and continue to stir until the roux is light brown. Add the onions, green bell pepper, and celery and cook about 3 minutes. Add the garlic and cook until the vegetables are soft. Add the tomatoes and their juice and cook, stirring constantly, until everything is blended. Add all the seasonings, the white parts of the scallions, and the Fish Stock. Cook gently, partially covered, until the liquid is reduced by half. The sauce should be quite thick. Stir in crawfish and simmer 5 minutes, then add the parsley and scallion tops.

Pile the mixture into the warm pastry shells, which have been prebaked for 12 minutes in a 400° F oven until golden brown at edges. Decorate with scallion brushes or whole boiled crawfish.

Makes 6 servings

Shrimp Rémoulade

Pay no attention to what this phrase means in classic French cuisine. This recipe is a good example of the sea change French underwent when it came under the influence of Caribbean blacks, southern Anglos, and immigrant Irishmen; this *is* true New Orleans rémoulade.

Rémoulade
1 bunch scallions
2 celery stalks, including leaves
¼ bunch fresh parsley
2 garlic cloves
1 teaspoon capers, drained
6 hard-boiled egg yolks
4 tablespoons Creole mustard
5 tablespoons paprika
1 teaspoon salt
½ teaspoon pepper
4 tablespoons tarragon vinegar
5 tablespoons lemon juice
½ teaspoon grated lemon zest
1 teaspoon minced fresh basil
2 teaspoons tomato paste
1 cup olive oil

1 pound whole fresh shrimp, boiled,
   peeled, and deveined
2 cups chiffonade of Romaine lettuce

Garnish
1 scallion, 1 celery stalk, 4 sprigs fresh
   parsley, chopped fine together
Tomato slices

With a sharp heavy knife, mince together the first 5 ingredients so finely that they are almost a paste. (Sorry, this can't be done in a food processor; for some reason, the scallions and garlic go bitter when chopped this fine.) Mash the egg yolks into a fine powder and add to the minced vegetables. Stir in all the other rémoulade ingredients except the olive oil. When everything is well blended, slowly whisk in the olive oil to create an emulsion.

Toss the rémoulade with the shrimp and chill 2 hours.

When ready to serve, divide the shrimp among 4 plates lined with the Romaine chiffonade. Sprinkle with the chopped scallion, celery, and parsley. Garnish with slices of tomato.

Makes 4 servings

Natchitoches Hot Meat Pies

Pronounced *Nackatosh*. Don't ask.

Meat Pie Pastry
4 cups all-purpose flour
2 teaspoons baking powder
1 teaspoon salt
½ cup melted shortening (not oil)
2 large eggs, lightly beaten
Cold milk

Sift together the flour, baking powder and salt in a large mixing bowl. Make a well in the dry ingredients and stir in the shortening and eggs. Add enough milk to make a stiff dough. Chill at least ½ hour or up to overnight.

Meat Filling
2 tablespoons fatty bacon, chopped fine
2 tablespoons all-purpose flour
½ pound ground beef
1½ pounds ground pork
2 large onions, chopped
3 celery stalks, chopped
1 bunch scallions, chopped
¼ cup chopped fresh parsley
½ teaspoon each pepper and cayenne
   pepper
1 teaspoon salt
1 teaspoon dried thyme
¼ teaspoon dried oregano
1 tablespoon Tabasco
Soy oil for deep frying

In a large cast-iron skillet over low heat, cook the bacon until all the fat is rendered. Add the flour and cook until golden brown, stirring constantly. Add the beef and pork, and cook until the pink color is gone and the roux is absorbed. Add the onions, celery, scallions, parsley, and seasonings and cook until the vegetables are limp. Set aside to cool.

Roll the pastry thin and cut out 6-inch circles using a saucer, and fill with about 1½ tablespoons meat mixture (don't overfill, or the pastry will split). Dampen the dough edges with water, then fold the pastry over the filling and crimp the edges with a fork.

Heat the soy oil to 375° F and fry the pies until golden brown, or bake in a 400° F oven.

Makes about 18

SOUPS

Avery Island Onion Soup

½ cup (1 stick) unsalted butter
½ cup all-purpose flour
5 cups thin-sliced quartered white onions
1 teaspoon each salt and white pepper
1 teaspoon white pepper
3 tablespoons Pernod
2 quarts milk
1 teaspoon Tabasco

Garnish
Fresh fennel sprigs

In a large heavy skillet, melt butter over medium heat. Whisk in flour and cook, stirring constantly, 5 minutes. Do not allow the roux to brown. Stir in the onion and toss with the roux. Lower the heat and cook until the onion is transparent, stirring from the bottom to prevent browning. Add the salt and white pepper, stir, then add the Pernod. Turn up the heat briefly and light the Pernod. Still stirring, add the milk and Tabasco. Bring the mixture to a simmer, and cook until well blended and slightly thickened. The soup should be rather thin. Correct the seasoning.

Serve in bowls garnished with sprigs of fresh fennel.

Makes 12 servings

Artichoke and Oyster Soup

As far as I know, Creole cooks in Louisiana discovered the affinity of artichokes and oysters. Creoles have always used both ingredients lavishly and well, but in combination they complement each other remarkably.

½ cup soy oil
½ cup all-purpose flour
½ cup minced onion
¼ cup minced celery
½ teaspoon dried thyme
Juice and grated zest of 1 lemon
4 large boiled artichoke bottoms, sliced
    thin, plus scrapings from their leaves
1 pint shucked oysters and their liquid
Tabasco to taste
Worcestershire sauce to taste
Salt and pepper to taste
2 quarts half-and-half

Garnish
Minced scallions

In a large heavy skillet, heat the oil until very hot, then briskly whisk in the flour and lower the heat. Cook 10 minutes, but do not allow the flour to brown. Add the onion and celery, and cook until the vegetables are limp and transparent. Add the thyme, lemon juice and zest, and artichoke bottoms and scrapings. Stir and cook briefly. Add the oysters and their liquid and stir until well blended. Add the seasonings. Slowly add the half-and-half (you may not need 6 full pints if the oyster liquid is abundant; the soup should be just thick enough to support the artichoke bottoms and oysters). Heat the soup through and correct the seasoning. Serve garnished with minced scallions.

Makes 12 servings

SALADS

Tomato Aspic

Americans have been eating and loving jelled salads ever since commercial gelatin starting coming in those conveniently premeasured little packages, but in higher culinary circles they are considered hopelessly low rent—especially those based on garishly colored packaged gelatin desserts. In Louisiana, aspics are almost never sweet, and are immensely popular as summer side dishes or as main courses at lunch. The sophistication and depth of flavor in this one may change your mind about jelled salads.

6 cups V-8 or tomato juice
6 fresh basil leaves
2 branches fresh thyme
3 envelopes unflavored gelatin
3 ounces cold lemon juice
1½ cups chopped celery
1½ cups chopped green bell pepper
2 teaspoons Worcestershire sauce
1 teaspoon Tabasco
Salt and pepper
1 cup peeled chopped cucumber
½ cup fine-chopped scallions

In a large saucepan heat V-8 or tomato juice with the basil and thyme until just below boiling. Dissolve the gelatin in the lemon juice. Strain the hot tomato juice into a large bowl and stir in the gelatin mixture. Immediately add the celery, green bell pepper, Worcestershire sauce, Tabasco, and salt and pepper to taste. Let cool slightly, then add the cucumber and scallions.

Pour the mixture into a greased 2-quart ring mold and chill 2 hours, or until set. Slice and serve on lettuce leaves with coriander or jalapeño mayonnaise. Serve in double slices on luncheon plates as a first course or for lunch.

For mayonnaise: To one cup Basic Homemade Mayonnaise (see page 4), add one tablespoon fine-chopped fresh coriander or 1 tablespoon fine-chopped pickled jalapeño.

VARIATION: Add 1½ cups small, boiled, and peeled shrimp when you stir in the cucumber and scallion.

Makes 6 to 8 servings

Peppery Greens with Blue Cheese and Pecans

The sweetness of the vinaigrette used here is another French culinary anathema, but the taste goes very well with the pecans and greens and makes a nice refreshment after the complex heat of Louisiana food.

A note on the minor misery of washing spinach and other sturdy greens: Use standing warm water liberally laced with salt, and be sure to break off any very sandy roots. Separate the leaves and swish them vigorously in the water, lifting the greens away from the water as you finish. Rinse the greens in cold water.

2 cups watercress, washed
2 cups young spinach, washed and
    stemmed
2 cups arugula, washed and stemmed
¾ cup Hot-Sweet Vinaigrette (recipe
    follows)
1 cup crumbled blue cheese
1 cup broken pecan meats

Mix the greens in a large bowl and toss with the vinaigrette. Sprinkle in the blue cheese and pecans, and toss again.

Makes 6 servings

Hot-Sweet Vinaigrette

2 teaspoons dry mustard
1 teaspoon honey
¼ cup cider vinegar
Juice of ½ lemon
¾ cup soy oil
Heavy dash of Tabasco
Salt and pepper to taste

Whisk together the mustard, honey, vinegar, and lemon juice. Add the oil, still whisking, to form a light emulsion. Add the Tabasco, salt, and pepper and mix thoroughly.

Makes 1 cup

MAIN COURSES

Crawfish Etouffée

2 cups soy oil
2 cups all-purpose flour
2 cups chopped green and red bell
   peppers
2 cups chopped onions
2 cups chopped celery
2 cups Fish Stock (see page 102)
2 tablespoons fresh thyme
1 tablespoon fresh basil
⅓ cup Worcestershire sauce
4 heavy dashes of Tabasco
4 large garlic cloves, chopped
4 cups chopped canned tomatoes
Salt and pepper to taste
2 pounds crawfish tails, thawed

In a large heavy skillet, heat the oil almost to smoking. Add the flour all at once, whisking quickly. Lower the heat to medium. Continue whisking as the flour gradually browns, about 30 minutes. When the flour is hazelnut brown (a shade darker than a good natural peanut butter), add the vegetables all at once. (Be sure not to add the vegetables until the flour is exactly the right color, and to add them all at once *as soon as* it is the right color. The vegetables will lower the temperature of the roux and keep it from cooking further.) Stir the vegetables briskly and add all the other ingredients except the crawfish tails.

Lower the heat and simmer 20 minutes, or until the vegetables are tender. Add the crawfish tails, stir until blended, and cook until heated through.

Turn off the heat and let stand 15 minutes before serving. Serve over Green Rice (recipe follows).

Makes 12 servings

Green Rice

A good green rice is so grassy-looking you want to lie down in it. The green should not be pastel but intense Irish green.

2¼ cups water
½ teaspoon salt
2 cups converted rice
1 large bunch fresh parsley, washed and stemmed (do not dry)
1 large bunch watercress, washed and stemmed (do not dry)
2 tablespoons fresh thyme leaves
¼ cup (½ stick) unsalted butter, melted

Bring the water to a boil in a large saucepan over high heat. Add the salt and the rice, lower the heat to medium and cook until tender, about 12 minutes. Turn the heat to low, cover the rice, and steam until fluffy, about 5 to 10 minutes, keeping an eye on it.

Meanwhile, process the parsley, watercress, and thyme into a fine purée in the bowl of a food processor fitted with a metal blade (add a little water if the mixture is too dry—only a thick liquid will properly distribute throughout the rice). Stir the butter into the purée and toss with the hot rice. Do not cook further. Serve at once, or the bright green will turn to khaki.

Makes 8 servings

Lucy-Mama's Eggplant

3 large eggplants
¼ cup (½ stick) unsalted butter, plus additional
¼ cup soy oil
1½ cups chopped celery
1½ cups chopped onions
1½ cups chopped green and red bell peppers
¼ cup chopped fresh parsley
2 tablespoons chopped fresh thyme
1 tablespoon chopped fresh basil
½ tablespoon chopped fresh oregano
2 large garlic cloves, chopped
3 tablespoons Worcestershire sauce
3 heavy dashes of Tabasco
1 teaspoon salt
1½ teaspoons pepper
2 cups grated sharp cheddar cheese
1½ cups crushed saltines

Trim off the tops and bottoms of the eggplants. Peel the eggplants lengthwise in strips, leaving about half the peel in place. Chop the eggplants in medium dice.

In a large heavy skillet over medium heat, melt ¼ cup butter in the oil. Sauté the celery, onions, and peppers until wilted. Stir in the eggplant and thoroughly toss the vegetables together. Simmer until the eggplant is thoroughly tender, about 45 minutes.

Add the herbs, garlic, and seasonings and continue cooking until the eggplant is done to the point of dissolving, adding water if the mixture gets dry.

(continued)

Preheat the oven to 400° F. Butter a 3-quart casserole.

Pile the eggplant into the casserole and sprinkle on the cheese and then the

cracker crumbs. Dot with butter. Bake 20 minutes, or until the cheese melts.

Makes 8 servings

Duck, Andouille, and Oyster Gumbo

1 4-pound Long Island duckling
2 tablespoons each fine-chopped garlic,
   cayenne pepper, pepper, and salt,
   mixed together
2 pounds andouille sausage
2 quarts Chicken Stock (see page 28)
2 cups soy oil
2 cups all-purpose flour
2 cups chopped celery
2 cups chopped onion
2 cups chopped green bell pepper
2 cups sliced okra
¼ cup Worcestershire sauce
4 heavy dashes of Tabasco
1 tablespoon chopped fresh thyme
4 large garlic cloves, chopped
4 ham hocks
Salt, pepper, and cayenne pepper to taste
1 quart shucked oysters and their liquid
Cooked white rice

Garnish
Scallions, chopped fine
Fresh parsley, chopped fine

Preheat the oven to 300° F.

Rub the duckling with the garlic mixture and bake in the oven 2 to 2½ hours. Meanwhile, cut the andouille into ½-inch slices and sauté briefly in a hot dry pan until just a bit brown. Deglaze the pan with a bit of stock and set aside.

In a large heavy Dutch oven, heat the oil until almost smoking and add the flour all at once, whisking madly. Lower the heat to medium and continue whisking constantly as flour browns, 30 to 40 minutes. When the flour is past hazelnut color and almost what my grandmother called a black roux—that is, just short of burned—add all the vegetables except the okra and stir briskly. (Be very careful at this point; the vegetables will boil up something fierce when they hit the hot roux.)

When the vegetables settle down, add the okra, Worcestershire, Tabasco, thyme, and garlic, cook briefly, then add the ham hocks and stock and simmer 1 hour. When finished, remove the ham hocks and cut up the cooked duck. Taste the gumbo liquid for seasoning and add more salt, pepper, and cayenne if necessary. Add the duck pieces, andouille, and oysters with their liquid and simmer 5 minutes.

Serve the gumbo over plain white rice, taking care to include duck, oysters, and sausage with each portion. Toss fine-chopped scallions and parsley together and garnish.

Makes 10 servings

Red Beans and Rice

I was raised on a Texas version of this dish that had chili powder in it. In fact, I was also raised on a version of spaghetti sauce that had chili powder in it. I don't shudder at the memory, but if you cook the version below, you may never want red beans any other way. I commend red beans and rice to you as a main course; it is too good to use as a side dish. Some Cajuns call red beans and rice Louisiana turkey.

2 pounds red kidney beans
1 gallon water
2 ham hocks
2 bay leaves
1 large onion, chopped coarse
1 teaspoon each salt and pepper
½ cup chopped bacon
1 cup chopped onion
1 cup chopped celery
1 cup chopped green bell pepper
1 teaspoon dried thyme
½ teaspoon dried oregano
2 small garlic cloves, chopped fine
1 cup chopped tasso
1 sliced andouille sausage
Tabasco to taste
Worcestershire sauce to taste
Green Rice (see page 129), Pink Rice with Herbs (recipe follows), or plain cooked white rice

Place the beans and the water in a large stockpot. Bring the water to a boil, turn off the heat, and let stand 45 minutes. Add the ham hocks, bay leaves, onion, salt, and pepper. Bring to a boil again and simmer 1½ to 2 hours, until the beans are almost tender.

Meanwhile, in a heavy cast-iron pan render the fat from the chopped bacon and sauté the vegetables until wilted. Add the thyme, oregano, and garlic, and toss briefly with the tasso and sausage. Add the vegetable mixture to the beans and stir.

Continue cooking the beans until just past tender. Remove the bay leaves and ham hocks. Cool the ham hocks, pick off their meat, and return the

(continued)

131

ham pieces to the pot. Season the beans lightly with Tabasco and Worcestershire sauce (this is not a hot dish). Remove 1½ cups beans from the pot and mash them to a purée. Return the bean purée to the pot and stir to blend.

Serve the beans over the rice of your choice.

Makes 8 to 10 servings

Pink Rice with Herbs

½ cup soy oil
½ cup chopped onion
½ cup chopped celery
2 cups long-grain converted rice
2 cups water
1½ cups puréed canned tomatoes and their
   juice
1 teaspoon salt
2 teaspoons paprika
¼ cup chopped fresh parsley
2 tablespoons chopped scallions, green parts
   only
1 teaspoon chopped fresh thyme
1 teaspoon chopped fresh oregano

Heat the oil in a large heavy skillet over medium heat. Sauté the onion and celery until wilted. Toss the rice with vegetables. Add the water, tomatoes, and salt and simmer until the rice is tender, about 20 minutes. Toss the rice with the parsley, scallion, and herbs.

Makes 8 servings

Lucy-Mama's Chicken Gumbo

When my grandmother's family migrated to Texas, their recipes came with them, but some of them changed to meet the tastes of Texans not yet accustomed to the intense roux and spices of southern Louisiana. This gumbo is wonderful, but a little like "white man's curry" in its mildness. Notice that the last recipe is okra-thickened; this gumbo uses filé, a powder made from sassafras bark. Lucy believed it produced an unpleasant texture when cooked in a dish, so she (and now I) always sprinkled it on the hot rice at serving time.

1 cup soy oil
½ cup (1 stick) unsalted butter
1 cup all-purpose flour
1 cup chopped onion
1 cup chopped celery
1 cup chopped green bell pepper
1 teaspoon dried thyme
1 garlic clove, minced
1 teaspoon each salt and black pepper
½ teaspoon white pepper
1 broiling chicken, cut at every joint
2 dashes of Tabasco
1 teaspoon Worcestershire sauce
6 cups Chicken Stock (see page 28)
Cooked white rice or Green Rice
4 scant tablespoons filé powder

In a large heavy saucepan, heat the soy oil until hot and melt the butter in it. Stir in the flour all at once, turn the heat to medium, and whisk briskly until the flour is a light golden brown, about 15 minutes. Stir in the vegetables, thyme, garlic, salt, and peppers all at once, being careful when the roux boils up. Stir briskly until everything is blended and the vegetables are limp, about 4 minutes.

Stir in the chicken pieces and toss with the vegetables and roux. Lower the heat and cook 5 minutes, or until the chicken looks a bit cooked. Add the Tabasco, Worcestershire sauce, and stock, and stir thoroughly until a sauce forms around the chicken. Cook over low heat just until the chicken is done.

Serve on fluffy white rice or with Green Rice (see page 129). Just before pouring the gumbo over the rice, sprinkle a scant tablespoon of filé powder over each portion.

Makes 4 servings

Redfish Court Bouillon with Spicy Fried Shrimp

Redfish is trash fish—at least in Texas, when I was growing up. Red snapper was stuffed with crabmeat for company and redfish was served in big fillets, baked, for Friday night supper. Now the demand for redfish has outrun the supply: It's no longer cheap, but I still enjoy big baked fillets.

The Court Bouillon, once again, has no resemblance to the poaching liquid of the same name found in classic French cuisine. The sauce is often diluted with fish or shrimp stock, enriched with hunks of fish and shrimp, and served as a soup.

1 3-pound redfish fillet, boned and
    skinned
½ cup white wine
2 tablespoons (¼ stick) unsalted butter
Salt and pepper to taste
¼ cup soy oil
1 cup chopped onion
1 cup chopped celery
1 cup chopped green bell pepper
1 teaspoon dried thyme
1 teaspoon dried basil
½ teaspoon dried oregano
1 curl lemon zest
2 fresh basil leaves
2 garlic cloves, minced
6 large ripe tomatoes, peeled and
    chopped, or 6 cups canned tomatoes
    with their juice
1 tablespoon Worcestershire sauce
2 teaspoons Tabasco
1 tablespoon lemon juice

Garnish
Spicy Fried Shrimp (recipe follows)

Preheat the oven to 425° F.

Place the redfish fillet in a large flat baking dish, and pour the wine over it.

Dot with butter and add salt and pepper to taste. Bake until done, about 30 minutes.

Meanwhile, in a large heavy skillet, heat the oil and sauté the vegetables until wilted. Add the seasonings and garlic and cook until the mixture is well blended. Add the tomatoes and simmer 10 minutes. Stir in the Worcestershire sauce, Tabasco, lemon juice, salt, and pepper and cook 5 minutes more.

When the fish has baked 25 minutes, remove from the oven and ladle the sauce over it. Return the fish to the oven and continue cooking until it is flake-tender and the sauce bubbles.

Serve with Green Rice (see page 129) and garnish with Spicy Fried Shrimp (recipe follows).

VARIATION: If you like shrimp better than redfish, as a main course, fry 6 or 8 shrimp per person and use the court bouillon to sauce them.

Makes 6 servings

Spicy Fried Shrimp

4 cups soy oil
2 cups all-purpose flour
1 teaspoon each salt and pepper
2 large eggs
1 cup half-and-half
1 tablespoon Tabasco
12 large shrimp, peeled

Heat the oil almost to smoking in a large deep frying pan.

Toss the flour together with pepper and salt. Beat the eggs and add the half-and-half and Tabasco. Dredge the shrimp in the flour, dip in the egg mixture, then dredge in the flour again (the shrimp should be completely covered and gooey).

Fry the shrimp quickly until golden brown. Use as a garnish for the redfish.

Makes 12

DESSERTS

Lucy-Mama's Favorite Dessert Pastry

My grandmother was very fond of desserts, but she didn't like them to be too sweet. She preferred to "cut the sweetness with a few egg yolks." This meant, for instance, that she used a scant cup of sugar to a quart of cream for ice cream—but a dozen egg yolks. Her desserts were always heady stuff, but with the suavity of any sweet that doesn't depend entirely on sweetness for its appeal.

Lucy was also fond of a dotty look in desserts; this one uses raw berries *on top* of a premade lattice, and so certainly qualifies.

Pie Crust

2 cups all-purpose flour
1 teaspoon salt
⅔ cup (1⅓ sticks) unsalted butter, cold
4 tablespoons ice water

Sift together the flour and salt. Blend in the butter until the mixture is fine and crumbly. Blend in the water with a fork, working lightly and quickly. Form the dough into a ball, cover, and refrigerate at least 1 hour.

Crème Anglaise

12 large egg yolks
½ cup sugar
Pinch of salt
1 quart half-and-half
1 vanilla bean, split lengthwise

In a large saucepan, beat the egg yolks until thick and lemony, adding the sugar and salt as you go. Scald the half-and-half with the vanilla bean. Add 2 teaspoons of hot half-and-half to the yolks and beat. Beat the rest of the half-and-half into the egg yolk mixture, whisking constantly. Place the mixture over very low heat, or in a bain marie with barely bubbling water, and cook, whisking, just until the custard heavily coats a wooden spoon. Strain and chill.

Filling

⅔ cup superfine sugar

6 cups berries (raspberries, blackberries, blueberries)

4 large bananas

1 tablespoon lemon juice

2 tablespoons red wine

1½ cups lightly sweetened whipped cream

Preheat the oven to 400° F.

Roll out the pastry ¼-inch thick on a floured board and cut out 6-inch rounds, using a saucer as a guide. (You should have about 6 rounds.) Cut the rounds into strips and weave as for small lattice-top pies. Place on cookie sheets. Sprinkle the lattices with a bit of sugar and bake 10 minutes, or until golden brown.

While the pastry browns, toss the berries and sliced bananas together with the remaining sugar, lemon juice, and wine, and let stand unrefrigerated.

When the pastry is brown, put a lattice on each of 6 dessert plates and pile the fruit mixture on top. Flood each plate with crème anglaise and top with dollops of whipped cream.

Makes 6 servings

Twice-Lemon Sponge Custard

2 tablespoons (¼ stick) unsalted butter
⅔ cup plus 1 cup sugar
2 large egg yolks, beaten
2 tablespoons all-purpose flour
Juice of 1 large lemon
1 tablespoon fine-grated lemon zest
2 large egg whites
1 cup milk
¼ cup water
1 large lemon

Preheat the oven to 350° F. Butter 6 4-inch custard cups.

In a large mixing bowl, cream together the butter and ⅔ cup sugar. While still beating, add the egg yolks, flour, lemon juice, and zest. Mix well. In a separate bowl, beat the egg whites until stiff. Blend the milk into the sugar/butter mixture, then fold in the egg whites. Divide the mixture among the custard cups and set in a pan of hot water. Bake about 40 minutes, or until the tops are golden brown and risen.

Meanwhile, boil the 1 cup sugar and water together until the sugar melts. Slice the lemon very thin and drop the slices into the syrup. Turn down the heat and cook gently 10 minutes, taking care not to let the sugar brown. Set aside to cool.

Turn the custards out of the cups into dessert dishes and top with lemon slices and syrup.

Makes 6 servings

Fig-Pecan Bread Pudding

6 large eggs
3 cups milk
1 cup packed dark brown sugar
½ cup fig preserves, chopped
2 cups chopped toasted pecans *
½ cup bourbon
2 cups 1-inch cubes of French bread
½ cup fig preserves, chopped, mixed
    with ½ cup brown sugar

* To toast pecans: Pour ¼ cup melted butter over
pecans and toss with ½ teaspoon salt. Spread in a
single layer on a cookie sheet and toast in a
400° F oven for about 15 minutes.

Preheat the oven to 325° F. Butter a
2½-quart pudding dish. Beat the eggs,
then add the milk and sugar and blend
well. Stir in ½ cup preserves, 1 cup
pecans, and the bourbon. Stir in the
bread and let stand 15 to 20 minutes.
Turn the mixture into the prepared
dish.

In a small saucepan over medium heat,
melt the brown sugar–fig preserves
mixture together and spread over the
top of the pudding. Bake about 45
minutes, or just until set.

Serve sprinkled with the remaining
pecans.

Makes 8 servings

Pecan Pie

Pecans and pecan pies are all over the South, but I strongly associate this dish with Louisiana because my grandmother talked so much about gathering pecans from the ground in Louisiana pecan groves. She set grandchildren, children, and anyone else she could recruit to picking pecans for pies, for hors d'oeuvres, or just to eat. Ready-picked pecans were a great luxury, and we had them only at Christmas.

1½ cups pecan halves
½ cup bourbon
1 cup packed dark brown sugar
2 tablespoons all-purpose flour
2 tablespoons (¼ stick) unsalted butter
3 large eggs, beaten
1 cup dark corn syrup
¼ teaspoon salt
Pastry with Vegetable Shortening (see
    page 80)

Preheat the oven to 325° F.

Toss together the pecans and bourbon and let stand until most of the bourbon is absorbed, about 1 hour. Blend the brown sugar with the flour, then cream with the butter. Add the eggs, syrup, and salt. Stir in the pecans and bourbon. Pour the mixture into the prepared crust and bake in the oven until set, about 45 minutes (you may want to protect the edge of the crust with an aluminum-foil strip during the first ½ hour of cooking).

Makes 8 servings

I had a literate uncle who used to say that Texas might not have a culture, but it sure as hell had a palate. Certainly, my own family was testament to this, since I grew up surrounded by good cooks. My paternal grandmother combined her Louisiana heritage with country cooking to produce great family meals of legendary variety and lusciousness. She argued always for small portions of many dishes—ham with biscuits, slivers of chicken with salad, baked eggplant with lamb and rice pilaf, all at the same meal, often on the same plate—almost as if she'd been an Indian cook. Rebecca Stringfellow, the woman who helped raise me and cooked for my family for years, saw to it that we ate, almost every day, the food of a deeper South: greens, black-eyed peas, ham hocks and broad beans, corn bread. And my mother cooked, too—the Texas version of the domestic-science, good-nutrition, ladies' magazine sort of cooking that was standard middle-class fare all over the country. But my mother's scrambled eggs with chili, huge, many-vegetabled salads served with every meal, dark, spicy gravies, and powerful garlic bread were a far cry from the meat-vegetable-starch-and-dessert pallidness of American cooking in the fifties.

Texans are often xenophobic, but never about food. Helen Corbitt, who was trained at Cornell, discovered in her migration from department store kitchens to hotel dining rooms all over the state that if it tasted good, Texans would eat it—and then go home and cook it. Probably, though, it wasn't the ladies she cooked for at Joske's and Neiman Marcus who were most influential in changing Texas tastes. It was the oilmen and railroad men and legislators she cooked for at the Driskill in Austin, whose wives found them suddenly amenable to a whole variety of things they would never have eaten before they started taking potluck with Miss Corbitt. She introduced the state to curry and many chutneys and pickles, to the first course (though it was often sneaked past us as cocktail food), and to fish cooked without a coating of fried cornmeal, and we Texans took to it all as if we'd been doing it forever. Of course, Corbitt started her career at a country club—that quasi-domestic bastion of good cooking where so many Texans eat out without going to a restaurant. Dues-paying members of Texas country clubs have had a far greater influence on their kitchens than even the most influential customer can have on a restaurant. For years, some of the best professional kitchens in Texas have been in country clubs, and they certainly have been the professional kitchens that most clearly reflect the best of Texas home cooking—which, as in most of America, has been much better than its restaurant food.

SMALL PLATES

Pimiento Cheese

Pimiento Cheese is a great beginning for a Texas meal, but its origins are not as an hors d'oeuvre; it began as a sandwich spread more popular than peanut butter all over the South. My sister and I were raised on it—in our lunch boxes, after school, for late-night snacks. It's good stuffed in celery, as a dip with vegetables, spread on crackers, and with lettuce and tomato on sandwiches.

2 cups grated sharp cheddar cheese
2 cups grated mild cheddar cheese
1½ cups Spicy Texas Mayonnaise (see
  page 149)
½ cup minced scallions
1½ cups chopped pimientos and their
  juice
Salt and pepper
2 tablespoons Worcestershire sauce
4 heavy dashes of Tabasco

Stir together all the ingredients. Chill until flavors are married, about 45 minutes.

Serve as a cocktail spread with crackers, or a sandwich spread accompanied by lettuce and tomatoes. Or use the spread to stuff celery, to top cucumber slices, or with vegetables as a dip.

Makes 1½ quarts

Danish Butter

Danish Butter, much more sophisticated than Pimiento Cheese, almost suave, is the recipe of Ernie Coker, the first Texas restaurateur who was really interested in food. He didn't just serve the Texas classics; he elaborated. His Ye Olde College Inn in Houston served Danish Butter as an hors d'oeuvre and followed it with the lethal Texas Stuffed Baked Potato, a 16-ounce steak, and pecan pie. These days, any such meal precedes a day or two of fasting—but my Uncle Gerard thrived on food like that and managed to live to a fairly ripe age.

½ pound Danish blue cheese
½ pound cream cheese
1 cup (2 sticks) unsalted butter
¼ cup good bourbon

Cream together all of the ingredients. Serve at room temperature on crackers or French bread as an hors d'oeuvre, or on dark bread with endive or red onion as a sandwich.

Makes 2 cups

SOUPS

Butter Bean Soup with Carrots

Butter beans are also called lima beans, and I don't know of any food that creates stronger reactions pro and con. I have some customers who remember limas as a warm and comforting side dish to ham or Swiss steak or smothered chicken; others are convinced that to serve a lima bean at all is to mount a personal attack. I love limas—they have a pronounced and charming shape; they're good fresh or dried; and they *are* as smooth as butter.

1 pound small dried lima beans
1 ham hock
2 carrots, diced fine
1 Spanish onion, diced fine
2 tablespoons fresh chopped parsley
Salt and pepper to taste
Heavy dash of Tabasco
Dash of Worcestershire sauce
1 tablespoon dark brown sugar
1 or 2 teaspoons cider vinegar

Garnish
½ cup chopped fresh parsley

In a large stockpot, soak the lima beans and the ham hock in water to cover overnight. After soaking, add water to the 1-gallon level. Bring the water to a boil and simmer until the beans are almost tender, about 1½ hours. Add the carrots and onion and cook until the carrots are almost tender. Add the remaining ingredients. Remove the ham hock from the soup and cool. Pick the lean meat from the bone and return it to the soup. Serve hot, garnished with lots of parsley.

Makes 8 servings

Cold Plum Soup

Not native to Texas, except that a native Texan invented it, Cold Plum Soup is a great antidote to July weather (which on the Gulf Coast runs from May to October) and the only good use for canned plums.

2 20-ounce cans purple plums
¼ teaspoon ground cloves
1 teaspoon allspice
Juice of ½ lemon
Juice of 1 orange
2 teaspoons grated lemon zest
1 quart grape juice
2 cups ice water
Plain yogurt

Stone the plums and purée with their juice in a food processor fitted with a metal blade until liquid. Add the cloves, allspice, citrus juices, and zest. Mix thoroughly. Add the grape juice and thin, if necessary, with ice water. Serve very cold with dollops of yogurt on top.

Makes 10 servings

SALADS

Big Texas Salad

½ head Romaine lettuce
Other crunchy greens, such as iceberg,
   chicory, escarole, spinach, or a
   combination, equal to half the amount
   of Romaine
3 firm ripe tomatoes
1 medium red onion
2 ripe avocados
Lemon juice
6 canned artichoke hearts
1 green bell pepper
1 red bell pepper
4 celery stalks
1 broccoli stalk
2 hard-boiled eggs
Texas Vinaigrette (recipe follows)
½ cup fresh-grated Parmesan cheese

Place the greens in a large wooden bowl. Cut the tomatoes into wedges; peel and slice the onion and separate it into rings; peel the avocados, cut them into slices, and dip in lemon juice to prevent discoloration; cut the artichoke hearts into quarters; cut the green and red bell peppers into rings; slice the celery in thin diagonals; separate the broccoli into small flowerets, peel the stalk, and slice it into shallow diagonals; cut the eggs into eighths. Add the prepared vegetables to the greens.

Dress with Texas Vinaigrette (recipe follows), toss, then toss again with Parmesan cheese.

Makes 6 servings

Texas Vinaigrette

½ cup cider vinegar
3 large garlic cloves, crushed
2 teaspoons dry mustard
⅓ cup Worcestershire sauce
2 heavy dashes of Tabasco
1 teaspoon dried basil
½ teaspoon dried oregano
Salt and pepper to taste
1½ cups vegetable oil

Combine all the ingredients except the oil and whisk well. Slowly add the oil, whisking all the while, until the dressing emulsifies.

Makes 2½ cups

Sliced Tomatoes and Onions

Large tomatoes
Bermuda or Vidalia onions
Chopped fresh parsley
Olive oil
Basil vinegar

Slice ripe firm tomatoes into thick rounds. Slice onions into thin rounds.

On a large platter, arrange slices of tomato and onion in an alternating pattern. Sprinkle the chopped fresh parsley over the slices, and sprinkle with olive oil and basil vinegar before serving. Or sprinkle with parsley and serve with Spicy Texas Mayonnaise (recipe follows).

Spicy Texas Mayonnaise

2 large egg yolks
1 teaspoon dry mustard
1 garlic clove, minced
1 teaspoon salt
1 cup soy oil
1 cup olive oil
Heavy dash of Tabasco
Heavy dash of Worcestershire sauce
2 teaspoons sweet paprika
Juice of 2 lemons

Whisk the yolks and mustard together until light and sticky. Add the garlic and salt. Add oils very slowly, whisking constantly. Add the Tabasco, Worcestershire sauce, paprika, and lemon juice, and stir to blend.

Makes 2½ cups

MAIN COURSES

Chicken-Fried Steak and Milk Gravy

Chicken-fried steak is an example of a whole principle of southern, and indeed American, cooking: the dish as part of a plate.

Chicken-fried steak is not a dish that belongs with any one or two of a number of side dishes. Though there can be small variations, the black-eyed peas, collard greens, mashed potatoes, and milk gravy are not optional but necessary components of a familiar plate. I can imagine chicken-fried steak served with stewed tomatoes, rice, and dark beef gravy: It would taste fine, but I would be disconcerted by it, and so would anyone else raised on it.

Of course, if you cook a dish long enough, you'll find yourself giving it other contexts, as good cooks always do (I've cooked chicken-fried steak in strips and served it as an appetizer with gravy or salsa to dip). But it's best to remember that chicken-fried steak is only the centerpiece of the plate as is the beef in a *daube;* the vegetables and gravy surrounding these meats are an essential part of the original *gestalt,* which you change when you alter the context.

1¾ pound bottom round, trimmed of fat,
  or 4 ½-inch thick boneless chuck
  steaks, trimmed
2 cups all-purpose flour
Salt and pepper to taste
2 cups milk, plus additional
1 large egg
1 teaspoon Tabasco
3 cups peanut or soy oil

Slice the bottom round into 4 ¼-inch steaks, or flatten the chuck steaks with the heel of your hand and place each in turn on a sturdy wood or marble surface. Using a hefty meat mallet or the back of a heavy knife, pound each steak evenly and vigorously on one side and then on the other until very thin. (The pounded steaks should be half their original thickness and almost twice their original surface area, with the natural resistance of the muscle completely broken down.) Set the steaks aside.

In a large mixing bowl, combine the flour and generous dashes of salt and pepper. In another bowl, beat together the 2 cups milk, egg, and Tabasco.

Pour the oil into a 12-inch cast-iron skillet. (Enamel on cast-iron will do, but cast-iron is preferable. Use nothing lighter.) Heat the oil almost to smoking. Test by dropping a smidgen of flour into the oil; if it dances, the oil is hot enough.

While the oil heats, first dredge the steaks in the flour mixture, being careful to coat the whole surface, then in the egg wash, and then in the flour again. The coating should be quite thick and sticky, completely covering the meat.

Fry the steaks one at a time, about 2 or 3 minutes per side. The flour should brown quickly, and steak juice should appear on the uncooked surface before the first turn. When the steak is golden brown on both sides, the meat will be done. Don't drain the steak on towels; by the time you place the steak on a platter, it should look dry and be almost board stiff. Hold the steaks in a warm oven until you've cooked all 4.

When the steaks are done, prepare the gravy: Drain all but 4 tablespoons oil from the skillet, carefully saving the browned crumbs. Whisk in 4 tablespoons of the leftover flour mixture and cook over medium heat, stirring constantly, until the roux is pale beige, about 5 minutes. Add the leftover egg mixture, whisk briskly to blend, and cook until the gravy thickens. If too thick, add more milk. Correct the seasoning, and serve over the steaks with Mashed Potatoes, Collard Greens, and Black-Eyed Peas (recipes follow).

Makes 4 servings

Mashed Potatoes

4 large Maine potatoes
1 cup hot milk
½ cup (1 stick) unsalted butter, melted
Salt and pepper to taste

Bring 3 quarts water to a rapid boil in a large saucepan.

Peel the potatoes and cut them into large chunks, then drop them into the boiling water. Cook the potatoes until tender, about 25 minutes, then drain. Return the potatoes to the pan and toss over low heat until completely dry.

Crush the potatoes with a potato masher, adding the milk and melted butter as you go. (In our family, we mashed until all lumps disappeared, but some people like sizable lumps.) Liberally salt and pepper the potatoes when they near the desired consistency. Texans prefer the pungent flecks of black pepper to the dusty suavity of white pepper.

Makes 4 to 6 servings

Collard Greens

½ pound salt pork, or 3 meaty ham hocks
4 quarts rough-chopped collard greens
Tabasco to taste
White or cider vinegar to taste
Salt and pepper to taste

Chop the pork, if using, into ⅛-inch cubes and place them in a large Dutch oven or heavy saucepan over medium heat. Cook until fat is rendered and the cubes are golden brown. Wash the collards and add them to the pot, along with 6 quarts water. (If you're using ham hocks, add them now.) Turn the heat to high and bring the greens to a boil, then reduce the heat and simmer briskly until the greens are tender and army green, about 2 hours. (Add water as necessary; when done, the greens should have a generous amount of pot liquid around them.)

When the greens are done, add Tabasco, vinegar, salt, and pepper as needed. (Tabasco is not a substitute for but a complement to pepper. The salt will depend upon the salinity of the pork or ham.)

Fish out the ham hocks, if used, pick off the lean meat, and return it to the pot.

Serve the greens at once, or let stand 1 day and reheat for even better flavor.

Makes 4 to 6 servings

Black-Eyed Peas

2 pounds dried black-eyed peas, washed and
*   picked over*
4 quarts water
3 ham hocks, or 4 ounces salt pork
Tabasco to taste
Salt and pepper to taste

Combine the peas with the water in a large stockpot and bring to a boil. Turn off the heat and let stand for 45 minutes. Meanwhile, chop the salt pork, if using, into ⅛-inch cubes and place them in a large Dutch oven or heavy saucepan over medium heat. Cook until fat is rendered and the cubes are golden brown.

Bring the peas to a boil again, then lower the heat to a brisk simmer. Add the rendered salt pork or ham hocks, and cook until the peas are done and just beginning to break open. Remove and cool the ham hocks; pick off meat and return it to beans.

Add a bit of water and stir; the peas should never be dry. Season with Tabasco, salt, and pepper.

Makes 6 to 8 servings

Texas Red

Chili in Texas is bigger than a bowl of chili. Texans like a broad range of choices at every meal, and no dish is complete without the side dishes and condiments that flank it. For us, the naked bowl of chili with crackers is lonesome-making. What we want is chili topped with onions and sour cream and cheddar cheese, and accompanied by saltines (the old way) and tortilla chips (the new way) and washed down with lemonade and good light pilsener (and, if you're a really old-fashioned Texan, milk). We add a Big Texas Salad (see page 148) and follow the whole Big Chili Deal with Leche Quemada (see page 184) or Lemon Ice with Strawberries (see page 162) or Houston Junior League Fudge Pie (page 161). For a Texan, *that's* chili.

¼ pound suet
3 pounds cubed top round steak
3 pounds Spanish onions, chopped rough
¼ cup dark red chili powder
2 teaspoons ground cumin
1 teaspoon each salt and pepper
½ teaspoon oregano
3 garlic cloves, chopped
2 cups canned crushed tomatoes, with
  their juice
6 cups water

In a cast-iron Dutch oven over medium heat, render the fat from the suet and brown the meat. Add the onions and cook until they begin to turn yellow. Add the chili powder, cumin, salt, pepper, oregano, and garlic. Stir, then add the tomatoes and water, and stir again. Cook gently 4 to 6 hours, or until the meat is tender and the sauce is thick.

The chili may be eaten alone, in the Texas fashion, or poured over Pinto Beans (recipe follows).

Makes 6 to 8 servings

Pinto Beans

¼ pound salt pork
2 quarts water
1 pound dried pinto beans
Salt and pepper

Cut the salt pork into ¼-inch squares, place in a heavy pot over low heat, and slowly render the fat. Add the water and the beans to the pot. Bring to a boil, then turn off the heat and let stand 45 to 60 minutes. Turn on again and simmer until tender, about 1½ hours. Add salt and pepper to taste.

Makes 4 servings

King Ranch Chicken

This wide-border dish—a marriage of Tex-Mex and southern—is so popular in central Texas that a friend of mine from Austin says that every third dinner party west of Hempstead features King Ranch Chicken.

Texans love the combination of mushroom-cream sauce—a favorite southern treatment for chicken and fish—with the tortillas, chiles, and cumin of Tex-Mex food, and not just because of the combination of flavors. Like a lot of other Americans, Texans like to combine favorite things in a casserole so that they come together in a single cloud of flavors. Such a robust way of combining foods—not reduced and invisible as in stock, or discreet as in ragout, but layered in solid and repeated strata—is satisfying and complex. Witness the Johnny Marzetti of Ohio, lasagna primavera of California, and tamale pie of New Mexico. King Ranch Chicken is the southern version of this idea with a southwestern accent.

½ cup (1 stick) unsalted butter
2 cups sliced mushrooms
¼ teaspoon dried oregano
½ cup all-purpose flour
2½ cups Chicken Stock (see page 28)
Salt and pepper
2 teaspoons ground cumin
2 cups sour cream
8 6-inch corn tortillas
2 2½-pound chickens, poached, with
    meat removed
1½ cups chopped canned green chiles
4 jalapeño peppers, canned or fresh,
    sliced thin
2 cups grated cheddar cheese

In a large skillet over medium heat, melt the butter and sauté the mushrooms until light brown, then sprinkle with oregano. Add the flour and stir, cooking until well blended. Stir in the chicken stock and blend until smooth. Add salt and pepper to taste.

Stir the cumin into the sour cream.

Preheat the oven to 400° F. Butter a large casserole. Line the dish with 2 tortillas, then with ¼ of the chicken. Top the chicken with ¼ of the mushroom sauce, then with ¼ of the chiles, jalapeños, sour cream, and cheese. Repeat 3 times, ending with cheese.

Bake 30 to 40 minutes, until the whole dish is hot and bubbling.

Serve with Big Texas Salad (see page 148).

Makes 6 servings

Pan-Fried Steak

Steak is a Texas tradition, but the backyard steak grill, oddly enough, is not very popular there, partly because the heat in most backyards drives everyone indoors, where air-conditioning makes life bearable. Most of us were raised on pan-fried steak, a method that sears the steak surface at a much higher temperature than any home-oven broiler can, approximating the temperature of a kettle grill or restaurant broiler.

The stuffed potato is a recipe from Ernie Coker, who for years ran Houston's best restaurant, Ye Olde College Inn. He served the stuffing ingredients on a carousel and the potato in its skin with a sign that said, "I've been tubbed and rubbed and you can eat my skin."

¼ pound suet
Salt
4 12-ounce New York–cut sirloin steaks,
    2 inches thick
Juice and zest of 1 lemon
Freshly ground black pepper
Cayenne pepper
½ cup soy sauce
½ cup Worcestershire sauce

Heat a 14-inch cast-iron skillet over high heat until *very* hot, rub the inside with suet, and sprinkle with salt. (Do not attempt to pan-fry steaks in anything but a well-seasoned cast-iron skillet; a lighter pan will cause steaks to stick at the high temperature needed to properly sear them.) Rub the steak with the lemon juice and zest, then pat with the pepper and cayenne. Mix together the soy and Worcestershire sauces.

Place the steaks, 2 at a time, in the hot skillet. Turn after 4 minutes and brush with soy-Worcestershire mixture. Cook the second side 4 minutes, turn, and brush with sauce, then cook 4 to 6 minutes longer until done but rare.

Serve the steaks with Lucy-Mama's Eggplant (see page 129), sliced tomatoes and onions with Spicy Texas Mayonnaise (see page 149), and Texas Stuffed Baked Potatoes (see page 157).

Makes 4 servings

Oven- or Kettle-Barbecued Ribs with Julia's Sauce

Barbecue is a Texas tradition—but Texas has a barbecue tradition different from that of other states, based on the rich, dark tomato concoction given here, which is disavowed by most other barbecue-loving southerners. Texans also like ribs better than most other barbecue, although they eat beef, pork, chicken, and sausage links with the same sauce. The advantage of barbecuing ribs is that they cook quickly because of their high ratio of bone to meat. Beef brisket or pork shoulder takes at least four hours, with constant turning and tending, to barbecue tender. By the way: No matter who recommends it, never, *never* parboil ribs before barbecuing. If you do, you'll have the disheartening taste of steamed meat, which no amount of broiling and saucing can eradicate, on your hands. Be brave and barbecue direct.

Julia's Sauce
2 cups ketchup
1½ cups cider vinegar
1½ cups Worcestershire sauce
1 large onion, sliced
½ cup dry mustard
¼ cup molasses
3 large lemons, sliced
3 bay leaves
½ teaspoon dried oregano
1 teaspoon dried basil
1 teaspoon Tabasco

6 racks meaty pork or beef ribs
Mesquite or hickory chips, soaked in
    water (for kettle grill method)
Sauce of 2 cups vinegar to 1 cup
    Tabasco (for kettle grill method)

To make the sauce: Combine all the ingredients and boil until the mixture thickens, about 1 hour.

To oven-barbecue the ribs: Preheat the oven to 425° F. Place salted and peppered ribs in a large roasting pan, and bake 40 minutes. Dip in barbecue sauce and bake 25 minutes longer, basting with sauce. Slice the ribs apart and serve with more sauce.

To barbecue the ribs in a kettle grill: Lay a bed of charcoal in the grill. Light the charcoal and, when the coals go gray, sprinkle with the wood chips. When the coals are good and smoky, dip each rack of ribs in the vinegar-Tabasco mixture and place on the grill 3 inches above the coals. Close the lid of the grill and cook 30 minutes, then turn the ribs. Cook 20 minutes longer, then baste the ribs on each side with Julia's Sauce. Cook 10 minutes longer, then slice the ribs apart and serve with more of Julia's Sauce, Texas Potato Salad, Sweet and Sour Coleslaw, and Barbecue Beans (recipes follow).

Makes 6 servings

Texas Stuffed Baked Potatoes

4 large baking potatoes
½ cup (1 stick) unsalted butter
2 cups grated cheddar cheese
2 cups sour cream
2 cups minced scallions
2 cups crumbled fried bacon
Salt and pepper

Preheat the oven to 425° F.

Wash and dry the potatoes, then bake on the oven rack 45 minutes. Remove from the oven and prick the potatoes, then continue baking until tender, about 15 minutes.

To serve, split potatoes lengthwise and spoon out the flesh. Toss together with all the other ingredients, then spoon the mixture into the skins and return to the oven to reheat. Or put the potatoes on the table with all the condiments and let diners help themselves.

Makes 4 servings

Sweet and Sour Coleslaw

1 head green cabbage, shredded
1 red onion, diced fine
2 large green bell peppers, diced fine
1 large red bell pepper, diced fine
1 teaspoon celery seed
1 teaspoon mustard seed
1 teaspoon each salt and pepper
¼ cup sugar
1 cup vinegar
½ cup water
½ cup oil

Toss the cabbage, onion, and peppers together. Combine the other ingredients in a medium saucepan and bring to a boil. Immediately pour the hot dressing over the cabbage mixture and toss. Chill at least 2 hours before serving.

Makes 4 servings

Texas Potato Salad

4 pounds waxy potatoes, boiled and cubed
1 green bell pepper, diced
1 red bell pepper, diced
4 celery stalks, diced
1 small red onion, diced
3 hard-boiled eggs, chopped
¼ cup pickle relish
1 dill pickle, minced
2 cups Spicy Texas Mayonnaise (see
    page 149)
¼ cup Worcestershire sauce
¼ cup Dijon mustard
Salt and pepper to taste
Dash of Tabasco
Dash of cayenne pepper
1 tablespoon chopped pickled jalapeño
    peppers

Garnish
6 to 8 radish roses
2 tomatoes, sliced

Combine all the ingredients except the radishes and tomatoes and toss lightly. Chill for 2 hours and serve garnished with radish roses and tomato slices.

Makes 8 to 12 servings

Barbecue Beans

1 pound dried pinto beans
2 quarts water
Salt and pepper to taste
2 cups Julia's Sauce (see page 156)
2 tablespoons chili powder
2 teaspoons ground cumin

Combine the beans and the water in a large pot and bring to a boil. Turn off the heat and allow to rest 45 minutes. Turn on the heat, bring to a boil again, then reduce heat to a brisk simmer. Cook until almost tender, about 1½ hours, then add the salt, pepper, barbecue sauce, chili powder, and cumin. Simmer until beans are meltingly tender, about 30 minutes longer.

Makes 4 to 6 servings

Green Pepper Hash

Texans love long-cooked, flavor-married, spicy dishes—and if some are twice cooked, all the better. This spicy Texas version of a classic American way of dealing with leftovers always made us as happy as the original roast beef. I never knew until I left Texas that a hash could be made with minced or ground meat; the chunked meat here makes the dish Texan—*and* southern.

⅛ pound suet or other beef fat
¾ cup cubed boiled potatoes
¾ cup green bell pepper chunks
¾ cup onion chunks
½ cup celery chunks
½ teaspoon dried thyme
½ teaspoon dried oregano
1 bay leaf
Salt and pepper
3 tablespoons Worcestershire sauce
Heavy dash of Tabasco
½ cup crushed canned tomatoes
4 cups cubed leftover roast beef
1½ cups beef gravy

In a large skillet, heat the suet or fat until it is rendered, about 10 minutes over medium heat. Toss the potatoes, pepper, onion, and celery with the fat. Cook until the onions are just translucent, then stir in the herbs, seasonings, and tomatoes. Add the roast beef and gravy. Stir and heat until the flavors marry, about 20 minutes. Correct the seasoning.

Serve over Rice Pilaf (recipe follows) with Big Texas Salad (see page 148).

Makes 4 servings

Rice Pilaf

½ cup (½ stick) unsalted butter
½ cup diced celery
½ cup diced onions
2 cups uncooked converted rice
1 bay leaf
½ teaspoon dried thyme
¼ teaspoon dried oregano
1 teaspoon salt
½ teaspoon pepper
3½ cups Beef Stock (recipe follows)
3 tablespoons chopped fresh parsley
2 tablespoons minced green scallions

In a large skillet over medium heat, melt 2 tablespoons of the butter and sauté the celery and onion until translucent. Add the rice and stir just until it becomes translucent. Add the bay leaf, thyme, oregano, salt, and pepper. Add the beef stock, and simmer until the rice is done and the stock absorbed, about 20 minutes. Stir in the remaining 2 tablespoons butter, and the parsley and scallions.

Makes 4 to 6 servings

Beef Stock

2 carrots, chopped coarse
1 large onion, chopped coarse
½ bunch celery, chopped coarse
2 pounds meaty beef shin bones, cracked and
  cut into 4-inch pieces
½ cup soy oil
3 cups water
2 bay leaves
½ bunch fresh parsley
Bouquet garni of thyme, rosemary, and
  summer savory
Handful cracked black peppercorns
1 cup canned tomatoes and their juice, or 1
  large fresh tomato, chopped

Preheat the oven to 400° F.

Spread the vegetables over the bottom of a shallow roasting pan. Arrange the bones over the vegetables. Sprinkle the oil over all and bake, uncovered, in the oven until the meat and vegetables are well browned (the more browned, the darker the stock will be).

Remove the bones and vegetables from the pan and deglaze with the water. Stir to loosen all the browned bits on the bottom. Place the meat and vegetables in a 4-gallon stockpot, and pour the pan juices over all. Add the parsley, herbs, peppercorns, and tomatoes and cover with water to 2 inches above the meat and vegetables. Bring to a boil over high heat, then lower the heat at once. Simmer (do not boil) 8 hours, skimming when the fat begins to surface.

Refrigerate overnight, and remove the congealed fat from the surface. Add more water if necessary, and repeat the process of boiling and simmering. Strain, chill, and skim the fat once more.

If you want to reduce the stock further at this point (you should have about 1 gallon), boil it over medium heat until reduced by ½ or ⅔. Use at once, or store in the refrigerator for up to 1 week. You may freeze the stock for as long as 3 months.

Makes 1 gallon

DESSERTS

Houston Junior League Fudge Pie

I found this recipe in an old cookbook of my mother's and made one salient and accidental change—the original called for baking at 350° F for 45 minutes, but my oven had a broken thermostat and we were desperate for desserts, so I chanced baking it at 500° F, watching it like a hawk. The pie was darkening at the edges after 20 minutes, so I pulled it out and cooled it and suddenly what had been a sort of superior brownie in all previous bakings had become a gooey-on-the-inside, crunchy-on-the-outside, heavenly piece of chocolate wickedness. Cooking is full of serendipities.

8 ounces unsweetened baker's chocolate
2 cups (4 sticks) salted butter
8 large eggs
4 cups sugar
1 cup all-purpose flour
1 teaspoon salt
1 teaspoon vanilla extract
3 cups broken pecans

Preheat the oven to 475° F. Grease and flour 3 8-inch pie pans.

In a large saucepan over low heat, melt the chocolate and butter together. Beat the remaining ingredients together until glossy. Add the melted chocolate and butter. Beat again until glossy. Pour the mixture into the prepared pans.

Bake 20 to 25 minutes, until puffy on top and just done. Cool before slicing.

Makes three 8-inch pies

Lemon Ice with Strawberries

1 cup water
1½ cups sugar and additional
Zest of 1 lemon
6 fresh mint leaves, crushed
½ cup lemon juice, strained
2 pints fresh strawberries

In a medium saucepan, boil the water, 1½ cups sugar, lemon zest, and mint leaves together. Add the lemon juice, then strain out the mint leaves and zest. Freeze the mixture in an ice-cream maker according to manufacturer's directions until scoopable, then set in the freezer for 2 to 3 hours.

Slice the strawberries and toss them with sugar. Serve with scoops of the ice.

Makes 6 servings

Northern New Mexico is as beautiful and remote as the mountains of the moon. For those who've lived there, though, it's hardscrabble country, difficult to pull a living out of. Even the establishment in the twenties of the millionaire art colonies, which have persisted and grown right down to the present, did not hide the bare hardness of the landscape.

The Indian diet, the original food of New Mexico, was corn, beans, and chiles—that's about all the near-desert land would support. Surprisingly, this food was not lost with the arrival of the Spanish and, later, the Anglo settlers. The primacy of Indian culture and the satisfactions of those basic raw materials were such that no succeeding people could, or would, dispense with them. Adobe is still the most effective and beautiful building material in New Mexico, and modern builders know this and remain faithful to it (Santa Fe's prettiest hotel is made of adobe). The same is true of the food: Chiles and corn and beans have been supplemented as modern transport has brought to New Mexico the varieties of food found in the rest of the country, but no one would think of substituting anything else for these staples.

New Mexican food has become an extraordinary amalgam of its historical and geographical culinary history. No modern New Mexican would live on beans and corn and chiles alone, but they are there in every New Mexican household, along with tomatoes, avocados, citrus fruits, chicken, pork, and a whole slew of ingredients and recipes borrowed from the Spanish that transformed Indian culture three hundred years ago. It is American culinary eclecticism with a vengeance, and its variety is what makes it our favorite American-Mexican cuisine. The food of New Mexico is its own self, solidly grounded in that bare and beautiful country.

SOME NEW MEXICAN BASICS

AVOCADOS

Not native to New Mexico, and in fact unsuited to the dry climate, the avocado was imported as part of the trappings of Cal-Mex cooking and has been completely adapted. No one believes that guacamole is not a New Mexican original.

BEANS

Talking about anything as basic as beans seems almost silly. Every culture uses beans; they are always peasant food, sometimes Lucullan (think of *cassoulet*), sometimes embarrassing (think of canned pork and beans). But there they are. In New Mexico beans are, with corn, the staff of life. By a happy ecological accident, both are available in the same environment and together provide a perfect protein for a poor people. By the same accident, one supposes, beans and corn are a perfect combination of flavors, almost entirely satisfying without the addition of meat flavoring or chiles. After living in New Mexico for a short time, it's possible to imagine living on corn and beans for an entire lifetime without feeling deprived. This is not an exaggeration. The primary types, normally used for boiled beans with pork and for refried beans, are pink beans and pintos, but red kidney beans turn up frequently and black beans, which are genuinely different in flavor and texture from the other three, are used as a change of pace and for their exotic color.

CHILES

A remarkably various family that makes the basic ingredients of corn and beans seem like a feast. From the mild and rich to the fiery and acidic, chiles transform even the most basic fare into something to celebrate. Reduced by American supermarket culture to the ubiquitous chili powder, they are a transcendent force in all Mexican-American cooking.

Anchos The large, dark-red peppers often seen in pepper wreaths (for which the longer but similar ristra (string) pepper is also used). Deep-flavored, rich, and mild, they are the chief flavor in supermarket chili powder and a basic element in all New Mexican cookery.

Chiles pequins Tiny red peppers that grow in clouds of bushes and are hotter, perhaps, than any other. Largely used steeped in vinegar for pepper vinegar. Not just a southwestern phenomenon, but used all over the American South.

Green chiles Both the New Mexico green and the Anaheim are varieties of this chile used to make the essential green chile sauce. Mild but pungent, large enough to roast and scrape for their pulp, these are used interchangeably.

Jalapeños Short, fiery green peppers, sometimes ripened to red, most often seen in Mexican restaurants as *jalapeños en escabeche* (pickled in brine). A fine flavoring element, fresh or pickled. A terrific variation: smoked and tomato-sauced *chipotles,* almost always found canned outside New Mexico; addictive.

Poblanos Small green chiles, quite hot but not lethal, used for sauces and to flavor any dish that needs mild heat and the color green.

CORN

This is the staple starch of New Mexican food and, together with beans, the staple diet of the old Indian cultures. In the new presentations, corn is a chief determiner of the look and taste of New Mexican food. Corn takes dozens of forms, some common to the whole country, such as cornmeal and fresh sweet corn, others peculiar to New Mexico, like posole and blue corn.

Blue corn A variety of Mexican corn, used to make masa. Mountain-of-the-moon stuff, nutty in taste, entirely typical of New Mexico.

Masa Very fine cornmeal made from dried hominy, used to make tortillas and tamales and to thicken chile preparations.

Posole Hominy, that is, lye-treated dried white, blue, or yellow corn, shorn of its skin.

Tamales Masa paste folded around pork, vegetables, chicken, or beef and steamed in corn husks.

Tortillas Mexican flat bread made of masa and water. One of the world's great basic carbohydrates.

H E R B S   A N D   S P I C E S

When I first came to New York in the late fifties, the city's one Mexican restaurant served only chili and a species of enchilada based on its chili. I realized I'd have to learn to cook Mexican food if I were going to stay in the city of my choice, so I went out and found some chili powder and meat and onions and assumed I could go home and make chili con carne, if nothing else. I was wrong. In the simplest Mexican dishes were ingredients I had never even thought of while eating those terrific Friday-night dinners in the Tex-Mex restaurants of my childhood. Since then, I've discovered these basic flavorings, and my pantry is never without them.

Cardamom A Spanish legacy, used often in sweets. Insinuating and not always pleasant, it grows in importance as you grow with the cookery.

Cilantro Or *fresh coriander,* or *Chinese parsley;* this too is used in a bewildering variety of cuisines. Until recently, it was never used in Tex-Mex, but it has always been a feature of New Mexican and Cal-Mex cooking. Best in raw salsas and for chopped and sprigged garnishes. Sometimes used dried, but in that form has a completely different flavor.

Cumin This was my first and most basic discovery; since then, I've realized it is also essential to Indian and West Indian cookery and a mainstay of Middle Eastern cuisine. Never be without cumin; with it, almost any dish will chime with a Mexican meal.

Oregano Oddly, this typical Italian herb doesn't taste remotely Italian in the New Mexican context. Very important for soups, meats, and even beans, it will never remind you of lasagna.

J I C A M A

A root vegetable with high water and low starch content not unlike the Jerusalem artichoke. Jicama is the perfect foil for the starchiness and heat of New Mexican food.

PEPITAS (PUMPKIN SEEDS)

Toasted and salted, these are used as a simple accompaniment to beer, as a background to any number of sauces, and to enrich stews, salads, and soups.

PIÑONS (PINE NUTS)

Native to New Mexico (as they are to Italy), these nuts are used in desserts and ground to provide a rich background for sauces. Almost pure oil and very mild in flavor, piñons are indispensable.

TOMATILLOS

Sometimes called *green tomatoes,* these are not even of the tomato family, and some cooks positively dislike them. I think they're great—citrusy, gutsy, providing exactly the right acid complement to the starchiness of corn and beans and the heat and sinuous pulp of chiles.

SMALL PLATES

Miss Ruby's Tostadas

My first restaurant in Berkshire County, Massachusetts, was founded on the tostada. At night, the menu changed from region to region, as it does now in New York, but at lunch we were obliged to keep tostadas on the menu all the time, day in and day out, in winter and in summer (although in the winter there were precious few people around to eat them). Our basics were refried beans and beef, but we soon discovered that tostadas were infinitely variable, and we played as many variations as we could think of. The rule below is general and includes many of the most successful ingredients we've hit upon in the last ten years.

Lots of customers at Miss Ruby's order tostadas in multiples, then have dessert and call it a day. Who could blame them?

Grated medium-sharp cheddar cheese
Grated mild white cheese, such as Muenster or Bel Pease
Refried Beans or Black Beans (see page 171)
8-inch corn tortillas, fried flat and crisp in corn oil
Tostada Beef, Sautéed Shrimp, or Chicken Tostadas (see page 172)
Cooked Salsa (see page 170)
Iceberg lettuce in chiffonade
Salsa Cruda or Summer Salsa (see page 170)
Sour cream

To assemble tostadas: All tostadas start with a layer of beans and a layer of cheese atop a crisp-fried flat tortilla. (If you are using beef, shrimp, or chicken, put it between the beans and cheese.) The tortillas then go into the oven (6 tostadas fit nicely on a cookie sheet) and bake at 400° F until the cheese melts—but no longer or you will toughen the protein and dry out the beans.

When the cheese melts, place each tostada on a big plate and top with 1 tablespoon Cooked Salsa, then a cloud of shredded iceberg lettuce (and no matter what your prejudices against iceberg lettuce, don't use anything else; iceberg is crunchy and watery and indispensable for this purpose), then 1 tablespoon Salsa Cruda or Summer Salsa. Top with 1 tablespoon sour cream.

The combinations I like best are shrimp and white cheese with Black Beans and Summer Salsa; chicken with

(continued)

Refried Beans and with Salsa Cruda instead of Cooked Salsa; plain Refried Beans with sharp cheddar and all the salsas; and beef with Refried Beans and everything else.

Salsa Cruda
4 cups fine-diced fresh tomatoes
½ cup fine-diced onion
¼ cup fine-chopped scallions
2 tablespoons fine-chopped fresh cilantro
1 large garlic clove, minced
Juice of 1 lime
Dash of Tabasco
Dash of ground cumin

Toss all the ingredients together and let stand at least 20 minutes, but not longer than overnight.

Makes 6 cups

Cooked Salsa
1 cup chopped onion
1 large garlic clove, chopped
2 tablespoons corn oil
1 tablespoon ground cumin
¼ teaspoon dried oregano
2 cups chopped canned tomatoes with their juice
¼ cup minced fresh jalapeño peppers

In a large skillet over a low heat, very slowly sauté the onion and garlic in corn oil until the onion is transparent but the garlic is not brown. Add the cumin and oregano and cook 2 minutes. Add the tomatoes and jalapeños and cook until the flavors are blended. Let stand in refrigerator overnight and serve at room temperature.

Makes 2½ cups

Summer Salsa
2 large peeled and seeded cucumbers
Juice of 1 lemon
Grated zest of 1 lemon

Chop the cucumbers into the bowl of a food processor fitted with a metal blade, add the lemon juice and zest, and blend until puréed.

Makes 1 cup

Refried Beans

2 cups fine-chopped onion
1 cup oil from fried tortillas
6 cups well-done pinto beans with their
    liquid
Salt and pepper
Ground cumin (optional)
Juice from canned pickled jalapeño
    peppers (optional)

In a large skillet over low heat, sauté the onions in the oil until limp and translucent. Add the beans and their liquid and simmer 2 to 3 hours, stirring and mashing as you go, and adding hot water regularly as the liquid evaporates—water is a major ingredient of refried beans. (The beans should have definition at the end of cooking to give them character; I do not like totally puréed refried beans.) Season the beans to taste with salt and pepper, and, if you like, cumin and jalapeño juice. I think you'll find, though, that these last ingredients are redundant. The simple bean-onion–tortilla oil taste is best.

Makes 2 quarts

Black Beans

½ cup fresh green chiles, diced
½ cup red bell peppers, diced
¼ cup pickled jalapeño peppers,
    chopped, with 3 tablespoons of their
    juice
1 teaspoon dried oregano
2 cups fine-chopped onion
1 cup oil from fried tortillas
6 cups well-done black beans with their
    liquid
Salt and pepper

Prepare the beans as described in Refried Beans (above), but sauté the chiles, bell peppers, jalapeños, and oregano along with the onion.

Makes 2 quarts

Tostada Beef

2 pounds ground chuck
2 cups chopped onion
¼ cup dark chili powder
1 tablespoon ground cumin
1 large garlic clove, minced
2 cups chopped canned tomatoes with
    their juice
Salt and pepper

Crumble the meat into a hot cast-iron skillet and stir, cooking just until the meat loses its pink color. Add the onions and cook until translucent. Add the spices and garlic and stir to blend. Add the tomatoes and salt and pepper to taste. Cook until all flavors are blended, about 20 minutes. If the beef throws off too much fat, skim before serving.

Makes 6 to 8 cups

Sautéed Shrimp

2 pounds medium shrimp
3 tablespoons soy oil
1 cup coarse-chopped tomatillos
2 tablespoons chopped fresh cilantro
1 tablespoon chopped fresh jalapeño
    peppers
Juice of 1 lemon
¼ cup white wine
1 medium red onion, slivered

Peel, devein, and coarse-chop the shrimp. Heat the oil in a large skillet and lightly toss the shrimp in the hot oil. Quickly add the tomatillos, cilantro, and jalapeños, and cook just long enough to blend the flavors. Add the lemon juice and wine and stir from the bottom. Cook until the alcohol in the wine evaporates, about 2 minutes. Remove the skillet from the heat, let cool 1 or 2 minutes, then add the red onion.

Makes 6 to 8 cups

Chicken for Tostadas

1 3-pound chicken, poached
2 tablespoons ground cumin
1 teaspoon each salt and pepper
1 cup Chicken Stock (see page 28)

Pick all the meat from chicken bones, tearing it into fine shreds as you go. Toss the chicken with the cumin, salt, and pepper, and moisten with chicken stock.

Makes about 4 cups

Sautéed Chorizo

This simple dish depends entirely on the flavor of the sausage. If you have a sizable Hispanic community in your town, you're likely to be able to find good locally made chorizo; the nationally available varieties are not as good.

*1 pound chorizo sausages, cut into ¼-
 inch slices
2 small garlic cloves, minced
2 cups canned chopped tomatoes, with
 their juice
Salt and pepper to taste
2 bay leaves
8 6-inch corn tortillas
Fresh cilantro leaves
Chopped scallions*

Heat a large cast-iron skillet to medium hot. Toss the sausage slices in the skillet until they begin to brown and render some fat. Add the garlic, tomatoes, salt and pepper, and bay leaves, and simmer gently, about 20 minutes, until the liquid is reduced by about ⅓ and the sauce is slightly viscous. Dip the tortillas in water and steam them briefly on the rack of a hot oven. Serve the chorizo on 2 overlapping tortillas, and top with cilantro and scallions.

Makes 4 servings

Guacamole

Guacamole is, of course, a national dish by now. Every cook in America probably has some version of it in his or her repertoire. But beware: Cutting the avocados with sour cream, cream cheese, or anything at all is not permissible; in New Mexico, the Tabasco and Worcestershire my Texas relatives always used is out, and cilantro is in. Make your own decisions.

*6 large ripe avocados, peeled and pitted
Juice of 2 lemons
1 small onion, minced
1 large tomato, chopped fine
1 garlic clove, minced
2 tablespoons chopped fresh cilantro
Salt and pepper
Warm deep-fried tortillas, quartered
Cooked Salsa (see page 170)*

Mash the avocados roughly with a fork. Stir in the lemon juice, onion, tomato, garlic, and cilantro, and toss with generous amounts of salt and pepper. Serve at once with warm deep-fried tortilla quarters and Cooked Salsa on the side.

Makes 3 cups

SOUPS

Tortilla Soup

If you cook enough Mexican food, you will eventually have a mess of stale tortillas around. This is what to do with them.

Corn oil for frying
10 6-inch corn tortillas
2 quarts Chicken Stock (see page 28)
Salt and pepper
Juice of 1 lemon
Dash of ground cumin
1 cup fresh raw corn kernels
½ cup fresh jalapeño peppers, minced
½ cup chopped fresh cilantro
1 cup toasted pepitas

Heat the oil in a large skillet. Cut the tortillas into thin strips and fry in the hot oil until just crisp. Remove from the oil and drain on paper towels. Heat the chicken stock with salt and pepper to taste. Add the lemon juice and cumin. Simmer the stock while you chop the condiments as necessary and put them in separate small bowls.

When ready to serve, put a handful of fried tortillas in each soup bowl, pour hot broth over them, and serve at once with the condiments on the table.

Makes 16 servings

Sopa de Albondigas
(Meatball Soup with Vegetables)

Meatballs

½ pound ground chuck
½ pound ground pork shoulder
1 large egg
⅓ cup milk
⅔ cup crushed saltine crackers
1 teaspoon salt
1 teaspoon ground cumin
½ teaspoon ground pepper
⅓ cup dried ancho chiles, blanched,
   skinned, and chopped
½ medium onion, chopped fine
2 garlic cloves, chopped

Combine the beef and pork in a large mixing bowl. Beat the egg with milk, stir in the crackers, then work the mixture into the meat. Add the seasonings, chiles, onion, and garlic, and evenly mix them through the meat. Shape meatballs by rolling 1 tablespoon of the meat mixture at a time between your hands.

Broth and Vegetables

6 cups Beef Stock (see page 160),
   skimmed
3 medium fresh ripe tomatoes, peeled
   and chopped
½ cup each zucchini, carrots, and
   turnips, cut into large julienne

Garnish

Chopped scallions
Chopped fresh cilantro

Bring the beef stock to a rolling boil in a large stockpot and add the tomatoes. Add the meatballs and vegetables to the broth all at once, cover, lower the heat, and simmer 10 to 12 minutes, or until the meatballs are done through and the vegetables are done but still crisp. Ladle the soup into bowls, with 4 or 5 meatballs per serving. Garnish with scallions and cilantro.

Makes 12 servings

SALADS

Pico de Gallo

This is my favorite New Mexican salad because it is the perfect refreshment from the hot, heavy flavors of beans and corn and chiles. I never use dressing with it because I think it should give a little pure shock to the palate without any oily intervention, but if you can't bear salad without dressing, try a light mustard vinaigrette with a touch of orange zest and 1 tablespoon tomato juice.

6 navel oranges, peeled
3 tablespoons bright-red New Mexican chili powder
½ cup fine-chopped scallions

Slice the oranges into circles, then arrange in overlapping circles on a glass plate. Sprinkle lightly with chili powder and then with the scallions.

Makes 4 servings

Avocados with Jicama

The avocado with its smooth dressing and the jicama, full of good, light crunch, make this another rich, fresh salad.

1 jicama, peeled and cut into 2-inch julienne
3 large avocados, peeled and cut into medium chunks
Dressing (recipe follows)
6 large Romaine lettuce leaves, in chiffonade
1 pimiento, cut into small dice

Plunge the jicama julienne into ice water 10 minutes. Drain, then toss the avocado and jicama with the dressing and pile onto beds of the Romaine chiffonade. Sprinkle with the pimiento.

Makes 6 servings

Dressing

2 teaspoons dry mustard
⅓ cup white vinegar
2 canned chipotle peppers and their sauce
Juice and grated zest of 1 lemon
1 cup good-quality olive oil
½ teaspoon each salt and pepper

Put the mustard, vinegar, chipotles, lemon juice, and zest in the bowl of a food processor. Mix for thirty seconds, then add the olive oil in a long stream. Stir in salt and pepper.

Makes 2 cups

MAIN COURSES

Pork with Green Chiles and Posole

There are New Mexicans who are subject to severe anxiety attacks if they don't eat this, the national dish of New Mexico, at least three times a week. I think we probably serve this menu as often as we do at Miss Ruby's because I yearn for posole.

1 3-pound pork shoulder, trimmed and cut into 1 inch pieces
2 tablespoons rendered pork fat or lard
1 onion, chopped
2 garlic cloves, chopped
¼ teaspoon dried oregano
1 teaspoon ground cumin
2 cups chopped green chiles
2 cups chopped fresh tomatillos
4 whole pickled jalapeños, chopped
Salt and pepper to taste
2 cups canned white hominy, or cooked dried hominy, rinsed
3 to 5 cups Chicken Stock (see page 28), degreased and strained

6 to 8 6-inch corn tortillas

In a large Dutch oven over medium heat, sauté the pork in the pork fat. Add the chopped onion and garlic and sauté until the onion is translucent, then stir in the oregano, cumin, pork, chiles, tomatillos, jalapeños, salt, pepper, and hominy and bring to a simmer; add 2 cups stock and simmer 1 hour, adding more stock as needed to keep the mixture moist. The meat will begin to shred. The dish should be dry enough to hold in a tortilla, and moist enough to eat as a stew. If at the end of 1 hour the dish doesn't seem thoroughly melded, simmer ½ hour or so longer, adding more stock.

Steam the tortillas: Dip in water briefly and place on rack of a 400° F oven for 2 or 3 minutes.

Serve the stew on steamed corn tortillas with Refried Beans (see page 171) and Spanish Rice (recipe follows).

Makes 6 to 8 servings

Spanish Rice

1 cup chopped onion
1 cup chopped pimiento or red bell pepper
1 cup chopped celery
¼ cup oil from fried tortillas
1 garlic clove, chopped
½ teaspoon dried oregano
2½ cups uncooked rice
4 cups water
1 cup tomato juice
3 tablespoons chopped fresh cilantro

In a large skillet over medium heat, sauté vegetables in the oil until the onion is translucent. Add the garlic, oregano, and rice, and stir until the rice and vegetables are well mixed. Add the water and bring to a boil, then turn down the heat and simmer, covered, until the water is absorbed and the rice is almost done. Add the tomato juice (if the rice is not pink, add a bit more juice), stir to mix thoroughly, and continue cooking until the rice is fluffy. Serve with chopped cilantro.

Makes 6 to 8 servings

Cheese Enchiladas with Red Chile Sauce

This is the Ur-enchilada: The sauce is basic, dark, and deep, the essence of New Mexico, and the filling is so simple it doesn't interfere in any way with the tastes of the sauce and the tortillas. It is possible to substitute Tostada Beef (see page 172) or shredded beef or pork for the cheese, but if you do, don't leave out the onion and 1 tablespoon cheese in the filling.

Enchiladas

8 6-inch corn tortillas
2 cups grated mild cheddar cheese (or, if
    you can get it, fresh Monterey Jack;
    the nationally available kind is
    tasteless)
1½ cups chopped onion
Salt and pepper to taste
Red Chile Sauce (recipe follows)
1 cup grated sharp cheddar cheese

Preheat the oven to 400° F.

Line each tortilla with ⅛ of the mild cheese and ⅛ of the onions, then sprinkle with salt and pepper and roll up. Place the tortillas in a single layer in a shallow baking dish, nap completely with Red Chile Sauce, and sprinkle with the sharp cheese.

Bake about 15 minutes, or just until the cheese inside the enchiladas melts.

Serve with Refried Beans (see page 171) and Spanish Rice (see page 179).

Makes 4 servings

Red Chile Sauce

6 cups boiling water
6 dried ancho chiles
1½ cups corn oil
1½ cups all-purpose flour
¾ cup dark chili powder
¼ teaspoon dried oregano
1 tablespoon ground cumin
1½ teaspoons salt
1 teaspoon pepper

Pour the water over the chiles and soak 10 minutes. Meanwhile, heat corn oil in a large skillet almost to smoking, then whisk in the flour quickly. Turn down the heat, and continue to cook, stirring constantly, 3 minutes. Cool 1 minute, then add the chile powder, oregano, cumin, salt, and pepper, whisking constantly. Drain the chiles, reserving the water, and scrape the chile flesh away from their skins. Chop the chile flesh, then add to the sauce and stir in 4 cups of the reserved water. Return the sauce to the heat and cook gently until thickened. If too thick to pour, thin the sauce with more of the reserved water.

Makes 2½ cups

Camarones Borrachos
(Drunken Shrimp)

This is real gringo food, based, nevertheless, on one of the great authentic New Mexican elements—Green Chile Sauce (recipe follows)—and devised on the spur of the moment by one of our waiters, Tony Ismail.

¼ cup soy oil
4 dozen medium shrimp, peeled and
   deveined, with tails on
1 cup slivered onions
2 cups fine-chopped ripe fresh tomatoes
1 tablespoon chopped jalapeños en
   escabeche
2 cups Green Chile Sauce (recipe
   follows)
Juice of 1 lime
Salt and pepper to taste
6 ounces tequila

Garnish
Avocado slices
Lime slices
Pimiento slivers

Heat the oil in a large sauté pan. When the oil is very hot, toss the shrimp and nions together in the oil until the shrimp begin to turn pink. Add the tomatoes and toss, then stir in the Green Chile Sauce, lime juice, salt, and pepper. Stir until the mixture is quite hot and bubbly to marry flavors. Pour on the tequila, light with a match, and flame until the tequila evaporates. Serve over Spanish Rice (see page 179) and garnish with avocado and lime slices and slivers of canned pimiento.

Makes 6 servings

Green Chile Sauce

2 tablespoons oil from frying tortillas
½ onion, chopped fine
1 large garlic clove, chopped
½ teaspoon ground cumin
½ teaspoon pepper
1½ cups water
2 cups diced fresh green chiles
1 cup diced tomatillos
¼ teaspoon dried oregano
½ teaspoon salt
2 chopped pickled jalapeños
½ cup fine-diced red bell pepper or canned
   pimiento
1 tablespoon cornstarch, dissolved in ¼ cup
   water

Heat the oil in a large cast-iron Dutch oven and add the onion and garlic. Cook until the onion is wilted, about 5 minutes. Stir in all the remaining ingredients except the dissolved cornstarch. Cook gently until a good deal of the liquid evaporates. Stir in the dissolved cornstarch and continue cooking over low heat until the mixture is slightly thickened.

Makes 4 cups

DESSERTS

Capirotada

(Bread Pudding with Wine and Cheese)

1 loaf good-quality French bread
1 cup sugar
1½ cups water
1 teaspoon ground cinnamon
¼ teaspoon ground cardamom
¼ cup (½ stick) unsalted butter
1 cup heavy cream
1 cup Madeira, Tokay, or port wine
¾ cup piñons (pine nuts)
¾ cup raisins
1 cup soft cream cheese or farmer
   cheese, or (if you can get it) grated
   fresh Monterey Jack cheese
2 cups unsweetened whipped cream

Preheat the oven to 350° F.

Remove the hard crust from the bread and tear it into bite-size pieces. Spread the bread on a cookie sheet and toast in the oven until lightly brown (watch carefully).

Put the sugar in a heavy enamel saucepan and heat over a medium heat, beginning to stir only when it begins to change color. Lower the heat and stir the sugar constantly until it is the color of maple syrup. Remove the pan from the heat and add the water 1 teaspoon at a time. This will cause the sugar to boil up fiercely, but keep adding water slowly, stirring constantly, until a thin caramel syrup forms. Whisk in the cinnamon, cardamom, and butter.

Butter a shallow baking pan.

Toss the toasted bread with the wine and cream, then put the bread in the prepared pan and sprinkle with the piñons and raisins. Evenly distribute the cheese over the surface, and pour the syrup over all. Cover with aluminum foil and place in the hot oven 20 minutes, or until the cheese melts down into the bread. Serve topped with whipped cream.

Makes 4 servings

Pumpkin Flan

We're especially fond of this New World hybrid. Flan, of course, is a Spanish custard dessert and the Mexican cinnamon and New Mexican pumpkin here are the New World touches.

½ cup plus ¾ cup sugar
2 tablespoons water
1¼ cups milk
1½ cups half-and-half
1 cinnamon stick
½ cup fresh pumpkin purée* or canned
    pumpkin
4 large eggs
2 large egg yolks
1 teaspoon vanilla extract
⅛ teaspoon salt

Garnish
Piñons (pine nuts) or slivered almonds

* To make fresh pumpkin purée: Cut into chunks a halved, peeled, and seeded 3-pound pumpkin. Steam the pumpkin chunks in a large covered pot with 4 cups of water until tender, about 20 minutes. Drain and mash with a potato masher.

Preheat the oven to 325° F.

Place ½ cup of the sugar in a heavy flame-proof 6-cup mold. Set over medium heat and cover. When the sugar goes straw-colored, begin stirring and continue until the sugar is dark brown. Add the water, and when the sugar stops boiling up, tilt the mold in all directions until it is completely coated with the caramel. Set aside to cool.

Scald the milk and half-and-half with the cinnamon stick. Whisk together the remaining ingredients and slowly blend in the hot milk.

Set the cooled mold in a heavy oven-proof skillet on a rack in the oven, and pour in the custard mixture. Fill the skillet with boiling water about ⅔ of the way up the side of the mold. Gently slide the rack into the oven, and bake the custard about 45 minutes, or until a knife inserted in the center comes out clean.

Remove the custard from the water bath and set in ice to cool. Refrigerate for at least 3 hours before serving. When ready to serve, invert the custard onto a plate and slice in wedges. Decorate with piñons or slivered almonds.

Makes 8 servings

Leche Quemada
(Caramelized Milk)

The original of this dessert was made by filling a rough cast-iron pot with rich milk and cooking it very slowly over a wood fire for three days. At the end of that time, a thick, caramel-flavored, custardlike mixture whose sweetness came from concentrated lactose had formed. Our version, a glorious fake, uses sweetened condensed milk and is wickedly sweet and rich.

Place 2 6-ounce cans (be sure the cans are sound and not dented or damaged in any way) sweetened condensed milk in a large saucepan and cover with boiling water. Simmer 3 hours, keeping the cans *covered* with water the whole time. Do not let the water get above a gentle simmer. Remove the cans from the water and cool, then open the cans and remove the contents. Eat the custard topped with heavy cream and toasted pecans, or use it as a topping for cheesecake.

Makes 3 servings

Carrie Waldman's Chocolate-Piñon Pie

For the first three years of Miss Ruby's life in New York, Carrie Waldman was our pastry cook, doing all our desserts, some of our breads, and the pastry that went into chicken pies, pâté en croute, and every other thing we asked her to do. Pastry cooks are a special breed, and Carrie was a special pastry cook: Tall, serene, and graceful, she wafted in in the early hours of the morning and wafted out again five or six hours later, leaving behind her a huge amount of good sweet stuff baked and ready. We miss her.

8 ounces piñons (pine nuts)
7 ounces unsweetened chocolate
1 cup (2 sticks) unsalted butter
1 cup plus 1 tablespoon sugar
4 large egg yolks
Zest of 1 orange
4 large egg whites

Preheat the oven to 300° F. Butter and flour an 8-inch layer cake pan and line it with parchment.

In the bowl of a food processor fitted with a metal blade or in a food mill, grind together the piñons and chocolate.

Cream the butter, then add the sugar and cream until the sugar dissolves. Add the egg yolks and mix. Add the orange zest and the chocolate-piñon mixture, and beat until well combined. Beat the egg whites until stiff, then fold in ⅓ at a time. Pour the mixture (a stiff batter) into the prepared pan and bake 45 minutes, or until the pie shrinks away from the edges of the pan. Cool, and slice with a wet knife.

Makes 10 servings

CALIFORNIA:
THE OLD TRADITION

O ld California cooking does not seem all that old to most of us. Growing up in Texas on traditional southern and Tex-Mex food, the food coming from California in the fifties seemed the newest and the freshest and not part of any past that I then recognized. We got avocados, oranges, and grapefruits, pineapple, Cobb salad, and Caesar salad —in fact, *salad*—from California in the fifties, and we were very happy to see them, too.

California was a postwar phenomenon. Restaurant tradition had been Continental—that is, western European—no matter how dimly. Home cooking was insular—English at least by aspiration—even if you were Italian, Polish, or Anglo-German. Strong ethnic enclaves existed, mostly in big cities, but the ladies' magazines made it clear that gravied meats, boiled vegetables, and apple pie were the wished-for norm. The changes wrought when all those soldiers and their families were exposed to the free-for-all culinary culture of the West Coast are still being felt. The Hispanic and Oriental influences, combined with a remarkably long growing season, made California cooking both American and exotic.

The California cooking that spread across the country then has by now become so traditional that almost all of us fail to think of it as Californian: quiche and a glass of wine for lunch; pineapple cheesecake; Caesar salad; avocado and sprouts in sandwiches; artichokes. The new-new California cooking has now arrived, and the old-new is fully part of the American culinary scene. Great

American raw materials and French techniques are serving an altogether more sophisticated palate than existed in the past and, as usual with California innovation, are working their way from coast to coast and then back to the center of the country.

But old-new California cooking still exists, and still tastes wonderful. Quite a lot has been inherited by the new cooks of California; grilling meats, tossing greens, lightening effects, and brightening the visuals were all parts of a tradition that these cooks have inherited and run with. For now, though, remember Fisherman's Wharf crowded with uniformed young men and pretty, shoulder-padded girls looking for their first cioppino.

Smoked Oyster–Stuffed Mushrooms

During a weird period in the fifties that seems to have had its origins in California, it was assumed that it was possible to can, dry, and freeze the "gourmet." Pantry shelves were suddenly full of canned pâté, dried mushrooms, soups that were destined to become dips and sauces, and, of course, smoked oysters. Well, I like smoked oysters, and they have an odd affinity with the mushrooms of this recipe that is even more pronounced if you can find the crimini mushrooms to use instead of the white cultivated ones.

16 medium fresh mushrooms
Juice of ½ lemon
2 cups heavy cream
⅛ teaspoon salt
Dash of Tabasco
½ teaspoon mild curry powder
1 8-ounce can smoked oysters, drained
1 cup grated smoked cheddar cheese

Garnish
Parsley sprigs
Pimiento strips

Remove the stems from the mushroom caps, wash and trim them, and wipe the caps with a damp towel to clean. Mince the stems very fine and toss with the lemon juice. Boil the cream until thick and quite viscous and reduced by ½. Stir in minced mushroom stems and seasonings and stir. Cook until the mixture is quite thick. Remove from the heat and stir in the smoked oysters.

Preheat the oven to 400° F. Butter a large baking dish and moisten the bottom with a little water.

Place an oyster and some sauce in each mushroom cap and top with grated cheese. Place the mushrooms in the prepared pan and bake until the cheese melts and bubbles slightly, about 15 minutes. Garnish with tiny parsley sprigs and pimiento strips.

Makes 4 servings

Poached Eggs on Greens and Tomato

This recipe seems contemporary—a restaurant in Los Angeles serves a version of it right now—but I got it out of an ancient cookbook. It has a number of characteristics of California cooking that haven't changed since the turn of the century: a willingness to try what sounds downright strange to the rest of America, a love affair with the light and flavorful, and a tendency to sneak salad ingredients into just about every course and every meal. The salad is less austere than it sounds; when cut, the poached egg, with the flavored vinegar, forms a lovely dressing.

4 warm soft-poached eggs
4 cups washed and dried dandelion
   greens, at room temperature
1 garlic clove, mashed
¼ cup good-quality red wine or
   balsamic vinegar, at room
   temperature
2 tablespoons fine-chopped fresh basil
4 thick slices peeled Beefsteak tomato, at
   room temperature

Drain the poached eggs on a towel. Tear the dandelion greens into pieces, and make a nest of them on each of 4 salad plates. Mash the garlic into the vinegar and toss with the basil. Strain into a small pitcher. Place a tomato slice on each plate, and a poached egg on top of each tomato slice. Pour the flavored vinegar over all and serve at once.

Makes 4 servings

SOUPS

Gazpacho Blanco

Californians have always loved surprises—in this case, a cold soup called gazpacho that *isn't* red. And, of course, it's part of the enormous tradition of Cal-Mex food that we can barely touch on here.

3 cucumbers, peeled and seeded
2 celery hearts with stalks, leaves and
    all, chopped
2 light green Italian frying peppers,
    halved and seeded
2 tablespoons California white wine
    vinegar
½ teaspoon salt
2 dashes of Tabasco
1 scallion, white and green parts,
    minced
1 garlic clove, minced
2 cups plain yogurt
2 cups Chicken Stock (see page 28)

Garnish
Chopped scallions
Extra-virgin olive oil

In a food processor fitted with a metal blade or in a blender, purée the cucumbers, celery, and peppers with the vinegar, salt, and Tabasco. Stir in the minced scallion and garlic, then the yogurt. Add the stock. Chill thoroughly and serve garnished with scallions and a drizzle of olive oil. Or top with avocado chunks or fresh garlic croutons or fine-chopped tomatoes.

Makes 6 servings

Zinfandel Beef Broth

This is light but rich and as heady as sake. I originally made this recipe a consommé, but decided the richness and roughness of an unclarified stock suited Miss Ruby's better.

1 fresh ripe tomato, chopped
1 tablespoon crushed black peppercorns
2 bay leaves
2 tablespoons fresh basil
2 tablespoons fresh thyme
8 cups Beef Stock (see page 160),
  strained and skimmed of all fat
1 cup water
2 cups red Zinfandel wine

Garnish
Italian parsley leaves

Stir the tomatoes and seasonings together with the beef stock and water in a heavy soup pot. Bring to a boil over high heat, stirring to prevent sticking. As soon as the stock boils, reduce the heat to a simmer, stop stirring, and allow the mixture to cook gently for 1 hour, then turn off the heat and let stand 5 minutes to allow the liquid to settle.

Strain the stock through 4 thicknesses of cheesecloth that have been washed in cold water. Cool the strained stock to room temperature, then refrigerate. When cold, skim any fat from the top.

To serve, reheat and add the wine. Do not boil. Garnish with Italian parsley.

Makes 6 servings

SALADS

Cobb Salad

It is not true that Californians invented salad; even the English eat greens, and the French, though austere about it, are devoted to salad and give it place as a separate course. But Californians are baroque in their taste for salad and were the first in this country to give it first-course status. Complexity and ingredients abound in the new California cuisine, but in the old—particularly its salads—there's a solid kind of richness unmatched anywhere today.

6 cups Romaine lettuce in chiffonade
2 cups slivered poached chicken breast
6 crisp-cooked bacon slices, crumbled
3 hard-boiled eggs, chopped
2 large fresh ripe tomatoes, chopped
2 large avocados, peeled and chopped
2 cups crumbled blue cheese
8 or 9 jumbo pitted California olives
1 cup fine-diced scallions, green and
    white parts
Spicy Vinaigrette (recipe follows)

Line a large oval platter with the lettuce. Arrange the chicken breast, bacon, eggs, tomatoes, avocados, and blue cheese in broad stripes on the lettuce. Garnish with the olives and sprinkle with the scallions.

Present the salad at the table, then toss in a large wooden bowl with Spicy Vinaigrette (recipe follows).

Spicy Vinaigrette
⅓ cup red-wine vinegar
2 tablespoons Worcestershire sauce
2 dashes of Tabasco
1 garlic clove, minced
1 teaspoon dry mustard
1 teaspoon salt
½ teaspoon pepper
1 cup olive oil

Combine all the ingredients but the oil in a small bowl. Gradually whisk in the oil to form a light emulsion.

Makes 6 servings

Caesar Salad

Not just a salad, but a dramatic tableside-created salad. Where could it have originated but in California?

1 garlic clove
1 cup olive oil
1 cup sourdough bread cubes
1 large egg
¼ teaspoon each salt and pepper
½ teaspoon Worcestershire sauce
1 head Romaine lettuce, washed and
    dried
Juice of 2 lemons
½ cup freshly grated Parmesan cheese
2 or 3 anchovy fillets, split

The day before serving, crush the garlic into the olive oil and let stand overnight.

Preheat the oven to 300° F. Toss the bread cubes with two tablespoons of the garlic oil and brown in the oven about 15 minutes, until crisp but light in color.

In a medium saucepan, bring several cups of water to a boil, then drop in the egg. Turn off the heat and let stand 1 minute. Remove the egg and plunge at once into cold water. Set aside.

In the bottom of a large wooden salad bowl, combine half the remaining garlic oil, salt, pepper, and Worcestershire sauce. Break the lettuce into the bowl in bite-size pieces, and pour the remainder of the oil over it. Toss lightly. Break the egg into the bowl and toss to coat the leaves. Add the lemon juice and toss again. Sprinkle in the Parmesan cheese and toss again. Add the croutons and toss again, then serve garnished with the anchovies.

Makes 4 or 5 servings

MAIN COURSES

Cioppino

Fisherman's Wharf in San Francisco gets the credit for this most satisfying fish stew, proving once again that a coastal town is a coastal town, whether in France or California.

2 large onions, chopped
2 bunches scallions, chopped
2 green bell peppers, seeded and chopped
4 garlic cloves, minced
½ cup olive oil
3½ cups California cabernet sauvignon
4 pounds ripe fresh tomatoes, peeled and
  chopped
1 bay leaf
1 tablespoon fresh oregano leaves
2 tablespoons chopped fresh basil
2 tablespoons chopped fresh parsley
1 tablespoon Tabasco
1 large whole lemon
Salt and pepper
2 dozen clams, scrubbed
2 pounds red snapper, skinned, boned,
  and cut into large chunks
1 pound mahimahi, skinned, boned, and
  cut into large chunks
2 dozen large shrimp, shelled with tails
  left on
½ pound scallops
2 Dungeness crabs, cooked, cleaned, and
  cracked

In a large Dutch oven over medium heat, sauté the onions, scallions, peppers, and garlic in the oil 5 minutes, stirring. Add the wine, tomatoes, herbs, and Tabasco. Cover and simmer about 40 minutes. Squeeze the lemon into the sauce, then add the rind along with salt and pepper to taste.

Add the clams to the sauce and simmer, covered, 3 minutes. Then add the fish and the shrimp, and simmer 3 minutes longer, or until the clams open. Add scallops. Add the crabs at the very end, and continue cooking just long enough to heat through. Remove the bay leaf and lemon halves. Serve in warm bowls with sourdough bread and a young red wine.

Makes 8 to 10 servings

Grilled Butterflied Lamb

Long before the current California dedication to indoor grilling, the outdoor grill was a way of life. In the South it's called barbecue, and it takes all day; in California, it's grilling, and it's much quicker and less dependent on sauces that alter the flavor of the meat. The grill is perfect for cooking lamb, so that its flavor is not disturbed.

1 small (15 pounds or less) lamb, split,
   with backbone broken
1 quart olive oil
1 pint lemon juice
1 bunch fresh rosemary, chopped
3 bay leaves, chopped
4 garlic cloves, minced
Salt and pepper

If the butcher has left the kidneys and liver attached to the lamb, remove them and save. Marinate the lamb overnight in the oil, lemon juice, herbs, and garlic.

Next day, prepare a large grill, or prepare coals in a pit two feet deep and wide enough to hold a large oven rack. Salt and pepper the lamb and, when the coals are medium-hot, place it over the heat in the prepared grill or pit. When the lamb begins to brown on one side, turn it and baste it with the marinade. Continue to turn and baste the lamb until well browned and medium-done—pink to dark pink—at the leg bone where the meat is thickest. This should take 1 to 1½ hours. If you like, you may dip the kidneys and liver in the marinade and grill them too: They should take about ½ hour. Serve them sliced with the lamb.

Carve the lamb and place directly on serving plates and serve with lemon wedges, tabouli, and any form of spinach. Offer plenty of good hot bread for mopping up the juices.

Makes 12 to 15 servings

DESSERTS

Avocado Ice Cream

I don't know whether California was the first state to grow avocados, but I always thought that all the avocados in the world came from there—in Texas, almost anything with avocados in it would be called Californian. Certainly avocado ice cream tasted exotic—and wonderful—enough to be from the exotic West Coast.

2 large Haas avocados, perfectly ripe
Juice and grated zest of 1 lemon
1 quart heavy cream
1 cup superfine sugar
½ teaspoon almond extract

Garnish
Grated orange and lemon zest
Orange slices

Peel and stone the avocados and then whizz in the bowl of a food processor with the lemon juice and zest. Meanwhile, heat the cream with the sugar until sugar is dissolved. Cool, and stir together with the avocado purée and almond extract. Freeze in an ice-cream maker according to manufacturer's directions. Serve with a sprinkle of grated orange and lemon zest, and orange slices.

Makes 1½ quarts

Pineapple Cream Pie

1 cup shredded fresh pineapple
2 tablespoons plus 1 cup granulated
　sugar
8 ounces softened cream cheese
1 cup Crème Fraîche (recipe follows)
3 large eggs
½ cup blanched almonds, toasted and
　ground
2 teaspoons vanilla
1 cup sour cream
1 tablespoon confectioners' sugar
Amaretti Crust (recipe follows)

Garnish
4 thin slices pineapple, cut in wedges

Preheat the oven to 350° F.

Combine pineapple and 2 tablespoons granulated sugar in a small nonreactive saucepan, and simmer until juice evaporates. Cool, then blend cream cheese, crème fraîche, and 1 cup granulated sugar until smooth; add eggs, almonds, and vanilla. Add pineapple to the cheese mixture and pour into Amaretti Crust (recipe follows). Bake for 30 minutes or until just set. Combine sour cream, confectioners' sugar, and vanilla and spread over the top of the pie. Garnish the edges with pineapple wedges. Chill for 2 hours to overnight and serve cold.

Makes 1 9-inch pie

Crème Fraîche
1 cup heavy cream
2 tablespoons buttermilk

Stir buttermilk into cream and leave, covered, at room temperature until the cream thickens, about 8 hours. Refrigerate.

Amaretti Crust
1 cup vanilla wafer crumbs
⅔ cup Italian amaretti cookie crumbs
¼ cup (½ stick) unsalted butter, melted

Blend ingredients together and press into the bottom and sides of a 9-inch pie pan. Bake for 8 minutes at 350° F. Cool.

Makes 1 9-inch crust

The Green Grape Dessert

This dessert appeared along with Beef Stroganoff in suburban dining rooms all over America in the fifties, and we all believed it came from California.

6 cups halved seedless green grapes
2 cups sour cream or plain yogurt
½ cup dark brown sugar

Put grapes in a shallow glass bowl. Spread sour cream evenly over the surface of the grapes, and sprinkle brown sugar over the sour cream. Serve at once.

Makes 6 servings

THE PACIFIC NORTHWEST

The Northwest is mother lode country—not that it's got everything, but if you don't want what it's got, what's wrong with you? Traveling up the coast from California, everything mellows out. Maybe it's the dampness in the air or the bigness of the country, with the great trees crowding down to the shore, but the atmosphere is almost always autumnal. My brother went to Puget Sound University, and even his mildewing shoes in the closet weren't enough to turn him against that quiet cool richness.

Certainly, for the cook there is almost everything—though, oddly, the great delicacy of the region, the salmon, whose season is spring, doesn't dispel the sense that the true spiritual season of the country is fall. Plums, apples, potatoes, mussels, pears, onions all contribute to a late-year kitchen nicely augmented by the crab, salmon, and berries of spring and summer. Nothing is more conducive to thoughtful good cooking than having good things to cook.

Though it's not just native plenty that attracts the cook—the Northwest is another of those cultural crossroads that seems to have made the most of every influence it's been heir to. Chicken and dumplings from Dust Bowl southerners, hearty stews and soups from across the border in Canada, and, nowadays, the light and intense work of the inventive northern California cooks have all found their way into the kitchens of the Pacific Northwest, and all have been welcomed and transformed.

SMALL PLATES

Bob Kanter's Warm Mussel Salad

Bob Kanter lives in New York and was born in Connecticut, but his recipe for mussels is a riff on the raw materials and influences of Pacific northwestern cooking that is irresistible—and exactly the kind of thing American cooks have been doing for our whole history: playing the changes, not just on our own mamas' food, but on everyone else's mamas' food too.

2 pounds mussels, soaked, scrubbed, and
    debearded
2 cups white wine
1 cup dried hijiki seaweed
4 shallots, minced
¼ cup rice wine vinegar
2 teaspoons dry mustard
1 tablespoon grated fresh gingerroot
¾ cup light olive oil
¼ cup fine-minced fresh cilantro
2 teaspoons soy sauce

Garnish
Fresh cilantro sprigs

Place the mussels, wine, hijiki, and shallots in a large Dutch oven over high heat, cover, and steam until the mussels are open wide. Discard any mussels that do not open. While the mussels steam, whisk together the vinegar, mustard, and gingerroot. Add the olive oil whisking all the while. Stir in the cilantro and soy sauce. Lift the mussels from the pot. Arrange the warm hijiki in the bottom of 4 pretty glass bowls. Remove the mussels from their shells, toss gently with the dressing, and pile on top of the seaweed. Decorate lavishly with fresh cilantro.

Makes 4 servings

Buckwheat, Black Bean and Dill Pancakes with Pacific Smoked Salmon and Caviar

Except for the pancakes, this is a perfect example of basic ingredients so good that almost nothing gets done to them. The pancakes here are, of course, a kind of American blini. There's not a thing wrong with any of this and, with a salad, it makes a fast but luscious lunch you can have ready in 15 minutes.

Pancakes (recipe follows)
4 ounces golden Pacific sturgeon caviar
4 1-ounce paper-thin slices Pacific smoked salmon, each rolled into a thin cylinder
Sour cream
Rough-chopped fresh parsley and dill, mixed
Capers, drained
4 tablespoons minced scallion, white part only
4 lemon wedges
Warm clarified butter *

* To clarify butter: In a small heavy saucepan, melt ½ cup (1 stick) unsalted butter over very low heat. When completely melted, skim off any solids on the top. Let settle briefly, then pour off clear yellow liquid, leaving solids behind.

On warm 8-inch plates, arrange 2 pancakes straight from the griddle. On 1 pancake place a pile of sturgeon caviar, on the other the rolled salmon slice. Beside the pancakes make a nest of the chopped herbs and nestle the capers and scallions in it. Place a dollop of sour cream and a lemon wedge near the parsley. Drizzle 1 tablespoon or so of the clarified butter over the pancakes and serve at once.

Makes 4 servings

Buckwheat, Black Bean and Dill Pancakes
1 cup buckwheat flour
1 cup unbleached white flour
2 tablespoons baking powder
1 teaspoon salt
2 tablespoons fine-chopped fresh dill
4 large lightly beaten eggs
2 cups milk
1 cup cooked black beans
¼ cup warm clarified butter, plus additional

Sift together the dry ingredients and toss with the dill. Stir in the eggs and milk and beat until the ingredients are mixed but not too smooth. Add the black beans and stir in the clarified butter. Drop the batter by 3-ounce ladlefuls onto a hot griddle greased with clarified butter and cook until the pancakes bubble. Turn and cook until golden.

Makes 8 to 12 pancakes

SOUPS

Mushroom and Potato Soup

Mushrooms and potatoes are both rich and earthy, but the flavors of the three mushrooms in this soup are full of lightness. This is a soup that will warm you up without weighing you down.

⅓ pound brown Roman mushrooms
⅓ pound chanterelles
⅓ pound shiitake mushrooms
½ cup (1 stick) unsalted butter
Salt and pepper to taste
½ lemon
2 leeks, cleaned and chopped fine
1½ cups fine-diced waxy potato
6 cups Chicken Stock (see page 28)
1 tablespoon chopped fresh fennel
1 cup sour cream

Wipe the mushrooms clean with a damp towel. Remove only the woody stems, and slice the mushrooms. Melt ½ the butter in a large heavy skillet and sauté the mushrooms, tossing constantly to keep them from browning. Add the salt and pepper, squeeze the lemon over the mushrooms, and add the whole half lemon. Cook just long enough for the mushrooms to release their juices, then remove the mushrooms with a slotted spoon and reserve the liquid, discarding the lemon.

Melt the remaining butter in a heavy enamel soup pot, add the leeks and potatoes, and sauté for 10 minutes. Add the mushroom juices, stock, and fennel, and bring to a boil. Reduce to a simmer, and cook 20 minutes, or until the potatoes are just tender. Add the mushrooms and cook 20 to 30 minutes longer. Serve in bowls topped with a dollop of sour cream.

Makes 8 servings

Donald Pratt's Three-Ingredient Onion Soup

1 gallon halved and very thin-sliced
   onions
1 cup good-quality dark soy sauce
Pepper or Tabasco to taste

In a large very heavy enamel-coated cast-iron pot, heat the onions over medium heat, stirring frequently, until translucent; reduce to lowest heat and cook, still stirring often, until caramelized to a dark brown and reduced to about ⅛ their original volume. (This may take up to 4 hours; you needn't be constantly attentive, but don't leave the kitchen.) Add 1 gallon water and the soy sauce, stirring the onions from the bottom. Simmer further until the flavors marry and the volume is reduced to one gallon. Season with pepper or Tabasco and serve plain or, as with French onion soup, with large croutons and melted Emmenthaler.

Makes 12 servings

SALADS

Fresh Vegetables with Egg and Anchovy Dressing

Coastal cooking is fearless cooking (they're even more reckless down the way a bit in California), and the anchovy has always been seen here for what it is: a gift from God, a way to add a mysterious richness to what otherwise would be just blandly charming.

12 Boston lettuce leaves
4 red radishes, sliced and iced
4 white radishes, grated lengthwise and iced
4 black radishes, sliced and iced
4 small unpeeled Kirby cucumbers, sliced and iced
16 snow peas, blanched 30 seconds and iced
Egg and Anchovy Dressing (recipe follows)

Break the spines of the lettuce leaves and arrange flat on 4 8-inch plates. Arrange the radishes, sliced cucumber rounds, and snow peas on the lettuce, garnish with ginger, and drizzle with Egg and Anchovy Dressing.

Makes 4 servings

Garnish
4 ounces pickled ginger

Egg and Anchovy Dressing
3 hard-boiled egg yolks
3 drained anchovy fillets
1 teaspoon fresh-ground pepper
⅔ cup light olive oil
⅓ cup balsamic vinegar

Mash the egg yolks and anchovy fillets together until thoroughly combined. Add the pepper, then work in the olive oil and then the vinegar. If necessary, add just enough warm water to make the dressing pourable.

Makes 1 cup

Shiitake and Watercress Salad

The trick here is to mash the shallots and red plum together so that they disappear into the dressing; even experienced cooks will find the flavor surprising.

2 bunches watercress, washed and dried
1⅓ pounds shiitake mushrooms
½ cup (1 stick) unsalted butter
4 shallots, minced fine
½ red plum, skinned, stoned, and diced fine
Salt and pepper to taste
2 tablespoons red wine vinegar

Arrange the watercress on 4 8-inch plates. Wipe the mushrooms clean with a damp towel, then remove the stems, and reserve for another use. Slice the mushroom caps.

In a medium saucepan, melt the butter until foamy. Mash the shallots and plum together until thoroughly blended, then sauté until limp; add the mushrooms and sauté until just beginning to brown. Add the salt and pepper and cook until the mushrooms just begin to release their juices. Toss with the vinegar and divide the mushrooms among the 4 plates of watercress. Sprinkle with the pan juices and serve at once.

Makes 4 servings

MAIN COURSES

Poached Whole Salmon with Dill and Caviar Hollandaise

One of the great illusory fears of the modern cook, professional or amateur, is the specter of banality, of being caught doing the less-than-original. I agree with Andy Warhol, who said that in most things he was a very progressive man, but that where food was concerned, he was deeply conservative. Warhol never wanted to go into a deli and ask for an orange and have the clerk say, "Orange what?" And—witness the following three recipes—I would never do a Pacific Northwest menu without making it a festival of salmon. What's good is good.

Court Bouillon
4 cups white wine
4 cups water
4 celery stalks
1 onion, chopped rough
2 bay leaves
2 cloves
10 whole black peppercorns

1 5-pound salmon, head and tail on,
*   boned*

2 peeled cucumbers, sliced thin
2 tablespoons (¼ stick) unsalted butter,
*   melted*
1 large red bell pepper, roasted and
*   peeled*
1 pimiento-stuffed olive
2 pounds tiny new potatoes, boiled and
*   tossed in hot butter*
Dill and Caviar Hollandaise (recipe
*   follows)*

Boil together the ingredients for the Court Bouillon in a large sauté pan or fish poacher. Reduce the heat and simmer 40 to 60 minutes.

Wrap the salmon in cheesecloth and carefully lower it into the simmering bouillon. Simmer gently about 30 minutes, or just until the salmon is flake-tender.

Lift the salmon carefully from the broth, unwrap, and roll the fish onto a warm platter, taking care not to dislodge the head or tail or tear the flesh. Carefully remove the skin and keep the fish in a warm place. Sauté the cucumber slices in warm butter 30 seconds. Slice the roasted pepper into slivers about the thickness of the cucumber slices. Pave the salmon with the cucumber slices, overlapping like

(continued)

scales, and highlight the slices with the pepper slivers. Cover the eye with a pimiento-stuffed olive slice. Serve

Dill and Caviar Hollandaise
2 large egg yolks
1 cup (2 sticks) unsalted butter, melted and hot
Juice of 1 lemon
½ teaspoon salt
1 tablespoon fine-chopped fresh dill
1 ounce fresh salmon caviar

with the hot new potatoes and Dill and Caviar Hollandaise.

Makes 8 servings

Beat the egg yolks with a whisk in a large saucepan until thick and lemony. Add the butter 2 tablespoons at a time until fully absorbed and the sauce is thick. Add the lemon juice and salt and gently stir in the dill and salmon caviar. Keep warm until ready to serve.

Makes 1½ cups

Grilled Salmon Steaks Teriyaki

¼ cup soy oil
¼ cup soy sauce
1 tablespoon superfine sugar
¼ cup plum wine
2 tablespoons rice wine vinegar
1 tablespoon grated fresh gingerroot
1 teaspoon fine-minced garlic
1 teaspoon sesame oil
4 1-inch thick salmon steaks

Garnish
Scallion brushes

Whisk all the ingredients together except the salmon. Pour the dressing over the salmon, cover, and refriger-

ate. Marinate at least 1 hour but not more than 3 hours.

Prepare the grill and, when coals are covered with a light gray ash, place the salmon steaks on the rack. Grill about 4 minutes to the side, or until the salmon is just short of flaking at the center.

Heat the marinade and drizzle over the steaks. Decorate with scallion brushes, and serve with brown rice and Daikon Slaw (recipe follows).

Makes 4 servings

Daikon Slaw

6 large daikon radishes
4 fine-minced scallions
2 tablespoons rice wine vinegar
6 tablespoons soy oil
2 or 3 drops sesame oil
Crushed red pepper

Grate the daikon and toss with the scallions. Dress with the vinegar and oils and season to taste with crushed red pepper.

Makes 6 servings

Chicken and Parsley Dumplings

I've always thought of this dish as southern—but for years I've been coming across accounts of the popularity of chicken and dumplings in Oregon and Washington state. This predilection finally was explained as part of the Depression migration phenomenon. Southern migrants took the recipe with them when they left the South and the southern Midwest for the golden West, where everything was supposed to get better. Eventually, it became a staple at church suppers and in small restaurants and diners all over the area.

2 celery stalks, with leaves
1 onion, quartered and stuck with 2
   cloves total
2 large carrots, quartered
2 bay leaves
1 small piece lemon zest
12 whole black cracked peppercorns
½ gallon water
1 5-pound stewing chicken, cut up
Unsalted butter
¾ cup all-purpose flour
Salt and pepper to taste
½ teaspoon ground nutmeg
2 cups light cream
1 cup onion slivers
1 cup celery cut into 2-inch julienne
1 cup carrot cut into 2-inch julienne
Parsley Dumplings (recipe follows)
1 cup asparagus tips or French-cut
   young green beans or young green
   peas

Place the celery, onion, carrots, bay leaves, lemon zest, peppercorns, and water in a large Dutch oven. Bring to a boil and boil furiously 10 minutes. Add the chicken and reduce the heat to a simmer. Cover and cook, never boiling, 2½ to 3 hours, or until the chicken is tender. Remove the chicken from the broth and keep warm. Strain

the broth and set aside 4 cups. Pour the remaining broth over the chicken and hold at a bare simmer. Let the 4 cups broth settle, then skim off and reserve the fat. Add butter to the fat, if necessary, to make ½ cup.

Heat the fat in an enamel Dutch oven and add the flour, salt, pepper, and nutmeg. Whisk over low heat 5 minutes, or until the flour is thoroughly cooked but not brown. Stir in the cream and 2 cups reserved broth. Add the onion slivers and the julienned celery and carrot, and simmer 5 minutes. Set aside.

Meanwhile, remove the chicken meat from the bones. Discard the bones and keep the chicken warm in the remaining 2 cups of previously reserved broth. Reserve and reheat the broth the chicken was simmering in and drop the dumpling batter by the tablespoonful into the hot broth being sure not to crowd the pot. Cover tightly and simmer 12 minutes, without checking the pot.

When the dumplings are done, reheat the vegetable sauce to a simmer and

(continued)

stir in the chicken pieces and asparagus or green beans or peas. Cook 3 minutes, or until the flavors are just married. Serve the chicken stew in soup bowls with the dumplings on top.

Makes 6 servings

Parsley Dumplings

2 cups all-purpose flour
1 generous tablespoon baking powder
1 teaspoon salt
2 tablespoons shortening
¼ cup fine-chopped fresh parsley
2 large eggs, well beaten
1 cup milk

Sift the dry ingredients together, and cut in the shortening with 2 knives or a pastry blender until the mixture is the texture of cornmeal. Toss with the parsley. Make a well in center of the mixture and drop in the eggs. Stir until the mixture begins to form a dough, then add just enough milk to absorb any dry particles. The dough should be quite moist and easily dropped from a spoon.

Makes 12 dumplings

Stuffed Whole Coho Salmon

4 10-ounce coho salmon, head and tail on, backbone removed
2 cups fresh buttered white French bread crumbs
1 medium red onion, quartered and sliced thin
12 large fresh basil leaves, sliced
4 medium ripe tomatoes, peeled and chopped coarse
½ cup (1 stick) unsalted butter, melted warm
1 cup white wine
Salt and pepper

Preheat the oven to 400° F. Butter a baking pan large enough to hold the salmon in a single layer.

Open out the salmon and pat bread crumbs onto the bottom halves, then layer with onions, basil, and tomatoes, in that order. Close the fish and place them, head to tail, in the prepared baking pan. Drizzle the butter over the fish, moisten the bottom of the pan with the wine, salt and pepper the fish to taste, and bake, covered, for 30 minutes, or until the fish just flakes. The vegetables should not be fully cooked, but hot and moistened by the fish juices and butter.

Makes 4 servings

DESSERTS

Three-Plum Tart with Plum Wine Pastry Cream

The basic tart recipe is French, the plums are native to the Northwest, and the plum wine is Japanese. America is a country of eclecticism, and the tendency is stronger as you go west.

Butter Pastry, for single-crust pie (see page 7)
2 greengage plums
2 Italian prune plums
2 red plums
1 cup plum wine
½ cup Mirabelle, or other plum eau-de-vie
1½ cups milk
1 vanilla bean, split
4 large egg yolks
⅓ cup plus ½ cup sugar
⅓ cup all-purpose flour
¼ cup water

Preheat the oven to 375° F.

Press the pastry into an 8-inch tin. Line the pastry with aluminum foil and weight with beans or pie weights. Bake the pastry until lightly brown. Cool.

Halve and stone the plums and slice them very thin. Spread the slices 1 or 2 slices thick in a large glass dish. Pour the plum wine and eau-de-vie over them and marinate while you make the pastry cream.

Scald the milk with the vanilla bean. Meanwhile, whisk the egg yolks with the ⅓ cup sugar until the mixture is thick and creamy. Sift in the flour a little at a time, beating constantly. Remove the vanilla bean from the hot milk, and add it to the yolk mixture, a little at a time, continuing to whisk. Strain the plums, then slowly add the liquid to the pastry cream. Cool the pastry cream slightly and strain through a fine sieve. Spread over the bottom of the cooled tart shell.

Melt the ½ cup sugar in the water and simmer briefly. Pour over the plum slices, then arrange them in concentric circles on the surface of the pastry cream, and drizzle with any leftover syrup.

Makes 8 servings

Poached Pears in Ginger Cream

Natural bounty and the Oriental influence again. The sharpness of the ginger spicy Gewürztralightens the earthy smoothness of the pears to great effect. Try a muscat d'oro with this dessert and you'll probably levitate.

1 quart white wine
2 cups water
1 vanilla bean, split
1 cinnamon stick
1 strip orange zest
1 cup granulated sugar
4 Bosc pears, cored and peeled, stems
   intact
2 cups heavy cream
2 ounces (3 tablespoons) grated fresh
   gingerroot
½ cup confectioners' sugar
2 ounces poire Willem, or other pear
   eau-de-vie
6 ounces slivered candied ginger

Boil the wine, water, vanilla, cinnamon, zest, and granulated sugar together 10 minutes in an enamel pot. Reduce the heat and set the pears upright in the liquid. Simmer about 40 minutes, or until pears are tender. Cool the pears in the syrup.

Reduce the cream by ½ over high heat. Stir in the gingerroot, confectioners' sugar, and eau-de-vie and simmer 10 minutes.

Remove the pears from the syrup, and set each one in a shallow glass dish. Strain the cream over the pears and sprinkle with the candied ginger.

Makes 4 servings

BIG SKY, BIG GAME:
MONTANA, IDAHO, AND WYOMING

When I was young and lived in Texas, I read a lot of grown-up biographies just to find out what my choices were. One of the books I read was about a lady who left a big city in the East and moved to Montana with her rancher husband. His house was much like a hunting lodge: a two-story log cabin with enormous porches, huge fireplaces, and great windows overlooking mountains and meadows. The house was sparsely furnished in wood and leather. Moved by an instinct for housewifery and gentility, she set about humanizing the place, finishing off with ruffled, flounced curtains on the windows. Six weeks later, while watching an elk and a pair of deer feeding outside, she was overcome with profound irritation at seeing them, with great mountains in the background, framed by organdy ruffles. She tore all the curtains down, heaved a sigh of relief, and from then on kept her eye on the picture instead of the frame.

The grand country that requires no setting, that diminishes lesser things to their proper perspective, and demands attention at a level most people never give a landscape, is what draws people to Montana and to the whole great West. There, it is still possible to imagine food taken straight from the land, as it certainly is in many ranch houses equipped with freezers, dryers, and huge cellars to hold the gardener's bounty, the fisherman's catch, and the game that hunters routinely bring in. The flavors are rich, immediate, and earthy, and sauces—a memory of the wild in sophisticated form—are designed to deepen the effect of elemental raw materials.

SMALL PLATES

Beef Pasties

These are hand food, fine for a first course or hors d'oeuvres, but even better to take out to the mountain to sit and look, or for picnicking with fruit, cheese, and a bottle of wine. There are some things restaurants can't provide: When I worked in Berkshire County, we made these in heart shapes each year for a couple to take out to an anniversary picnic on the lawn at Tanglewood. The food was good, but the love and longevity and music were even better.

5 cups all-purpose flour
1 teaspoon salt
2 cups shortening or lard
1 jumbo egg, well beaten
2 teaspoons vinegar
2 slices bacon, minced
1 pound ground chuck
1 large potato, grated
1 medium onion, minced
Salt and pepper to taste
1 teaspoon ground allspice
1 teaspoon dried thyme
2 large egg yolks
½ cup water

Sift the flour with the salt and rub in the shortening until the mixture resembles fine oats. Put the egg in a measuring cup and add the vinegar, then fill with ice water to 1 cup. Add the egg to the flour and mix just until the flour is absorbed and the dough forms a rough ball. Cover and refrigerate 45 minutes.

Meanwhile, fry the bacon in a heavy skillet until the fat is rendered and the

bits are almost crisp. Crumble in the beef and stir until the meat loses its pink color and begins to brown. Add the potato and onion, and cook until the onion is translucent. Add the salt, pepper, allspice, and thyme. Cool to room temperature.

Preheat the oven to 400° F. On a well-floured board, turn out the pastry and roll out ¼ inch thick. Cut out 4-inch circles and fill with 1 heaping table-spoonful of the meat mixture. Do not overfill. Paint the pastry edges with an egg wash made of the egg yolks and water beaten together; then fold in a half circle and crimp the edges closed. Prick the pasties on top and bake about 45 minutes. Serve warm or cold with Pickled Onions (recipe follows).

Makes 12 pasties

VARIATIONS: Substitute any of the following, if you prefer not to use the beef filling.

Potato Pasties

Omit the ground chuck and instead use 2 potatoes and 2 onions for the filling. Add 1 teaspoon dried rosemary, along with the other seasonings. Fill the pasties as described above.

Cabbage Pasties

2 slices bacon, minced
2 medium onions, minced
3 cups sauerkraut, soaked, washed, and
    chopped
1 bay leaf
1 teaspoon crushed juniper berries, tied
    in cheesecloth
1 teaspoon dried dill

Render the bacon fat as for Beef Pasties. Add the onion and sauté until translucent. Stir in the sauerkraut, bay leaf, and juniper berries. Add about 1½ cups water and simmer until the water is almost all evaporated. Fill the pasties as described above. These are wonderful with sour cream.

Pickled Onions

½ gallon vinegar
1 tablespoon mustard seed
1 tablespoon whole black peppercorns,
    cracked
1 teaspoon crushed red pepper
2 bay leaves
10 whole cloves
3 quarts water
2 quarts pearl onions, peeled

Boil the vinegar with the spices about 30 minutes. Chill the vinegar thoroughly. Boil the water and add the onions. Cook until just translucent, about 10 minutes; they should not be entirely done. Drain the onions and, while still boiling hot, transfer directly to the cold vinegar mixture. Refrigerate in glass or stainless steel containers. The pickled onions will keep, refrigerated, up to 6 weeks.

Makes ½ gallon

Venison Loaf with Spiced Lady Apples

In this country, we just don't call such concoctions as this pâtés; we call them meat loaves, we usually eat them hot with potatoes and vegetables, and they're supper. Meat loaves are wonderful, and I don't want to hear another word about it. But this one is really meant to be eaten with pickles, or the Spiced Lady Apples here, and at room temperature, and before supper. Call it venison terrine if it makes you feel better.

1 pound ground venison
¾ pound ground pork
1 large onion, minced
1 garlic clove, minced
1 carrot, minced
1 tablespoon Worcestershire sauce
1 teaspoon dried thyme
Dash of ground cloves
2 tablespoons chopped fresh parsley
1 large egg
¾ cup bread crumbs
Salt and pepper to taste
Salt pork cut into 2- by 4-inch paper-
*   thin slices, or approximately 8 thin*
*   slices blanched bacon*

Preheat the oven to 350° F.

Thoroughly mix together all the ingredients except the salt pork or bacon. Line a 2-pound loaf pan with the salt pork or bacon and tightly pack the venison mixture into it. Top with 3 additional slices pork or bacon, then seal the pan with foil and weight with a brick.

Bake for about 2 hours, or until pâté is firm to the touch. Cool completely with the weight on top, then turn out of the pan and slice. Serve with Spiced Lady Apples (recipe follows).

Makes 8 servings

Spiced Lady Apples

1 gallon Lady apples, stems on if possible
½ gallon fresh apple cider
½ gallon cider vinegar
2 cinnamon sticks
¼ cup whole cloves, tied in cheesecloth
4 large curls lemon zest
4 cups sugar

Wash the apples and prick them at both ends.

Boil together all the other ingredients until reduced by ½. Add the apples, then simmer just until tender, about 20 minutes.

Cool the apples in the syrup, and store in a crock in the refrigerator. The apples will keep up to 1 month, refrigerated.

Makes 1 gallon

SOUPS

Oxtail Soup

This is deep-of-winter soup. Except for the tomatoes (and you can substitute canned tomatoes), it has only ingredients that can be found in the freezer or root cellar all year round. In the vastness of the west, this is great comfort food.

3 pounds oxtails, cut in 1½-inch sections
¼ pound suet
2 bay leaves
2 tablespoons chopped fresh parsley
1 teaspoon dried thyme
3 quarts Beef Stock (see page 160)
1 cup diced carrot
1 cup diced onion
1 cup diced celery
1 cup diced rutabaga
1 cup diced white turnip
1 cup diced peeled fresh tomatoes
Salt and pepper to taste

In a large Dutch oven, brown the oxtails in the suet. Add the bay leaves, parsley, and thyme, then stir. Add the stock and simmer until the meat falls from the bones. Remove the oxtails from the broth, then add vegetables and tomatoes and cook until tender, about 1 hour.

When the oxtails are cool, remove the meat from the bones. Discard the bones. When the vegetables are done, add the meat to the soup, season with salt and pepper, and serve with Sourdough Rolls (recipe follows).

Makes 12 servings

Sourdough Rolls

1 cup buttermilk
1 cup all-purpose flour
1 cup warm water
4½ cups all-purpose flour
1 large egg
3 tablespoons salad oil
⅓ cup milk
1 teaspoon salt
2 tablespoons sugar
Melted unsalted butter

To make the sourdough starter: Mix the buttermilk and 1 cup flour and let stand at least 48 hours, or until the mixture has a pleasing sour odor (many people compare this to the smell of a good beer gone flat). After the bubbling of the fermentation begins, refrigerate the starter and use as needed. (Each time you use the starter, replenish it with equal parts flour and condensed milk. Allow the starter to stand at room temperature 12 hours before returning to the refrigerator.)

The night before you plan to make rolls: Mix 1 cup starter with the warm water and 2½ cups flour in a large bowl. Mix thoroughly, cover the bowl, and let stand in a warm place.

Next day, add to the sponge the egg, oil, and milk, and beat thoroughly. Mix together the salt and sugar, sprinkle over the sponge, and stir, then let stand for a few minutes. Stir in the remaining 2 cups flour to make a stiff dough. Knead the dough until a smooth ball with satiny finish forms.

Place the dough in a greased bowl, brush with melted butter, and allow it to rise in a warm place 1 hour. Punch down the dough, turn it out onto a floured board, and knead again, adding more flour if needed. Roll out the dough ¾ inch thick and cut out rolls with a biscuit cutter, dip each side of the rounds in melted butter and tuck them into muffin tins. Cover and let rise until nearly doubled, about 1 hour.

Preheat the oven to 400° F. Bake the rolls 15 to 18 minutes. The rolls will be brown and lightly speckled. Serve hot.

Makes 2 dozen

Beet and Buttermilk Soup

More roots. A form of borscht, of course, good cold or hot—as good in Montana as it was on the steppes.

1 pound beets
2 cups buttermilk
2 tablespoons dark brown sugar
1 tablespoon lemon juice
1 teaspoon each salt and pepper

Garnish
6 scallions

Scrub the beets and cut off the stalks, leaving 2 inches of tops. Place the beets in a large pot, cover with water, and boil until the beets are tender, about 40 minutes. Cool and peel the beets, then slice into small julienne. Measure 2 cups of the beet water, and add to the buttermilk. Stir in the brown sugar, lemon juice, salt, and pepper. Stir in the beets. Serve hot or cold with minced scallions for a garnish.

Makes 4 servings

SALADS

Hot Red Cabbage Salad

1 medium head red cabbage, shredded
2 teaspoons salt
1 teaspoon pepper
¼ cup sugar
8 slices bacon, minced
½ cup vinegar
¼ cup water
1 teaspoon caraway seeds

Toss the cabbage with the salt, pepper, and sugar. Fry the bacon just until crisp. Heat the vinegar and water together to the boiling point. Pour the bacon and its fat and the hot vinegar over the cabbage at once. Add the caraway seeds and toss together. Serve immediately.

Makes 6 to 8 servings

Warm Fruit Salad with Greens

Oh, all right. I made this up. The salad tastes great with all the northern, dark, wintry flavors that make Montana food so memorable. It lightens the heaviness, adds to the richness, and gives some crunch at the edges. Very nice, very Western, and—oh, all right, I made it up.

1 tablespoon brown sugar
2 teaspoons lemon juice
½ cup orange juice
1 tablespoon hazelnut oil
3 fresh apricots, peeled, halved, and
    stoned
1 fresh peach, peeled, halved, and stoned
⅓ head chicory, washed, dried, and cut
    in bite-size pieces
⅓ head escarole, washed, dried, and cut
    in bite-size pieces

Boil the sugar, lemon juice, and orange juice together in a medium saucepan. Stir in the oil and slice the fruits into the pan. Stir until everything is well mixed, then simmer until the fruit is tender, about 5 minutes. Toss at once with the greens and serve on the same plate with game or roast pork.

Makes 4 servings

MAIN COURSES

Grilled Buffalo Steaks with Onion-Oregano Butter

I spent a lot of time resisting buffalo, which sounds like an endangered species, even though it's all raised on farms these days and meant for slaughter. Besides, it's designer food—meant to be exploited for its nostalgia and novelty and a lot of other things I am not remotely interested in. Then I tasted it—and decided the buffalo people were right: This was the meat beef wanted to be. I would use it instead of beef all the time if it weren't so expensive and scarce—and that, of course, is all that makes it designer meat. With luck the guys who produce buffalo will produce more and promote better. Maybe we'll all be eating buffalo in a few years.

1 medium onion, grated
½ cup water
2 tablespoons minced fresh oregano leaves
¾ cup (1½ sticks) unsalted butter, at room temperature
6 8-ounce buffalo sirloin steaks, 1 inch thick
2 cups soy oil
Salt and pepper

In a small enamel pan, simmer the onion in the water until the water evaporates; do not allow the onions to brown or discolor. Cool the onions, then mash with the oregano into the butter. On wax paper, pat the butter into a long roll, and gently fold the paper around it. Chill.

Prepare the grill.

At serving time, dip the steaks into the oil. When the coals are very hot, grill the steaks on a rack at the closest setting to the fire, 5 minutes on each side for medium-rare. Salt and pepper the steaks to taste as they cook. Top the steaks with a slice of the herbed butter, and serve with Confetti Fried Corn (recipe follows).

Makes 6 servings

Confetti Fried Corn

Kernels cut from 6 ears fresh corn
1 large red bell pepper, diced
1 medium green bell pepper, diced
1 celery stalk, diced
1 medium red onion, diced
1 small carrot, diced
1 cup water
3 tablespoons bacon grease
Salt and pepper to taste

Stir the vegetables together in a saucepan and add the water; add the bacon grease, salt, and pepper. Simmer the vegetables very gently, stirring from the bottom from time to time, about 15 minutes, until the water has evaporated and the vegetables are tender.

Makes 6 servings

Woodsman's Venison Stew

Salt and pepper to taste
2 cups all-purpose flour
2 pounds venison shoulder, cubed
4 slices bacon, minced
1 large onion, chopped
2 tablespoons cider vinegar
1 teaspoon ground allspice
1 teaspoon dried thyme
2 cups hard cider
1 large curl lemon zest
1 tablespoon Worcestershire sauce

Salt and pepper the flour, then dredge the venison in the mixture. Render the fat from the bacon in a heavy cast-iron skillet. Remove the bacon bits and reserve. Brown the venison in the bacon fat. Remove the meat from the pan, and add the onion and leftover flour. Stir until all the flour is absorbed, then cook gently 5 minutes.

Return the meat to pan with all the other ingredients and simmer about 1½ hours, or until the meat is fork-tender. Serve the stew with Mashed Potatoes (see page 151) or Deep-Skillet Potatoes (recipe follows).

Makes 6 servings

Deep-Skillet Potatoes

4 cups soy oil
10 medium red-skinned potatoes, unpeeled, halved, and blanched
Salt and pepper to taste

Heat the oil until almost smoking in a deep cast-iron skillet. Add the potatoes, being sure not to crowd the pan (you may have to cook them in 2 batches). Fry until light brown and crunchy. Season with salt and pepper.

Makes 6 servings

DESSERTS

Carrot Cookies

These big, soft, fluffy cookies go beautifully with ice cream, vanilla pudding, or lemonade on the porch.

1 cup (2 sticks) unsalted butter
1 cup sugar
1 jumbo egg
1 teaspoon vanilla extract
2 cups all-purpose flour
¼ teaspoon salt
2 teaspoons baking powder
1¼ cups cooked carrots, mashed and
    cooled

Preheat the oven to 350° F.

Cream together the butter and sugar, and beat in the egg and vanilla. Sift together the flour, salt, and baking powder, and add to the butter mixture, alternating with the carrots. Mix the dough well until all the dry ingredients are absorbed.

Drop the dough by the teaspoonfuls on cookie sheets lined with parchment. Bake 15 minutes, or until lightly browned. Cool on a rack.

When cool, dip cookies into the icing and allow to harden.

Makes 2 dozen

Orange Icing
1 cup confectioners' sugar
⅛ teaspoon salt
1½ teaspoons unsalted butter, softened
1 teaspoon lemon juice
Juice and grated rind of ½ orange

Beat together all the ingredients. The icing will be runny.

Dried Apple and Rhubarb Pudding

2 cups dried apples
1 cup chopped fresh rhubarb
1 cup sugar
½ cup raisins

Simmer the chopped apples in about 2 cups water until the fruit is almost falling apart. Meanwhile, in a separate saucepan, add 1 cup water to the rhubarb and simmer 30 minutes. Add the sugar and raisins to the rhubarb and simmer until the raisins are plumped.

Strain the apples, mash lightly, then add to the rhubarb mixture.

Serve the pudding warm with cream, or use as a pie filling.

Makes 6 servings

THE MIDWEST:
DAVID BLACKBURN'S OHIO

*T*he moment is lost in the dim reaches of the past, but David Blackburn once thought cooking chicken-fried steak was a task too demeaning for a self-respecting cook. He was trained by Frenchmen in New York long after he'd been raised by that formidable Ohio cook, Mary Ruth Smith Blackburn, within visiting distance of his grandmother, Mary Elizabeth Biracree Smith. Finally David realized that these women hadn't just raised him, they'd fed him, and fed him well. When the penny dropped, he started making long-distance phone calls to his mother, who got out her files and sent him her best recipes, reminding him that she had "a million of 'em." Now David can be seen dredging cream-and-Tabasco-soaked chicken in flour in almost any kitchen he cooks in, and muttering, "Born to fry."

This change of heart led David to do our Ohio menu, braving the weird New York parochialism imbued with the suspicion that any food from west of the Hudson is dry, tasteless, sauceless, and probably conducive to coma. Here's what David wrote about Ohio cooking at the time:

I've been asking around, and guess what? For a lot of people, Ohio just isn't as *palpable* a presence as, say, New Orleans or the Lower East Side. If it were, no one would ask me, "What *do* you eat out there?" "And where *is* it, anyway?"

Let me put it this way. The *where* is relatively unimportant, it being a matter of some indifference anyway—especially to anyone who has ever passed through Akron. We'll just say Ohio's out there in the middle of our great low-profile heartland, and let it go at that. Ohio is where Thurber's aunt, Sarah Shoaf, lay awake nights, terrified in her certainty that at any minute burglars would break in and blow chloroform under her door through a tube. I've long felt the official state motto should be changed to Mark Twain's "It isn't always easy being eccentric, you know."

The *what* is something else again. *What* covers a good deal more ground than we could do justice to on one menu, or even several. Ground like green tomato mincemeat pie with fresh ham and corn pudding, and pineapple upside-down cupcakes, and roast turkey with three stuffings, and sweet-and-sour braised venison, and cheese dreams, and chicken-in-a-pot, and strawberry-rhubarb pie. And have some more Johnny Marzetti, and get your elbows off the table.

I once told a cab driver in Boston that I'd grown up in Columbus, Ohio, and, after a long pause he smiled and said, "Oh, yeah, Ohio. That's out there next to Mississippi." I laughed, of course, but then became very sad, thinking, *That poor slob! He's never once in his whole life had a slice of Mary Blackburn's sour milk banana nut bread.*

And that is a large part of what Miss Ruby's is all about. It is engaged in teaching cooks—even cooks as gifted as David Blackburn—as well as diners that the food they were raised on has the same esthetic and emotional weight as the food they've learned to eat in most restaurants.

SMALL PLATES

Corn Pudding

Just another of the 827 ways Americans deal beautifully with our greatest native ingredient. What makes this recipe midwestern is the sugar, bell pepper, and the pinch of mace. Don't hold this dish. It longs to be served at once, and it goes beautifully with the spiciest and most distinguished Gewürztraminer you know of. How's that, Columbus?

6 tablespoons (¾ stick) unsalted butter
2 cups minced onion
2 cups minced green and red bell pepper
5 tablespoons all-purpose flour
1½ cups milk
8 large eggs
8 cups corn kernels, cut from the cob
    with their milk
4 tablespoons sugar
4 teaspoons salt
2 teaspoons pepper
6 dashes of Tabasco
Pinch of mace
2 cups grated cheddar cheese

Preheat the oven to 325° F.

In a large skillet over medium heat, melt the butter and cook the onion and bell pepper until limp. Add the flour and milk and cook a bit more. Starting with the eggs, mix the remaining ingredients together. Slowly, bit by bit, add the egg mixture to the pepper and onion mixture.

Pour the mixture into 6 2-cup baking dishes or 1 4-quart casserole. Bake 20 minutes for the small casseroles, 40 minutes for the large.

Makes 12 servings

Ham Balls

If you had to think of just one thing that Americans do well and variously and persuasively, it might be curing and smoking and cooking pork. Good American ham in dozens of versions is great just off the bone, boiled, baked, fried, or frizzled —and, for some of us, it is even better in croquettes, loaves, patties, or, as here, in the simplest formation, the venerable and charming Ohio ham ball. Don't be embarrassed. Just eat 'em with the pickles and be grateful.

2 pounds cooked water-added ham,
   ground
1 cup bread crumbs
1 cup minced onion
2 tablespoons paprika
2 teaspoons Dijon mustard
2 teaspoons prepared horseradish
2 large eggs

Glaze
1 cup dark brown sugar
3 tablespoons cider vinegar

Preheat the oven to 375° F. Lightly grease several baking sheets.

Mix together all the ingredients and roll into 1-inch balls. Place on the prepared baking sheets and bake 15 to 20 minutes, until lightly browned and sizzling. Glaze: melt the brown sugar over a low heat with the cider vinegar until reduced to a syrup. Drizzle over ham balls. Serve with Mary Ruth Smith Blackburn's Bread and Butter Pickles (recipe follows).

Makes 2 dozen

Mary Ruth Smith Blackburn's Bread and Butter Pickles

1 gallon medium Kirby cucumbers
8 small white onions, or 2 large Spanish
   onions, sliced
3 red bell peppers, cut into narrow strips
1 cup kosher salt
Cracked ice
5 cups sugar
1½ teaspoons ground turmeric
½ teaspoon ground cloves
2 tablespoons mustard seed
5 cups white or cider vinegar

Slice the cucumbers thin, then combine with the sliced onions and peppers. Add the salt, cover with cracked ice, mix thoroughly, and let stand 3 hours. Drain the vegetables. Combine the remaining ingredients, bring to boil, and pour over the vegetable mixture. Bring to a boil once more. Seal in sterile jars (see page 72) or store in a crock in the refrigerator for 6 weeks or more.

VARIATION: If desired, add any of the following, singly or in combination: 5 bay leaves; 1 tablespoon coriander seeds; 8 to 10 sliced fresh jalapeño peppers.

Makes 1 gallon

SOUPS

Vegetable-Beef Soup

Versions of this soup are all over the country (my Texan mother put more tomatoes and a good deal of chili powder in hers). The important point here is to make the beef stock (Mary Blackburn would call it a broth), chill it, skim it, and reduce it to something dark and flavorful. Use bones and carrots and celery and onions. Brown and simmer them, and let them fill the house with their odor. Then you'll have a stock worthy of this soup. Coma on the prairie? Oh, no.

*2 pounds boneless chuck or top round in
    4 pieces*
1 cup chopped onion
1 cup chopped celery
½ cup chopped green bell pepper
1 cup diced peeled potatoes
½ cup chopped carrot
½ cup chopped turnip
6 cups Beef Stock (see page 160)
*1 cup canned chopped tomatoes with
    their juice*
Salt and pepper to taste
1 bay leaf
1 teaspoon dried basil
½ teaspoon dried oregano
1 teaspoon Worcestershire sauce
1 garlic clove, minced
1 cup corn kernels, cooked
1 cup green beans or lima beans, cooked

In a large Dutch oven, brown the meat in its own fat, then remove it from the pot and add the onion, celery, and bell pepper. Cook until the onion is translucent. Return the meat to the pot and add all the other ingredients except the corn and the beans or limas. Simmer until the meat is fork-tender, about an hour.

Remove the meat from pot and chop. Return it to the pot with the corn and green beans or limas and cook until just heated through.

Makes 12 servings

Corn and Chicken Chowder

Landlocked but delicious. The red bell pepper is light and lovely with the corn, and the tarragon tastes terrific but isn't at all midwestern. We're a nation of innovators, though, so try it sometime.

¼ pound bacon, diced fine
1 medium onion, diced
1 cup diced red bell pepper
2 tablespoons all-purpose flour
1 cup diced peeled waxy potatoes
4 cups Chicken Stock (see page 28)
1 quart light cream
2 cups poached chicken, diced
2 cups corn kernels cut from the cob,
  with their milk
Salt and pepper to taste

Garnish
1 thin-sliced red bell pepper

In a large Dutch oven over medium heat, sauté the bacon until the fat is rendered. Remove the bacon from the pan and reserve. In the fat, sauté the onion and the red pepper until the onion is translucent. Stir in the flour and cook 5 minutes, until flour is thoroughly absorbed. Stir in potatoes. Add the stock and light cream and whisk to distribute the flour evenly. Simmer until the potatoes are almost done, then add the chicken, corn, salt, and pepper. Cook until the potatoes are tender and the flavors marry. Stir in the reserved bacon and serve garnished with thin slices of bell pepper.

Makes 12 servings

SALADS

Three-Bean Salad

American salads have a hard time. Sometimes they're not really salads but part of that great side-dish tradition that reaches its apex in the seven sweet and seven sour of Amish cooking. This one might be best as lunch, with tomatoes, hot rolls, and lots of iced tea.

2 cups cooked kidney beans
2 cups blanched cut string beans
2 cups cooked garbanzos
1 cup sweet pickle relish
1 cup sliced pimientos
1 cup green olives
1 large red onion, sliced thin
1 cup vegetable oil
⅓ cup red wine vinegar
1 tablespoon minced garlic
1 tablespoon sugar
Salt and pepper to taste
1 tablespoon chopped fresh basil
2 tablespoons chopped fresh parsley
Lettuce leaves

Garnish
Tomato slices

Combine the beans, relish, pimientos, olives, and onion in a large bowl. Mix oil, vinegar, garlic, sugar, salt, and pepper, and toss with the bean mixture. Let stand at least 2 days in the refrigerator, stirring occasionally. Just before serving, add the basil and parsley. Serve the salad on lettuce leaves garnished with tomato slices.

Makes 8 servings

Five-Cup Salad

If you're really embarrassed by the marshmallows, you can substitute fresh pitted cherries, cantaloupe pieces, or peach slices. On the other hand, if the idea turns you on, you might really go bonzo and buy the *pastel* miniature marshmallows. In any case, taken with a good slab of cold ham and a piece of Grilled Banana Bread (see page 281), this makes another great lunch.

1 cup miniature marshmallows
1 cup chopped mandarin oranges
1 cup pineapple chunks, drained
1 cup shredded coconut
1 cup sour cream
Iceberg lettuce in chiffonade

Garnish
Pimiento slivers

Combine the first 5 ingredients and let stand in the refrigerator at least 3 hours. Serve on beds of the lettuce and garnish with pimientos.

Makes 4 servings

MAIN COURSES

Swiss Steak

Once again, the trick is to make and cherish your own stock; what's your own will taste like your own.

Salt and pepper to taste
2 cups all-purpose flour
4 pounds boneless bottom round, cut into
    8 2-inch-thick steaks
4 tablespoons bacon grease
1 cup chopped onions
1 cup chopped carrot
½ cup chopped green bell pepper
4 cups Beef Stock (see page 160)
2 cups tomato sauce
2 branches fresh thyme
2 bay leaves

Salt and pepper the flour, then dredge the steaks in the mixture. Pound the steaks in the flour, until they're almost as thin as for Chicken Fried Steak (see page 150). Melt the bacon grease in a large ovenproof skillet, brown the steaks very well and lift out. Sauté the vegetables in the remaining fat until limp. Return the steaks to the pan, heaping the vegetables around and on top of the meat.

Preheat the oven to 325° F.

Add the stock, tomato sauce, and herbs to the steak pan. Bake, covered, 1½ hours, or until the meat is fork-tender. Strain the sauce; add more liquid if too thick, and adjust the seasoning. Serve with Mashed Potatoes (see page 151) or Scalloped Potatoes (recipe follows).

Makes 8 servings

Scalloped Potatoes

Large Maine potatoes
Salt and pepper
Garlic powder
Grated cheddar cheese
Heavy cream

Slice peeled Maine potatoes (1 large potato per person) about ⅛ inch thick on a mandoline. Toss the potato slices with a mixture of salt, pepper, and garlic powder (do not rinse the potatoes before seasoning). Layer the potatoes three slices deep in a shallow roasting pan and sprinkle with grated cheddar cheese (about ½ cup per potato). Alternate layers of potatoes and cheese almost to the top of the pan, ending with cheese. Fill the pan about ⅔ full with heavy cream. Bring the cream to a boil on top of the stove, then bake about 1 hour, covered, in a 350° F oven removing the cover for the last 20 minutes of cooking.

Johnny Marzetti

Marzetti's is the oldest restaurant in Columbus. In the tradition of so many Italian restaurants in America, it's not quite Italian, very American, and often the only restaurant everyone goes to year in and year out. Recipes for Johnny Marzetti are all over Ohio—and they all start with what Peter LaRiviere, a tireless student of American cooking, calls Irish lady's tomato sauce. Note the bay leaf; note the Worcestershire sauce; note the taste, which is wonderful.

1 pound ground chuck
1 cup minced onion
1 cup minced green bell pepper
1½ cups fresh mushrooms, sliced
2 cups chopped ripe fresh tomatoes or
    canned tomatoes
2 cups tomato sauce
1 tablespoon chopped fresh basil
½ teaspoon dried oregano
1 bay leaf
Salt and pepper to taste
1 tablespoon Worcestershire sauce
3 quarts salted water
4 cups medium egg noodles
¼ cup (½ stick) unsalted butter
3 cups grated cheddar cheese
2 cups fresh buttered bread crumbs

Crumble the meat into a heavy skillet over high heat and stir until it loses its red color. Add the onion and pepper and cook until the onion is translucent. Add the mushrooms and cook 5 minutes longer. Add the tomatoes, tomato sauce, herbs, salt, pepper, and Worcestershire sauce, and simmer gently 30 minutes. When the sauce has simmered 15 minutes, boil the salted water and cook the noodles until just tender. Drain, and toss with the butter.

Preheat the oven to 350° F.

To assemble the casserole: Place half the noodles in a 3-quart casserole and top with half the cheese and half the sauce. For the second layer, add remaining noodles, sauce, and cheese then top with the buttered bread crumbs. Bake until cheese melts and the flavors marry, about 30 minutes. Let the casserole sit for 10 to 15 minutes to make serving easier.

Makes 6 to 8 servings

DESSERTS

Mary Elizabeth Biracree Smith's Green Tomato Mincemeat Pie

(with David Blackburn's Glosses)

This is how American cooking is really done: from generation to generation, not necessarily consciously, not necessarily with intent, but with the receipts passed down anyway, and sooner or later a comment or two added. In this case, for the latter part of the twentieth century, David has halved the sugar and the raisins and added a little citrus zest—and recognized the true idiosyncrasy of the green tomato by doubling the amount. The original was good; its descendant is even better.

1 quart chopped peeled tart apples
1 quart chopped green tomatoes
2 teaspoons ground cinnamon
1½ teaspoons ground cloves
1½ teaspoons salt
1½ teaspoons ground allspice
1½ cups sugar
½ pound raisins
¼ cup vinegar
1½ cups chopped suet
1 teaspoon grated orange zest
Pastry with Vegetable Shortening (see
   page 80)
¼ cup bourbon

Combine all ingredients except pastry and bourbon in a large Dutch oven and bring to a rapid boil. Reduce the heat, then simmer gently until thick, stirring often to prevent sticking. Cool and refrigerate the filling in a glass or stoneware crock for up to 6 weeks or more, or seal in sterilized jars (see page 72).

Make Pastry with Vegetable Shortening for a double-crust pie. (Or make Butter Pastry, page 7, using ½ butter, ½ lard.) Line an 8-inch pie plate with half the rolled out pastry. Fill with 3 cups mincemeat; sprinkle with the bourbon. Top with a lattice of ¼-inch pastry strips.

Preheat the oven to 400° F.

Bake until crust is golden brown, about 30 minutes.

VARIATION: Use the mincemeat as a topping for ice cream or as a pudding with heavy cream. Always sprinkle with a tablespoon or two of bourbon before reheating to serve.

Makes 6 servings

Lemon Meringue Pie

6 tablespoons cornstarch
1 cup sugar, plus 8 tablespoons
¼ teaspoon salt
1½ cups hot water
3 large egg yolks, well beaten
2 tablespoons (¼ stick) unsalted butter
1 teaspoon grated lemon zest
½ cup fresh lemon juice
Pastry with Vegetable Shortening (see
   page 80)
3 large egg whites, at room temperature
¼ teaspoon cream of tartar

Roll out a single-crust pastry. Line a 10-inch pie plate with foil and fill with raw rice or dried beans for weight. Bake at 400° F for 12 to 15 minutes, or until lightly brown. Mix the cornstarch, 1 cup sugar, and the salt in a saucepan. Stir in the hot water. Simmer the mixture over direct heat, stirring constantly, until thick and clear, about 10 minutes. Remove the mixture from the heat and stir ½ cup of the hot mixture into the egg yolks, beating constantly. Stir the yolk mixture back into the hot mixture. Cook over low heat, stirring constantly, 2 to 3 minutes. Remove from the heat and beat in the butter, then add the lemon zest and juice, stirring until smooth.

Pour the filling into the baked pie shell and let cool briefly.

Preheat the oven to 350° F.

Beat the egg whites with the cream of tartar until frothy. Sprinkle the whites with the 6 tablespoons sugar as you continue to beat. Beat until the meringue stands in glossy peaks. Spread the meringue on top of the filling, making sure it covers the edges of the crust. Swirl the meringue toward the center of the pie into a tent-shaped peak and sprinkle with remaining 2 tablespoons sugar. Bake the pie in the oven 15 minutes, or until the meringue is delicately browned. Cool the pie and serve at once (it is better not to refrigerate meringues; they begin to weep easily).

Makes 8 servings

THE OLD NORTHWEST: MINNESOTA AND MICHIGAN

Coastal dwellers may believe nothing is going on out there—but believe me, the culinary scene, at least, is hopping. Of course, restaurants were not discovered in the heartland until about 1974. Before that, you'd better have known someone if you planned to eat. Now, young chefs are beavering away, imitating Alice Waters and sending minions out to the marshes of the Great Lakes to look for mushrooms in the spring. All very well—but all those folks eating at home for the last couple of hundred years were onto something too.

The raw materials are, of course, wonderful—this is the home of watercress and wild rice and freshwater bass—and the cultural heritage is just as rich. Garrison Keillor, raised among Lutherans in the heart of this country, seems to have had some terrible experiences with *lutefisk,* that odd fermented holiday fish from Scandinavia, but most of the Norwegian and Swedish settlers who ended up in the Old Northwest had a benign influence on the cooking of the region, bringing with them dark sour rye bread, smoked fish in endless variety, and rich coffee cakes to go with the bottomless northern taste for strong coffee. And the Germans who settled the cities brought a solid culinary heritage to help get through those winters at forty below zero. (David Holupchinski, that gifted cook who left us for Eveline's in New York, used to brag about the cold weather—he loved going home to St. Paul for Christmas, so that he could flex his muscles against the icy blasts. They are giants of fortitude out there.)

SMALL PLATES

Steak Tartare

My father called this dish a cannibal sandwich, and it may be that we get it from the smorgasbord of northern Europe rather than from the smooth decadence of France. It's good stuff, though, as unlikely as it seems having come out of the long-cooking far north.

1 pound absolutely lean sirloin
1 tablespoon Worcestershire sauce
1 teaspoon each salt and fresh-ground
  pepper
2 heavy dashes of Tabasco
1 tablespoon extra-virgin olive oil
Squeeze of lemon
1 cup minced onion
½ cup tiny capers, drained
½ cup minced fresh parsley
4 small raw egg yolks

Cut the sirloin into 4 or 5 pieces and place in the bowl of a food processor fitted with a metal blade. Using the on-off switch, chop the steak just until it reaches ground-meat consistency (it shouldn't be too fine). With your hands, mix the Worcestershire, salt, pepper, Tabasco, olive oil, and lemon juice into the beef. Divide the mixture into 4 helpings on chilled plates and distribute the onion, capers, and parsley around each serving. Make a depression in each portion of meat and drop an egg yolk into each. Serve at once with black bread and butter.

Makes 4 servings

Janssen's Temptation

I had thought this was a Danish dish, but a Danish customer recently told me it is Swedish. Every Scandinavian customer I've ever had loves it like candy. Oh, the North.

4 Maine potatoes, sliced very thin
2 medium onions, halved and sliced very thin
1 can flat anchovies, well drained and lightly rinsed
½ cup (1 stick) unsalted butter, melted
2 teaspoons fresh-ground pepper
Light sprinkle of salt
2 cups heavy cream
4 tablespoons minced fresh parsley

Preheat the oven to 400° F.

Butter a deep 10-inch pie plate and line with half the potatoes, sprinkle half the onions on top of the potatoes, then add a layer of half the anchovies and sprinkle with half each of the melted butter, pepper, and salt (remember that the anchovies are salty). Repeat the layers, ending with onions. Fill the dish to the top with heavy cream.

Bake until the potatoes are tender and the cream is almost absorbed, about 45 minutes. Cut in slices and serve heavily sprinkled with parsley.

Makes 8 servings

SOUPS

Minnesota Wild Rice and Turkey Soup

From the superb cook David Holupchinski, whose native Minnesota gave him all the ingredients for what is very much his own dish.

1 turkey carcass
2 quarts Chicken Stock (see page 28)
2 bay leaves
½ turkey breast, about 1 pound
2 medium onions, diced fine
1 medium carrot, diced fine
2 celery stalks, diced fine
2 tablespoons (¼ stick) unsalted butter
1 cup uncooked wild rice
1 branch fresh thyme
Salt and pepper to taste
Chopped watercress

Simmer the turkey carcass in the chicken stock with the bay leaves for about 1 hour. Strain.

Poach the turkey breast in the stock until just tender but still a little pink in the center (about 30 minutes). Sauté the vegetables very gently in the butter, until the onion is translucent. Wash and stir in the wild rice. Add thyme, salt, and pepper. Add the stock and simmer until the vegetables are tender and the rice is done, about 40 minutes. Cut the turkey breast in slivers and add to the soup. Serve hot with the watercress on top.

Makes 8 to 10 servings

Cauliflower Soup

Okay, it's a white vegetable cream soup and couldn't be more wintry—but taste it, and winter almost seems worth it.

2 quarts milk
1 head cauliflower, cut into flowerets
1 onion, chopped coarse
1 celery stalk, chopped coarse
¼ cup (½ stick) unsalted butter
3 tablespoons all-purpose flour
1 quart Chicken Stock (see page 28)
1 teaspoon ground nutmeg
½ teaspoon cayenne pepper
Salt and white pepper to taste

Garnish
Paprika
Minced fresh parsley

In a large Dutch oven, bring the milk to a boil over medium heat, then add the cauliflower, onion, and celery. Lower the heat and simmer until the vegetables are very tender. Drain the vegetables, reserving the milk. Purée the vegetables in the bowl of a food processor fitted with a metal blade until very fine. Strain.

In a large Dutch oven over medium heat, melt the butter, then whisk in the flour, and cook, without browning, 10 minutes, stirring constantly. Whisk in the stock, then the vegetable purée, nutmeg, cayenne, pepper, and salt. Thin the mixture to soup consistency with the reserved milk. Serve sprinkled with paprika and minced parsley.

Makes 12 servings

SALADS

Spinach Salad

1 pound young spinach
6 hard-boiled eggs
8 slices crisp-fried bacon
¼ cup cider vinegar
2 tablespoons Dijon mustard
Pinch of ground rosemary
Salt and pepper to taste
1 cup olive oil
Pimiento strips

Wash the spinach (immerse in *warm, salted* water first, swishing madly, then immerse again in very cold unsalted water), remove the stems, pat dry, and tear into bite-size pieces. Chop 4 hard-boiled eggs, crumble the bacon, and toss both with the spinach. Whisk the vinegar, mustard, rosemary, salt, and pepper together, then drizzle in the oil, a bit at a time, still whisking. Toss the salad again with just enough of the dressing to coat. Garnish the salad with slices of the remaining hard-boiled eggs and strips of pimiento.

Makes 4 servings

Perfection Salad

Not a salad. Not a weird Jell-O half-confection. A really good aspic that won a Knox gelatin contest in 1905, and may in part be responsible for all those terrible sweet things in lurid colors. But parents can't always be responsible for their children's faults, so just try this and leave snobbery behind.

1 cup small carrots, cut into thin slices
    and cooked
French Dressing (recipe follows)
1 envelope unflavored gelatin
¼ cup sugar
½ teaspoon salt
¾ cup boiling water
¾ cup cold water
¼ cup lemon juice
5 stuffed green olives, sliced
1 cup shredded cabbage
½ cup chopped celery
¼ cup chopped green bell pepper
¼ cup chopped pimiento

Garnish
Ripe olives

Marinate the carrot slices in the French Dressing (recipe follows). Blend the gelatin, sugar, and salt, and add ¼ cup cold water. Let stand until the gelatin softens. Add the boiling water, stir until gelatin dissolves, and stir in remaining ½ cup cold water and the lemon juice and allow to cool.

Place the olives in an even pattern in the bottom of a greased 3½-cup ring mold. Add the cabbage, celery, bell pepper, and pimiento to the gelatin mixture, and carefully turn into the mold. Chill until set, at least 3 hours or overnight. When ready to serve, unmold the salad and fill the center with the carrots. Garnish with the ripe olives.

Makes 6 servings

French Dressing

¼ cup cider vinegar
1 teaspoon Dijon mustard
2 tablespoons ketchup
Salt and pepper to taste
1 teaspoon sugar
1 cup soy oil

Whisk the vinegar, mustard, ketchup, salt, pepper, and sugar together. Add the oil in a slow drizzle, continuing to whisk until the mixture emulsifies.

Makes 1½ cups

MAIN COURSES

Swedish Roast Leg of Lamb

David Fetherolf, who points out that in parts of the country his Norwegian name is quite common, has cooked for us in New York since we opened. He calls this "leg of lamb with regular coffee." The dish, part of a Scandinavian-American menu David did for us, deserves only praise.

1 4-pound leg of lamb, boned and tied,
   bones reserved
1 carrot, chopped coarse
1 onion, chopped coarse
2 celery stalks, chopped coarse
2 teaspoons salt
1 teaspoon pepper
1 quart red wine
1 bunch parsley
1 bay leaf
1 branch fresh rosemary
2 cups strong coffee
1 tablespoon sugar
½ cup heavy cream
3 tablespoons all-purpose flour
1 tablespoon red currant jelly

Preheat the oven to 400° F.

Place the lamb bones and any excess fat trimmed from the leg in a roasting pan with the vegetables, salt, and pepper. Roast 1 hour, or until the bones are good and brown, turning from time to time. Remove the bones and deglaze the pan with the red wine on top of the stove, stirring from the bottom to dislodge all the browned bits. Pour the pan juices and vegetables into a stockpot and cover with water. Add the parsley, bay leaf, and rosemary. Bring the liquid to a boil, reduce the heat to a simmer, and cook slowly 6 to 8 hours. Remove the stockpot from the heat, chill, skim, and strain. Return to the heat and reduce at a brisk boil to 1 quart and reserve.

Preheat the oven to 450° F.

Salt and pepper the lamb, place it in a roasting pan, and roast about 30 minutes. Pour the coffee, sugar, and cream over the lamb, lower the heat to 350° F, and continue cooking until the

(continued)

lamb is dark brown outside and pink in the middle, about 40 minutes longer.

Remove the lamb from the roasting pan and keep warm. Skim the fat from the pan and reheat it in a saucepan. Add the flour and whisk over medium heat until hazelnut brown. Add 2 cups of the reserved stock and cook about

10 minutes, until thickened and bubbly. Add this mixture to the liquid in the roasting pan, then whisk in the red currant jelly. Strain and serve hot with the sliced lamb.

The lamb is wonderful with lightly cooked kale and boiled potatoes.

Makes 8 to 10 servings

Roast Loin of Pork with Dried-Fruit Dressing

The bounteous use of simple ingredients is what the old North is all about—and this recipe seems to combine the Scotch-Irish, German, and Scandinavian strains that settled the country.

1 quart Chicken Stock (see page 28)
1 3-pound pork loin, boned and butterflied, bones reserved
1 bay leaf
1 garlic clove, minced
1 branch fresh thyme
1 teaspoon dried thyme
¼ cup (½ stick) unsalted butter, softened
Salt and pepper to taste
2 cups dried apricots, chopped coarse
1 cup dried peaches, chopped coarse
2 cups sliced peeled apples
½ cup currants
2 cups fresh apple cider
1 cup orange juice
¼ cup (½ stick) unsalted butter, melted

Bring the stock to a boil and add the reserved bones. Simmer with the bay leaf 1 hour or so.

Preheat the oven to 400° F.

Meanwhile, rub the inside of the pork loin with the garlic, thyme, and the soft butter. Roll and tie the loin, then salt and pepper it. Place it in a large roasting pan and roast about 1½ hours.

Toss the fruit with 1 cup cider and ½ cup orange juice.

Lift the roast from the pan and line the bottom with the fruit. Return the roast to the pan, lower the temperature to 350° F, and continue cooking ½ hour longer. Strain the stock and skim.

Measure out 2 cups stock; add the remaining cider, orange juice, and melted butter, and baste the roast frequently with this mixture.

When the roast is done, remove it from the pan and set aside to keep warm. Spoon the fruit from the bottom of pan, scraping if necessary. Deglaze the pan with the remaining stock and any leftover basting mixture. Stir from the bottom of pan to dislodge all the good bits.

Let the roast stand for 10 minutes, then serve the meat sliced with the fruit on the side and the sauce on top. Wonderful with Mashed Sweet Potatoes (recipe follows).

Makes 6 to 8 servings

Mashed Sweet Potatoes

6 large sweet potatoes
1½ cups milk
½ cup (1 stick) unsalted butter
Salt and pepper to taste

Peel and cut up the sweet potatoes. Bring a large pot of water to a boil, add the potatoes, cover, and cook until tender but not falling apart. Scald the milk and melt the butter in it. Mash the potatoes, and blend in the milk, butter, salt, and pepper. Add no sugar.

Makes 8 servings

DESSERTS

Raisin Pudding Cake

1 cup all-purpose flour
1 cup sugar
2 teaspoons baking powder
¼ teaspoon salt
½ cup milk
3 large eggs, beaten
1 cup raisins
½ cup chopped walnuts
1 cup packed dark brown sugar
1 teaspoon unsalted butter
1½ cups boiling water

Preheat the oven to 350° F. Grease a 9-inch-square baking pan.

Sift the flour, sugar, baking powder, and salt together into a large mixing bowl. Add the milk, eggs, raisins, and walnuts. Mix until well blended. Spread the batter in the prepared pan.

Combine the brown sugar, butter, and water and stir well. Pour the mixture over the batter, but do not mix together. Bake 35 minutes, or until a straw inserted in the center comes out clean. Serve warm with applesauce.

Makes 6 servings

German Chocolate Cake

4 ounces German sweet chocolate
½ cup hot coffee
1 cup (2 sticks) unsalted butter
2 cups sugar
4 large egg yolks
1 teaspoon vanilla extract
2½ cups sifted cake flour
1 teaspoon baking soda
½ teaspoon salt
½ cup buttermilk
4 large egg whites, stiffly beaten

Preheat the oven to 350° F. Grease and flour 3 8-inch cake pans.

Melt the chocolate in the hot coffee and allow to cool. Cream the butter and sugar, then add the egg yolks, one at a time, beating well. Blend in the vanilla and the chocolate-coffee mixture. Sift together the flour, baking soda, and salt, then add to the chocolate mixture, alternating with the buttermilk. Fold in the egg whites.

Pour the batter into the prepared pans. Bake 30 to 40 minutes, or until a straw inserted in the center comes out clean. Cool the cake layers on racks.

To assemble the cake: Spread frosting between layers and over the top. When completely cooled, sprinkle chocolate curls over the cake.

Makes 10 servings

Coconut-Pecan Frosting

1 cup sweetened condensed milk
½ cup sugar
3 large egg yolks, slightly beaten
½ cup (1 stick) unsalted butter
1 teaspoon vanilla extract
1½ cups shredded coconut
1 cup chopped pecans

1 cup sweet chocolate curls

Combine the milk, sugar, egg yolks, butter, and vanilla in a large saucepan. Simmer over low heat until thickened, about 10 minutes. Stir in the coconut and pecans. Cool the frosting just until spreadable, beating as it cools.

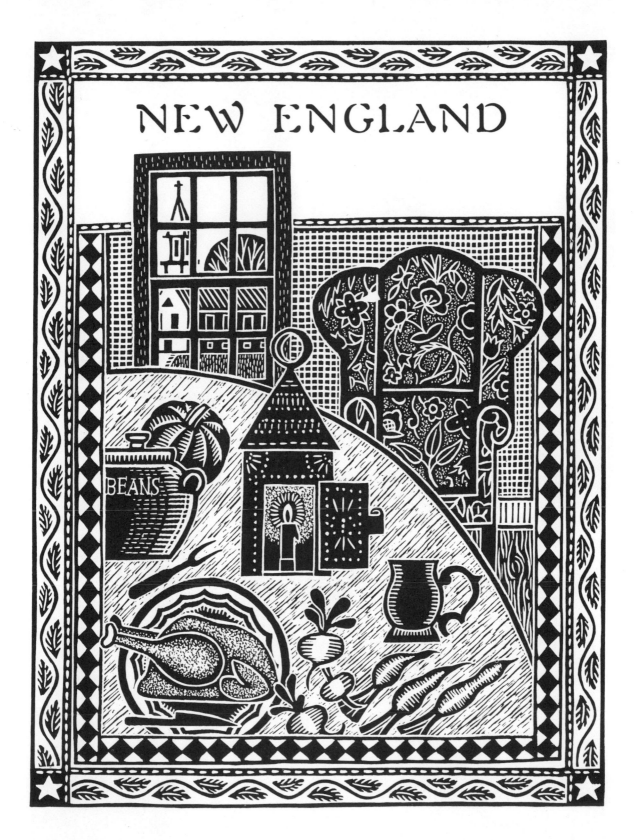

Oh, all right. New England is rockbound and very, very cold. It was not settled by easygoing, freewheeling second sons with a genial allegiance to the squirearchy, but by stiff-necked Puritans prepared to fight it out winter after winter in the Spartan Atlantic Northeast rather than turn back to the spiritually soft English Southeast. The Puritans' reputation for dourness has persisted right down to the present and makes it almost impossible to cook New England food in a restaurant without being accused of an almost Puritan stubbornness.

Nevertheless, the effort is worth it. The Indians taught the Puritans to farm a difficult land during a short growing season, and the combination of native materials and English love of plenty added up to a cookery that is satisfying to this day. The Atlantic is as bountiful on this side as it was in England, and new experiences in a new land seemed to open the settlers' minds to brighter and broader tastes than they had experienced in the Old Country. New England's cookery is still very basic, but the flavors chime together, making winter a lot warmer and the landscape a lot softer.

SMALL PLATES

Ritz Fish Balls

Salt cod is simple stuff and a very good way of having fish through the winter if you don't want to head out into the freezing Atlantic. Typical of New England is that this simple stuff is served in Boston's most venerable classy hotel, the Ritz, overlooking the lyrically pretty Common. The Ritz's ground-floor luncheon room also offers that homely noontime ladies' treat, the tongue sandwich.

1½ large potatoes, peeled
2 quarts Fish Stock (see page 102)
1 pound salt cod, soaked in water
   overnight then drained
2 tablespoons (¼ stick) unsalted butter,
   melted
1 teaspoon Worcestershire sauce
1 teaspoon dry mustard
1 teaspoon pepper
3 large egg yolks
2 cups all-purpose flour
Soy oil for deep frying

Garnish
Lemons
Parsley sprigs

Bring a large saucepan of salted water to a boil and cook the potatoes until tender. Drain the potatoes and rice them into a warm bowl. In a large skillet containing the fish stock, simmer the fish 5 minutes, then drain on a tea towel. Flake the fish into the hot potatoes, then add the butter, Worcestershire sauce, mustard, pepper, and egg yolks. Gently toss together, being careful not to let the mixture pack down. Shape the mixture quickly into 2-inch balls and roll in flour. In a large deep pot, heat the oil to 375° F. Gently lower the balls into the fat and fry until golden, about 2 minutes. Serve with quartered lemons and parsley sprigs.

Makes 6 servings

Creamed Turkey and Oysters

Well, there was the turkey, inland, and there were all those oysters, right off shore. The combination makes the best and mildest of first courses, the two flavors marrying in an almost exotic simplicity that wouldn't hurt a baby.

¼ cup (½ stick) unsalted butter
4 tablespoons all-purpose flour
1 cup light cream
1 teaspoon salt
½ teaspoon white pepper
Dash of Tabasco
½ teaspoon Worcestershire sauce
1 pint fresh shucked oysters, with their
   liquid
4 large slices cooked turkey breast
4 thick slices good white bread, toasted
   and buttered

Garnish
Watercress

In a large skillet over medium heat, melt the butter until it froths. Add the flour and cook, stirring constantly, 5 minutes. Add the cream, salt, pepper, Tabasco, and Worcestershire. Simmer 5 minutes, or until thickened. Add the oysters and their liquid and cook 2 minutes, then add the sliced turkey, tucking it just below the surface of the sauce, and simmer until the turkey is heated through. Lift out the turkey slices, and place them on the toasted bread on individual serving plates. Pour the oysters and sauce over all, and garnish with watercress.

Makes 4 servings

SOUPS

Clam Chowder

Some regional American dishes are still current in their regions of origin but not necessarily all that popular. The homogenization of American culture by television, national magazines, and a constantly shifting population has seen to that. Among the exceptions, though, clam chowder is queen. In fast-food franchises, local diners, major hotels, fine traditional restaurants, and even French houses of impeccable lineage, it's impossible to avoid the cup of chowder, and no New Englander would want to. Clam chowder is not a cliché but a tradition. It tastes wonderful, whether you have it the old-fashioned way, as a Friday night supper with cold salads, or as a first course before dinner.

¼ pound fatty salt pork
1 cup (2 sticks) unsalted butter
2 celery stalks, diced fine
3 large onions, peeled and diced fine
2 tablespoons all-purpose flour
4 medium potatoes, peeled and diced fine
1 quart milk
1 quart shucked hard-shell clams, with
    their liquid
2 cups light cream
1½ teaspoons salt
1 teaspoon pepper
Heavy dash of Tabasco
½ teaspoon dried thyme

Crackers*

Cut the pork into fine dice and cook over medium heat in a large enamel-covered cast-iron Dutch oven until brown and crackly. Lift out the pork and melt ½ cup butter in the pan. Add the celery and onions and cook until slightly yellowed. Sprinkle on the flour and cook 4 minutes, stirring constantly. Do not let the mixture brown.

Stir in the potatoes, add the milk, and simmer until the potatoes are tender. Chop the clams and add with their liquid and simmer a few minutes longer, then add the cream and all the seasonings. Stir, and allow to cool. Chill the

(continued)

* "Common crackers," once the most ordinary cracker in New England, are now made only by George H. Bent, 7 Pleasant Street, Milton, Massachusetts 02186—the oldest and original makers of common crackers—and by the Vermont Country Store, Route 103, Rockingham, Vermont 05101. The crackers are available by mail, in retail amounts, from both. If you don't want to send for them, substitute saltines.

chowder at least 2 hours, then reheat and correct the seasonings. Serve with a lump of butter in each bowl and plenty of crackers.

SATURDAY-NIGHT CHOWDER: To leftover clam chowder, add corn kernels and flaked fish. Reheat and serve as above.

Makes 10 servings

Northern Border Yellow Split Pea Soup

2 cups yellow split peas
1 ham bone
2 celery stalks, diced fine
1 onion, diced fine
1 carrot, diced fine
2 whole cloves and 1 large bay leaf, tied
    in cheesecloth
1 large potato, diced fine
Salt and pepper to taste

Pick over the peas and soak overnight in cold water to cover. Drain the peas and place them in a heavy pot with water to cover. Add the ham bone, all the vegetables except the potatoes, and the spice bouquet. Simmer gently until the peas are tender, about 2 hours. Add the potatoes and cook 30 minutes longer, or until done. Remove the ham bone and bouquet. Season with salt and pepper and serve. You may want to purée the soup for a finer texture.

Makes 10 servings

Old-Fashioned Herring Salad

Victor Hugo said of the herring that it would be a delicacy if it weren't so cheap. Hardly any fish is cheap these days, but the herring still has a proletarian reputation that is hardly deserved. This is a kitchen-sink salad, with the unexpected combination of apples, beef, and fish coming together with greater felicity than you'd suppose. One of the pleasures of serving it is watching people try to sort out the flavors.

1 large salt herring, soaked in water
  overnight
1 cup diced cooked peeled potatoes
1 cup diced peeled Cortland or Rome
  Beauty apples
2 tablespoons tiny capers, drained
2 hard-boiled eggs, chopped
1 cup diced cooked roast beef
1 cup diced cooked beets, well drained
½ cup diced cucumber
½ cup Mustard-Garlic Vinaigrette (see
  page 105, but omit garlic and add 1
  teaspoon sugar)
Boston lettuce in chiffonade

Clean the herring, remove its skin and bones, and cut into small dice. Combine the fish with all other ingredients except vinaigrette and lettuce, toss with the dressing, and let stand 1 hour in the refrigerator. Serve on a chiffonade of Boston lettuce.

Makes 6 servings

Cabbage-Cheddar Salad

Cabbage suffers from bad press and a long popularity in American cookery. Some people raised without recourse to lettuce have eaten hundreds of pounds of coleslaw and been all the better for it. This variation is enriched and smoothed by the cheddar cheese, a trick New Englanders are very fond of.

3 cups fine-shredded cabbage
1 cup fine-shredded carrots
1 green bell pepper, diced fine
1 red bell pepper, diced fine
1½ cups fine-diced fresh ripe tomato
¾ cup grated cheddar cheese
¾ cup Curry Mayonnaise (see page 4)

Lightly toss the vegetables, tomato, and the cheese together with 2 forks. Toss with the mayonnaise, chill briefly, and serve on chilled plates.

Makes 8 servings

MAIN COURSES

Baked Scrod with Bacon

This is a great dinner dish, typical not only of New England but of the whole country in its use of bacon to enrich fish. What is peculiar to New England is the habit of eating this dish at breakfast. In some old-fashioned inns baked fish still appears on the menu each morning.

2 cups medium-fine bread crumbs
½ teaspoon dried thyme
1 tablespoon chopped fresh parsley
¼ pound salt pork, diced fine
1 large onion, diced fine
1 sour dill pickle, diced fine
½ cup white wine or water
4 8-ounce scrod fillets, skinned
Salt and pepper to taste
8 thick slices bacon

Preheat the oven to 350° F. Heavily butter a large baking pan.

Toss the bread crumbs with the thyme and parsley. In a large skillet over medium heat, fry the salt pork until the fat is rendered and the pork is brown and crackly. Add the onion and cook briefly until transparent. Add the bread crumb mixture and remove the skillet from the heat. Toss to combine, then add the pickle. Moisten with the wine or water.

Pat the crumb mixture into 4 mounds and place on the prepared baking pan. Place the scrod fillets on the mounds, then salt lightly and pepper heavily. Place 2 bacon slices across each fillet, and bake in the oven until the bacon is done and the fish flakes when probed with a fork, about 25 minutes.

Makes 4 servings

New England Boiled Dinner

Properly cooked and served, this is a great *pot au feu*, its various mild flavors augmented by pungent sauces and its own rich broth. We serve it with cornbread and dark rye and sweet butter.

5 pounds corned beef
2 quarts Beef Stock (see page 160), or to cover)
1 bay leaf, 2 whole cloves, and 1 bunch parsley, tied in cheesecloth
½ pound salt pork
8 carrots, peeled and quartered
8 parsnips, peeled and quartered
8 small white turnips, peeled
1 large rutabaga, peeled and cut into large chunks
8 medium onions, peeled
8 small beets, unpeeled
4 potatoes, peeled and halved
1 medium head cabbage, trimmed and quartered, core in
Salt and pepper to taste
1 tablespoon good-quality cider vinegar

Place the corned beef in a large Dutch oven and cover with the stock. Add the herb bouquet, and bring to a boil over high heat. Lower the heat, cover, and simmer 2 hours. Add the salt pork and simmer 2 hours longer, skimming from time to time. Skim once more, then add the carrots, parsnips, turnips, rutabaga, and onions. Cover and simmer 30 minutes. Meanwhile, place the beets in a separate pot with water to cover and boil 30 minutes.

Add the potatoes to the beef and cook until almost tender, about 20 minutes.

Add the cabbage and cook just until tender, about 10 minutes longer. Remove the beef from the first pot and place on a large warmed platter. Drain the beets and slip off their peels. Surround the beef with the vegetables, including the beets, well-drained potatoes, and the cabbage.

Remove the herb bouquet from the pot and thoroughly skim the broth. Season the broth with pepper and salt, if needed (be cautious with the salt), and add the vinegar. Bring the broth to a boil again, and serve the broth in bowls as a first course. Keep the meat and vegetables warm on their platter, and serve after the broth with Sweet and Sour Mustard, Sour Cream and Horseradish Sauce, and Orange-Cranberry Relish (recipes follow).

Makes 10 servings

Sour Cream and Horseradish Sauce

Mix 2 cups sour cream with ¼ cup freshly grated horseradish. Add salt to taste.

Makes 2 cups

Sweet and Sour Mustard

4 tablespoons dry mustard
¼ cup sugar
½ teaspoon dried marjoram
½ teaspoon each salt and pepper
Dash of cayenne pepper
¼ cup good-quality cider vinegar
¼ cup white wine

Combine all the ingredients in the bowl of a food processor fitted with a metal blade and blend until smooth.

Makes 1½ cups

Orange-Cranberry Relish

1 large seedless orange
1 pound cranberries
1½ cups sugar
½ cup Cointreau liqueur

Cut the orange into 1-inch chunks. Put all ingredients into food processor bowl fitted with a metal blade and pulse-stop until reduced to a very rough purée. Do not overprocess. Let stand, refrigerated, about 2 hours to marry flavors.

Makes 2½ cups

Boston Baked Beans

It's important to remember that this dish, like numerous other American classics, is never meant to be served alone, but as part of a complex of dishes that add up to a much more interesting set of flavors than the central dish, taken singly, suggests. Eaten with brown bread, Piccalilli (recipes follow), and perhaps a slice of ham or a sausage, this is a serious and solid dish. Alone, its position as a classic would puzzle anyone.

2 pounds dried pea beans
1 medium onion, peeled and stuck with 3 cloves
½ pound salt pork
½ cup molasses
½ cup soy sauce
½ cup ketchup
½ cup cider vinegar
1 teaspoon pepper
1 tablespoon dry mustard
1 teaspoon salt

Preheat the oven to 300° F.

Soak the beans overnight in cold water to cover. Rinse and pick over the beans, then add water to cover the beans by 2 inches. Bring to a boil, lower the heat, and simmer until the bean skins split when blown on hard, about 2 hours. Using a slotted spoon, place about 2 cups of beans in the bottom of a heavy, small-mouthed bean pot or in a heavy casserole with a close-fitting top. Add the onion, then the remaining beans (draining them with the slotted spoon, until the pot is almost full. Tuck the salt pork down into the beans, allowing it to protrude above the beans.

(continued)

Combine the remaining ingredients and drizzle over the beans

Bake the beans in the oven 6 to 8 hours, adding water as necessary to keep the beans moist. Serve the beans with Massachusetts Brown Bread and Piccalilli (recipes follow).

Makes 6 servings

Massachusetts Brown Bread

¾ cup graham flour
¾ cup yellow cornmeal
¾ cup all-purpose flour
¾ fine dry bread crumbs
1 cup molasses
2 cups buttermilk
2 teaspoons baking soda
1 teaspoon salt
¾ cup chopped raisins

Grease 2 1-quart coffee tins. Combine all the ingredients and mix well. Fill the prepared coffee tins about ⅔ full, cover tightly with aluminum foil, and tie securely with string to seal.

Set the coffee cans on trivets or racks inside a large Dutch oven. Fill the Dutch oven ⅔ of the way up the coffee cans with boiling water. Cover the Dutch oven tightly and steam at a simmer about 2 hours.

Makes 2 loaves

Piccalilli

1 pound green tomatoes, chopped
1 pound firm ripe tomatoes, chopped
1 large onion, chopped coarse
1 large green bell pepper, sliced
1 large sweet red bell pepper, sliced
½ cucumber, chopped
½ bunch celery, chopped coarse
⅓ cup salt
1½ cups cider vinegar
½ pound dark brown sugar
1 teaspoon dry mustard
1 teaspoon pepper

Combine the tomatoes with all the vegetables and sprinkle with the salt. Let stand at least 12 hours. Drain well in a colander, pressing out the salty brine. Place the vegetables and tomatoes in a large pot, add the vinegar, brown sugar, mustard, and pepper, and cook over low heat 1 hour. Chill the piccalilli and serve (it will keep at least 2 weeks in the refrigerator), or seal in clean hot jars (see page 72).

Makes 3 quarts

DESSERTS

Blueberry Slump

The names of New England dishes, even the very best, have a kind of antipoetic ring to them. It's all part of the heritage of old England, I suspect, where names like toad-in-the-hole and bubble-and-squeak are used to describe food that people actually like to eat. This slump is not just good, it's luscious, and the name just has to be taken as part of the territory. (Maybe a New England strategy for protecting it from outsiders?)

4 cups fresh blueberries
1½ cups sugar
1 whole lemon, chopped fine
⅛ teaspoon ground cloves
1 cup milk, plus additional
½ cup cornmeal
1 cup all-purpose flour
¼ teaspoon salt
½ cup sugar
2 teaspoons baking powder
1 tablespoon unsalted butter
Heavy cream

Wash and pick over the blueberries, then combine with the sugar, lemon, and cloves in a large saucepan. Simmer until the blueberries are tender and become liquid.

Meanwhile, scald the milk. Sprinkle the surface of the milk with cornmeal, whisk in, then cook until the milk thickens slightly. Sift together the remaining dry ingredients and cut in the butter with 2 knives or a pastry knife. Stir in the cornmeal mixture, and moisten with additional milk, if necessary, to create a soft biscuitlike dough.

Drop the dough into the simmering blueberries by teaspoonfuls, leaving 1 inch or so of space between each dumpling. Tightly cover the pot and continue simmering 15 minutes, or until the dumplings are done. Spoon the hot dumplings into bowls and spoon the blueberries over them as a sauce. Serve with heavy cream.

Makes 8 servings

Indian Pudding

This simple-tasting dessert is so deeply imbued with New England tradition that eating it is like eating history. The corn we had from the Indians, the molasses from the rum trade with the Caribbean islands. Our dessert cook, Carrie Waldman, likes it so much that she sometimes makes it just to comfort herself; never mind, our patrons always buy it—to comfort themselves. Taken with cream, and without the ice cream, Indian Pudding makes a wonderful breakfast.

4 cups milk
⅓ cup yellow cornmeal
½ teaspoon ground ginger
½ teaspoon ground cinnamon
½ cup brown sugar
½ teaspoon salt
½ cup unsulphured molasses
Unsalted butter

Scald 3 cups milk in a large saucepan, then sprinkle the cornmeal over the milk and whisk in. Simmer 20 minutes, stirring frequently.

Preheat the oven to 300° F. Butter a 1½-quart casserole.

Combine the spices, sugar, salt, and molasses and stir well. Stir into the cooked cornmeal mush. Pour the cornmeal mixture into the prepared casserole. Gently pour the remaining milk over the top of the pudding but do not stir in. Dot the pudding with butter. Place the casserole inside a shallow pan filled with water, and bake for 2½ hours. An hour into the baking, check pudding. If the milk is absorbed, stir and add another cup of milk and dot again with butter.

Serve the pudding with ice cream, Hard Sauce (see page 19), or heavy cream. I like chopped candied ginger on top too.

Makes 6 servings

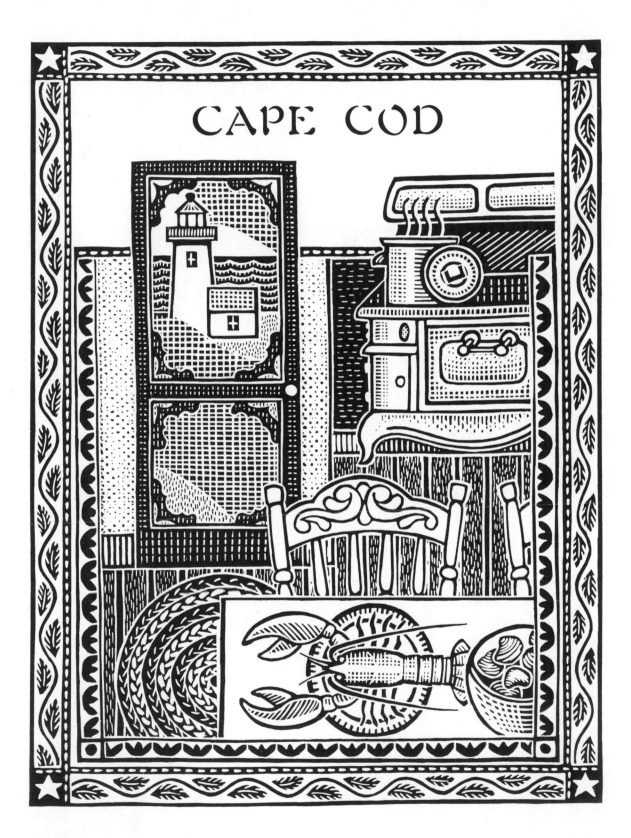

CAPE COD

Cape Cod curls out into the Atlantic like a tornado brought to earth. It is a cornucopia, too, proving my dictum that the more cultures we pack into any given location, the better the food is likely to be. Cape Cod, whose food has influenced the Massachusetts coast as far north as Gloucester, is a happy amalgam of Puritan WASPs, long-term tourists, market gardeners, and Portuguese fisherman. And its raw materials—some of them common to the whole of the East (corn, tomatoes, beans, oysters, clams, raspberries, blueberries), others the peculiar province of Cape Cod (steamers, cranberries, salt cod, and that great invention of Paul's in Falmouth, *linguiça* [Portuguese sausage] pizza).

Cape Cod invites cooks—the tourist community of Provincetown will drive you crazy in summer with great food aromas, from simple hibachi cookouts to lobster Marengo, floating away from each cottage. And the year-round gay community of P-town has in its number some of the best cooks in the country—I got the bluefish recipe in this chapter from one of them. Cape Cod is one of the few beach resorts in the world where cooking seriously threatens to cut into beach time. People actually pick themselves up off the sand before three in the afternoon to put the fish under marinade.

The inducements are strong. Cranberries, for instance, are taken out of their familiar saucy Christmas and Thanksgiving context entirely, and run into muffins, roasts, chicken dishes, even Hollandaise. Cranberries are among our raw materials on the "native and neglected" list: They are high in pectin and so thicken a sauce naturally; they have a wonderfully astringent acidity that doesn't distort with cooking; and their color is constant even with long cooking. I use cranberries in dozens of recipes and expect them to explode into the culinary mainstream any minute.

SMALL PLATES

Stuffed Quahogs

Quahogs are huge, tough, and full of flavor. Ground, they make great chowders and fritters, but on Cape Cod, they most often get tossed with a mess of good things and stuffed back into their shells. One of them is a substantial appetizer; three are a quite large meal.

12 large quahog clams
2 cups white wine
3 ounces salt pork, diced fine
1 small onion, minced
½ green bell pepper, minced
1 large celery stalk, minced
1 tablespoon Worcestershire sauce
3 to 4 drops of Tabasco
Pinch of dried sage
Pinch of dried thyme
Pinch of dried oregano
1 bay leaf, crushed
Smidgen of ground cloves
1 garlic clove, minced
2 cups day-old bread crumbs
Salt and pepper
12 lemon wedges

Place the clams in a large Dutch oven with the wine and steam until opened. Remove the clams from their shells, reserving the clam juice. Twist the shells to loosen the hinges, but do not separate. Then wash the shells and let them drain.

Preheat the oven to 350° F.

Chop or grind the clams (a food processor is good for this). Cook the salt pork in a heavy cast-iron skillet until the fat is rendered and the pork is browned. Remove the pork and reserve. Add the vegetables to the skillet and sauté until limp; add the ground clams, seasonings, garlic, and bread crumbs, turn off the heat, and stir together until well mixed. Add the clam juice to moisten. If the mixture is still too dry, add more wine. The mixture should be moist but not gummy. Add salt and pepper as needed, and pack lightly into the clean clam shells. Close the shells, and place the clams on a cookie sheet. Bake 20 minutes. Serve at once with lemon wedges.

Makes 12 servings as an appetizer, or 4 as a main course

Fish Salad

This is good old-fashioned New England cooking: using leftover fish for a cold lunch or first course. The modern twist is in the olive oil and lemon juice; fifty years ago, it would have been mayonnaise, and fifty years before that, boiled dressing.

4 cups flaked cooked fish
1 cup chopped celery
¼ cup chopped green bell pepper
¼ cup minced scallion, green and white
    parts
¼ cup sour dill pickles, minced
⅓ cup olive oil
¼ cup lemon juice
¼ cup chili sauce
1 teaspoon paprika
½ teaspoon pepper
Greens

Garnish
6 hard-boiled eggs, sliced

Toss the fish and vegetables together. Mix the oil, lemon juice, chili sauce, paprika, and pepper together, and toss with the fish mixture. Chill thoroughly, and serve on greens garnished with the sliced hard-boiled eggs.

Makes 4 servings

Fava Beans with Linguiça

Every warm climate seems to give birth to bean salads. This wonderful Portuguese version, combining beans and sausage, is entirely satisfying hot or cold.

¼ pound salt pork, diced fine
½ cup onion, chopped
1 garlic clove, minced
½ cup dry white wine
½ cup water
1 pound linguiça, sliced thin
1 bay leaf, crumbled
½ teaspoon each salt and pepper
4 cups cooked fava beans
2 tablespoons chopped fresh parsley
1 tablespoon balsamic vinegar

Sauté the diced salt pork in a heavy cast-iron pot until the fat is rendered. Remove the pork and reserve. Add the onion and garlic to the skillet and cook 5 minutes, or until the onion is wilted.

Add the wine, water, sausage, salt pork, bay leaf, salt, and pepper.

Bring to a boil and simmer 10 minutes. Add the beans, parsley, and vinegar, and cook until hot and the flavors marry, about 10 minutes longer.

Serve on small plates with sliced black olives and garlic toast.

Makes 8 servings

SOUPS

Pilgrim Winter Vegetable Soup

This recipe has such an old feeling to it that the orange seems an exotic addition, as in fact it was until the late nineteenth century. A great soup with a solid, simple taste.

¼ cup fine-diced salt pork
2 onions, chopped coarse
1 orange, sliced
6 cups boiling Chicken Stock (see page 28), enriched with pork bones and ham hocks
2 cups cubed unpeeled waxy potatoes
2 cups cubed winter squash
1 pound kidney beans, cooked tender
Salt and pepper to taste
¼ teaspoon cayenne pepper
¼ teaspoon ground allspice

Garnish
Chopped fresh parsley
Chopped fresh scallions

To enrich chicken stock: Add a ham hock and half a pound of raw pork bones to 7 cups of chicken stock. Bring to a boil and reduce to 6 cups. Strain.

Heat the salt pork in a large cast-iron Dutch oven and remove the pork bits when browned. Add the onions and the orange and cook until the onion is tender and beginning to yellow. Remove the orange slices, pressing out the juice as you remove them from the pan.

Remove the ham hocks and bones from the stock. Cook, then pick the meat from the bones and reserve.

Stir the potatoes and squash into the pot, add the boiling stock, and cook just until the vegetables are tender. Add the kidney beans and the reserved meat. Add the salt, pepper, cayenne, and allspice, adjust the seasoning, and serve with generous sprinklings of chopped parsley and scallions.

Makes 12 servings

Portuguese Calda Verde

This good-for-a-meal soup is almost as popular on Cape Cod as chowder.

¼ pound fine-diced salt pork
¾ pound linguiça
1 onion, diced
6 waxy potatoes, unpeeled and diced
   coarsely
6 cups Chicken Stock (see page 28)
1 pound fresh kale, washed and chopped
1 cup water
1 tablespoon white vinegar
¼ teaspoon cayenne pepper
Salt and pepper to taste
2 cups cooked kidney beans

Cook the salt pork in a large Dutch oven over medium heat until lightly browned. Mince ¼ pound linguiça, add to the pork, and cook gently 5 minutes. Add the onion and cook until wilted. Add the potatoes, stock, and kale, and simmer just until the potatoes are done.

Meanwhile, cut the remaining linguiça into ¼-inch slices and sauté in a large skillet until lightly browned. Deglaze the pan with the water, scraping the brown bits from the bottom. Add the linguiça and its pan juices, vinegar, seasonings, and beans to the soup and cook just until heated through.

Serve with soft Portuguese bread drizzled with garlic butter.

Makes 8 servings

SALADS

Scallop Salad

The sweet Cape Cod assumption that anything at all is better with a little seafood in it is perfectly illustrated by this salad. The alabaster whiteness and smooth roundness of the scallops make a good foil for the grapefruit and onion.

½ head Romaine lettuce, in chiffonade
½ cup Mustard-Lemon-Honey
   Vinaigrette
1 pound scallops, lightly poached in
   white wine with bay leaf and cloves
2 large grapefruits, peeled and sectioned
   into supremes
1 red onion, sliced

Arrange the lettuce on a large platter. Slice the scallops and toss them with the vinaigrette, then arrange them on the lettuce. Arrange the grapefruit on the scallops and the red onions on top.

Mustard-Lemon-Honey Vinaigrette
1 tablespoon dry mustard
1 tablespoon honey
Juice and zest of ½ lemon
⅓ cup cider vinegar
½ teaspoon each salt and pepper
1 cup soy oil

Combine first 4 ingredients in a bowl. Add salt and pepper; whisk in soy oil.

Makes 4 servings

Cauliflower Salad

This is one of those salads invented in the days when the lettuce ended early in the season, but you could count on the crucifers until late fall. The carrot and radishes relieve the whiteness.

1 medium cauliflower, trimmed and
    broken into flowerets
½ cup Lemony Mayonnaise (see page 4)
½ cup sour cream
1 tablespoon grainy mustard
1 teaspoon paprika
Salt and pepper to taste
Lettuce leaves
1 carrot, cut into julienne
6 radishes, cut into julienne

Blanch the cauliflower in boiling salted water 2 minutes, or until no longer raw. Drain well, then toss with the other ingredients except carrot, radishes, and lettuce. Add with salt and pepper, and chill. Serve on lettuce leaves sprinkled with carrot and radishes.

Makes 6 servings

MAIN COURSES

Salt Cod with Tomatoes and Onions

This recipe owes a good deal to the Mediterranean Cape Codders, but in its simplicity and depth it has a real New England quality.

1 pound salt cod
3 cups waxy potatoes, peeled and cubed
3 tablespoons olive oil
2 onions, chopped
1 green bell pepper, chopped
1 10-ounce can Italian tomatoes
1 tablespoon chopped fresh parsley
Salt and pepper
Oyster cracker crumbs

Soak the cod overnight in cold water. Change the water and soak 2 hours longer, then shred the fish. Simmer the fish and potatoes in lightly boiling water until the potatoes are tender, then drain.

Meanwhile, heat the olive oil in a large skillet and sauté the onions and bell pepper until soft. Add the tomatoes and their juice and simmer 10 minutes, then add the parsley and salt and pepper to taste.

Preheat the oven to 350° F. Butter a 2-quart casserole dish.

Put ½ the fish and potato mixture in the bottom of the buttered casserole, and add ½ of the tomato mixture. Repeat the 2 layers and sprinkle crumbs over the top. Bake for 30 minutes, or until bubbly and thick.

Makes 6 servings

Cranberry Pot Roast

The cranberry sauce for this recipe has just enough sugar to keep the cranberries from puckering your mouth. It makes for a very sparky pot roast, good with dark red wine or hard cider.

½ cup all-purpose flour
1 teaspoon salt
1 medium onion, grated
1 garlic clove, minced
½ teaspoon pepper
1 3-pound pot roast
¼ pound suet
Dash of cloves
Dash of cinnamon
2 cups red wine
2 cups Beef Broth (see page 160)
Cranberry Sauce (recipe follows)
1 tablespoon red wine vinegar

Combine the flour, salt, onion, garlic, and pepper and rub into all surfaces of the roast. Melt the suet in a large skillet over medium heat and gently brown the roast on all sides. Add the cloves, cinnamon, wine, and broth. Cover and simmer 3 to 3½ hours, until tender. Skim the fat, then add the Cranberry Sauce, vinegar, and ½ cup water. Cover and cook 30 minutes longer.

Serve with Mashed Sweet Potatoes (see page 249) or David Raney's Stir-Fried Parsnips (recipe follows).

Makes 6 servings

Cranberry Sauce

2 cups cranberries
1 small whole orange, diced fine
½ cup sugar

Wash the cranberries and pick off the stems. Put the orange, cranberries, and sugar in a heavy enamel or stainless-steel pot. Cover, and cook over low heat until the ingredients are well blended and the cranberries split. Add water, if necessary, to thin, and continue cooking 15 minutes longer. Set aside.

Makes 2½ cups

David Raney's Stir-Fried Parsnips

Though it's so simple it has only five ingredients, this recipe is deeply mysterious —one of my favorite qualities. No one can believe that anything so sweet contains no sugar. The flavor comes from the natural sugars in the parsnips, which caramelize in the high heat of the wok.

1 pound parsnips
½ cup (1 stick) butter, clarified (see page 202)
2 ounces gingerroot, grated
Salt and pepper to taste

Garnish
Scallions
Pickled ginger strips

Peel the parsnips and cut them into 2-inch long strips (avoid the woody section running down the middle). Heat the butter in a wok, and when it's almost smoking add the parsnips. Toss the parsnips to coat with butter, and continue tossing until the parsnips begin to brown. Cook until almost tender, then add the ginger and cook 5 minutes longer. If the parsnips become too brown before they're tender, add ½ cup water and allow the liquid to cook down. Just before serving, add the salt and pepper, toss again, and serve with scallions and pickled ginger.

Makes 4 servings

Provincetown Bluefish

I had this recipe from a great gay cook in Provincetown, who was out to prove that bluefish was no common catch.

1 tablespoon paprika
1 tablespoon pepper
1 teaspoon cayenne pepper
½ teaspoon dried thyme
2 1-pound bluefish fillets, skinned
4 tablespoons olive oil
1 green and 1 red bell pepper, cut into
   julienne
4 anchovy fillets, drained and chopped
2 teaspoons balsamic vinegar

Combine the paprika, pepper, cayenne, and thyme, then dredge the fish in the mixture. Heat 2 tablespoons olive oil in a large skillet until smoking. Sear the fish in the hot oil on both sides, cooking until just tender. Transfer the fish to a warm platter.

Sauté the bell pepper in the remaining 2 tablespoons oil until it begins to brown. Turn down the heat and add the anchovy fillets. Cook until the anchovy dissolves, then add the vinegar, stir, and remove quickly from the heat. Dress the fish with the pepper sauce and serve at once with boiled potatoes.

Makes 4 servings

DESSERTS

Grilled Banana Bread

American quick breads are one of our singular contributions to world cookery, but they don't have much of a shelf life. This is a great way to use them the day after.

¾ cup walnuts, chopped
⅓ cup golden raisins
2 cups all-purpose flour
1 tablespoon baking powder
½ teaspoon grated gingerroot
1 teaspoon ground nutmeg
½ teaspoon salt
1 teaspoon vanilla extract
2 large black-ripe bananas, mashed
½ cup (1 stick) unsalted butter, softened
⅔ cup brown sugar
1 large egg, beaten
2 tablespoons dark rum

¼ cup (½ stick) unsalted butter
½ cup toasted grated coconut

Preheat the oven to 350° F. Grease and flour a loaf pan. Toss the nuts and raisins with 1 tablespoon flour and set aside. Sift the remaining flour, baking powder, ginger, nutmeg and salt together and set aside. Add the vanilla to the bananas. Cream ½ cup butter and the brown sugar until light and fluffy. Add the egg and rum and blend well.

Add the dry ingredients to the butter mixture, alternating with the bananas, beating until smooth after each addition. Stir in the nuts and raisins.

Pour the batter into the prepared pan. Bake 50 minutes, or until a straw inserted in the center comes out clean. Let stand 5 minutes, then turn out onto a wire rack to cool.

Serve at once, cut into ½-inch-thick slices or let stand overnight or longer, slice and serve as follows: Melt the ¼ cup butter and sauté the slices until lightly brown. Sprinkle with the coconut and serve warm.

Makes 1 loaf

October Pie

There's nothing at all wrong with this pie for dessert, but it's in its glory as breakfast, served warm with coffee and lots of hot milk.

Pastry with Vegetable Shortening (see
*   page 80)*
2 tablespoons all-purpose flour
1 cup chopped cranberries
½ cup chopped walnuts
1 cup chopped apples
1 cup raisins
1 cup dark brown sugar
½ cup cranberry juice
¼ cup (½ stick) unsalted butter

Preheat the oven to 425° F. Line a 10-inch pie plate with ½ the pastry and sprinkle with 1 tablespoon of the flour.

Toss the cranberries, walnuts, apples, and raisins together, then add the sugar, the remaining 1 tablespoon flour, and the cranberry juice. Mix well.

Turn the filling into the prepared crust. Dot with butter. Roll out the remaining pastry and cut into ¼-inch strips. Place the strips across the pie filling in a lattice pattern and crimp the edges to secure.

Bake 30 to 40 minutes, or until the crust is brown and the juices are bubbling.

Makes 8 servings

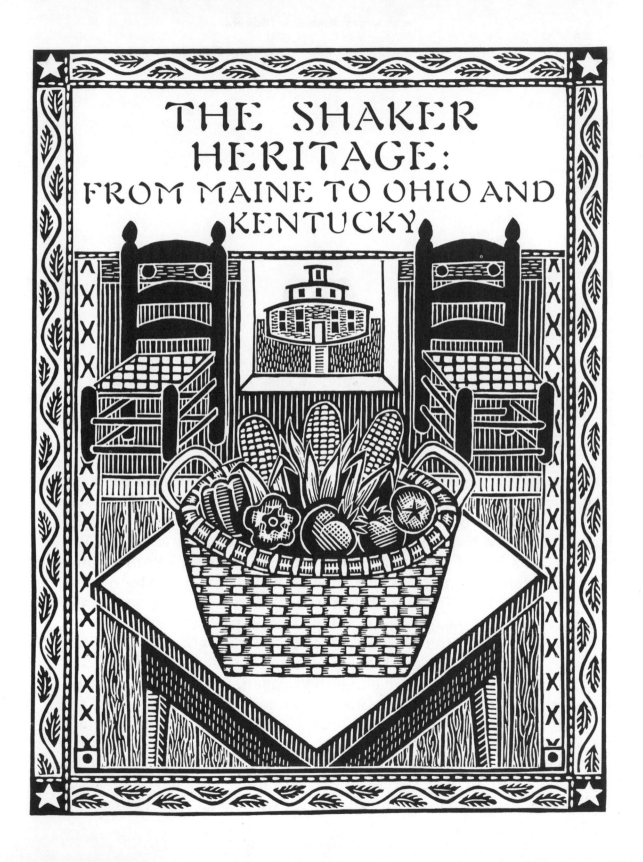

THE SHAKER HERITAGE: FROM MAINE TO OHIO AND KENTUCKY

To call American cooking regional for convenience sake, is to ignore whole sections of well-organized, discrete cuisines, and at Miss Ruby's we've pledged to cover the food of America from coast to coast and border to border. Ethnic groups, for instance, often cook in the same way all over the country, leaving their legacy in dozens of regions. Italian-American food has developed into a cooking subgenre that reveals its history in its flavors but is very different from the food eaten in Italy, and, in the same way, the German food of Pennsylvania Dutch country is not the same as the food now eaten in Bavaria. Even more specific to America is sectarian cooking. We are a nation of associations and sects and religious enthusiasms that often last more than a generation and involve whole communities. The Grahamites, the Amish, C. W. Post's group of dietary maniacs—all have developed eccentric cuisines, some of them best forgotten as soon as possible. Other groups have given us an enduring legacy of ingenious and exciting food.

Probably the most distinguished American sect from the aesthetic point of view is the Shaker community of Mother Ann Lee, which lasted in force for a hundred years in outposts as far-flung as Sabbathday Lake, Maine; Kentucky; and Ohio. Through correspondence and newsletters, the various Shaker farms kept in touch and in effect were one community. In their egalitarian ideals, the Shakers did not change the traditional roles of men and women, but valued women's work equally with men's. Shaker kitchens were light and bright and beautifully equipped in a time when most kitchens were damp, dark, and primitive. And Shaker cooks were invited to be inventive and eclectic: The farm-based Shakers were the first growers and sellers of cooking herbs in the United States, and Shaker women were charged with the responsibility of devising recipes that would help promote herbs. They stole freely from the English (sage-and-thyme pork pie) and the French (tarragon chicken) and created their own formulas such as rosemary jelly and chicken-herb soup.

At Miss Ruby's, we cook in the Shaker style four times each year in order to take advantage of their broad palette of vegetable recipes, developed in part because of the abundant produce from the community's farms and partly because of its twenty-year period of vegetarianism, inaugurated by Mother Ann Lee's son William. We ignore first courses in favor of vegetable dishes and encourage multiple ordering, so that customers can approximate the heavily laden table of the Shaker community.

SMALL PLATES

Sherried Mushrooms

This simple sauté is meaty, rich, and simple—lovely on toast and austere and delicious as a first course.

½ cup (1 stick) unsalted butter
6 cups sliced fresh mushrooms
4 tablespoons fine-chopped fresh dill
Salt and pepper to taste
⅔ cup amontillado sherry

Garnish
Fresh dill sprigs

Melt the butter in a large skillet over high heat, and when the butter is very hot sauté the mushrooms until light brown. Add the dill, salt, and pepper, and toss the mushrooms until very hot.

Pour the sherry over the mushrooms and ignite with a match. When the alcohol has been consumed, serve garnished with dill sprigs.

Makes 4 servings

Green Bean Casserole

This goes well with meats like ham and pot roast but is even better as a main course, served in combination with two or three other vegetable dishes.

¼ cup (1 stick) unsalted butter
2 onions, diced
1 tablespoon all-purpose flour
¼ teaspoon ground nutmeg
½ teaspoon chopped fresh thyme
4 cups green beans, stemmed, washed, sliced, and blanched
2 cups sour cream
2 cups grated cheddar cheese
½ cup fine bread crumbs

Preheat the oven to 400° F. Butter a 2-quart casserole.

Melt the butter in a large skillet over medium heat. Sauté the onions until wilted and almost transparent. Sprinkle on the flour, nutmeg, and thyme, and cook very slowly 5 minutes. Do not brown.

Add the beans and toss thoroughly. Let cool slightly, then add the sour cream and toss. Place the mixture in the prepared casserole dish, sprinkle on the cheese and then the bread crumbs. Bake 20 minutes, or until the cheese is melted and the beans are heated through.

Makes 4 servings

Yellow Velvet

When I first read this recipe in Amy Bess Miller's *The Best of Shaker Cooking*, I was surprised I'd never thought of it myself—the combination of summer flavors and textures is so logical. In this recipe there is no substitute at all for fresh corn, preferably from your own backyard.

*4 cups corn kernels, scraped from young
 and tender ears*
*4 cups small young yellow squash,
 halved and sliced thin*
½ cup (1 stick) unsalted butter
2 onions, grated
Salt and pepper to taste
1 cup heavy cream

Garnish
Chopped fresh chives
Fine-chopped red bell pepper

Steam the corn and squash together very gently in no more than 4 table-spoons water until the squash is tender, about 10 minutes, then drain.

Melt the butter in a large skillet and gently cook the onions until wilted and translucent. Add the corn and squash and cook slowly until almost dissolved, about 45 minutes. Add the salt, pepper, and cream and simmer until heated through.

Serve with a sprinkle of chopped chives and fine-chopped red bell pepper.

Makes 6 servings

Baked Tomatoes and Corn

I serve sliced tomatoes and boiled corn as a first course all summer, but every now and then during a long season, cooking them together seems like a good idea. In fact, almost anything we do with corn and tomatoes seems like a good idea. And just think: We're just about the only people in the world who use this remarkable combination.

10 large ripe fresh tomatoes
10 cups corn kernels, scraped from
  young and tender ears
2 cups (4 sticks) unsalted butter, melted
Salt and pepper to taste
½ teaspoon ground nutmeg
2 cups Chicken Stock (see page 28) or
  heavy cream
2 cups fine bread crumbs

Preheat the oven to 400° F.

Plunge the tomatoes into boiling water 30 seconds and slip off the peels. Core and slice the tomatoes and line a 3-quart baking pan with the slices. Spread some corn over the tomatoes. Mix together the butter, salt, pepper, and nutmeg, and drizzle some over the tomatoes. Continue layering until the corn and tomatoes are used up, but save a little of the butter mixture for the top.

Pour the broth or cream evenly over the tomato-corn layers, then sprinkle bread crumbs over the top and drizzle with the remaining butter mixture. Bake 30 minutes, or until the crumbs are brown and the casserole is bubbling.

Makes 12 servings

SOUPS

Herb Soup

Using fresh herbs, homemade broth, and good bread is important for this peculiarly Shaker recipe.

1 tablespoon unsalted butter
2 tablespoons fine-chopped chives
2 tablespoons minced chervil
2 tablespoons minced sorrel
½ teaspoon fine-chopped tarragon
1 cup fine-chopped celery
1 quart Chicken Broth (see page 28)
Salt and pepper to taste
6 slices dry white toast
Dash of ground nutmeg
Grated cheddar or Parmesan cheese

Garnish
Fresh herbs

Melt the butter in a large saucepan, then add the herbs and celery and simmer very slowly 5 minutes. Add the broth and the salt and pepper. Cook gently 20 minutes. Pour the soup into bowls over slices of toast. Sprinkle cheese and nutmeg over the top and garnish with fresh herbs in any combination.

Makes 4 servings

Cranberry Bean Soup

Cranberry beans are striated with pink and available dried. They form a hearty base for this deep-flavored soup that gets it meaty flavor from mustard and sherry.

2 cups cranberry beans, picked over and
   soaked overnight in water to cover
1½ quarts water
1 teaspoon each salt and pepper
2 tablespoons soy oil
2 tablespoons (¼ stick) unsalted butter
2 onions, minced
1 garlic clove, minced
1 small carrot, chopped fine
1 tablespoon minced fresh basil
1 teaspoon minced fresh thyme
1 teaspoon minced fresh summer savory
1 cup tomato juice
1 tablespoon Worcestershire sauce
1 tablespoon dry mustard
⅓ cup dry sherry

Garnish
3 tablespoons fresh summer savory
   leaves

Drain the beans and add the water, salt, and pepper. Simmer, covered, 2 hours, or until just tender. Meanwhile, heat the oil in a frying pan and add the butter. When the butter melts, add the onion and garlic and cook gently 10 minutes, or until the onion begins to yellow. Do not allow the garlic to brown. Add the carrot and herbs. Cook 5 minutes longer and add the tomato juice to the pan. Add the mixture to the cranberry beans.

Cover and simmer slowly until the beans are tender and falling apart, about 1 hour longer. Stir in the Worcestershire sauce, mustard, and sherry, and keep warm until ready to serve. Sprinkle the soup with fresh summer savory leaves as a garnish.

Makes 8 servings

SALADS

Celery with Mayonnaise

Crunchy and watery, this salad is good with garlicky or peppery main courses.

4 cups chopped celery
2 cups chopped cucumber, well drained
1 small onion, grated
1 teaspoon salt
½ teaspoon pepper
½ teaspoon dry mustard
1 cup Tarragon Mayonnaise (see
  page 4)
Lettuce

Garnish
Fresh tarragon

Blanch the celery 30 seconds in rapidly boiling water, then drain and cool. Toss the cucumbers with the grated onion and salt, and let stand 10 minutes in a sieve over a bowl. Toss the celery with the cucumber and onion mixture and the remaining seasonings, then mix well with the mayonnaise. Serve on a bed of lettuce, garnished with fresh tarragon.

Makes 8 servings

Tomatoes

The simplest of Shaker salads is the best of all American summer salads:

Take the ripest and juiciest of fresh tomatoes—this can really only be done in the summer, when you have a source for local tomatoes—and peel them with a sharp paring knife. Slice the tomatoes and serve plain or with a light sqeeze of lemon or orange juice and bit of zest. There is no reason to be more elaborate, but abundant summer tomatoes may lead you into the following decadences:

VARIATIONS: Alternate tomato slices with slices of Vidalia or Bermuda onion (see page 149), and sprinkle with scallions and citrus juice, or with olive oil and chopped basil. Or serve the tomato slices with fresh farmer cheese, mozzarella, or homemade yogurt.

But, really, the Shakers were right the first time: Just slice them and eat them, and if you have fresh boiled corn and newly baked bread, you won't need anything else for supper.

MAIN COURSES

Chicken Shortcake

1 5-pound chicken
1 onion, chopped rough
3 celery stalks, broken up
1 large carrot, chopped in 3 pieces
2 whole cloves
2 bay leaves
½ bunch fresh parsley
Curl of orange zest
2 quarts of Chicken Stock (see page 28),
*   or enough to cover chicken*
1 onion, quartered and sliced
4 celery stalks, sliced diagonally
1 large carrot, cut in large julienne
½ cup (1 stick) unsalted butter
½ cup all-purpose flour
1 teaspoon each salt and pepper
½ teaspoon ground nutmeg
2 cups heavy cream
1½ cups sliced mushrooms
1 cup fresh or frozen peas, or 1 cup
*   sliced fresh green beans*

Put chicken, onion, celery, carrot, cloves, bay leaves, parsley, and orange zest in a 6-quart stockpot. Cover with chicken stock and bring to a boil, then lower to a simmer and cook for 1½ hours, or until chicken is tender, almost falling from the bone. Lift the chicken out of the stock to cool. Strain and skim the stock and simmer the sliced onion, celery, and julienned carrot until tender. Meanwhile, melt the butter in a large saucepan until frothy; add the flour and whisk, cooking over low heat for 5 minutes, taking care not to brown the flour. Add the salt, pepper, and nutmeg. Pour the hot stock and vegetables into the roux, and whisk until smooth. Simmer until the sauce thickens, then add the heavy cream and simmer again briefly. Remove meat in large pieces from the cooled chicken, and add it to the sauce. Add the mushrooms and peas or beans and simmer just until chicken is heated through and the peas or beans are tender.

(continued)

Biscuits
6 cups all-purpose flour
1 tablespoon salt
3 tablespoons baking powder
1 cup shortening
2 teaspoons chopped fresh tarragon
1 teaspoon chopped fresh thyme
2½ cups milk

½ cup fine-chopped fresh parsley

Preheat the oven to 400° F.

Sift flour, salt, and baking powder to-gether. Work in vegetable shortening until the mixture is the consistency of oatmeal. Toss with herbs. Add milk until you have a soft dough. Do not overmix. Turn out the dough onto a floured board and pat or roll to about a ½-inch thickness. Cut with a 3-inch diameter biscuit cutter and bake, sides touching, on a cookie sheet until golden brown, about 17 minutes.

Split and butter the biscuits, and lay 2 bottom halves on each serving plate. Spoon the hot chicken mixture over the biscuit bottoms, then cover with the biscuit tops. Sprinkle generously with chopped parsley.

Makes 6 servings, with plenty of biscuits to spare for sopping up gravy

Cidered Beef Stew with Herbed Dumplings

We like the dryness of bottled hard cider in this recipe, but the Shakers probably used fresh sweet cider. If you like the flavor of the latter, you might want to try it that way.

3 tablespoons rendered suet
4 pounds bottom round, cut in 1-inch
   squares
2 tablespoons (¼ stick) unsalted butter
6 large onions, halved and sliced
Salt and pepper to taste
1 quart English or French hard cider
1 quart Beef Stock (see page 160)
2 cups cubed peeled carrots
2 cups halved peeled turnips
3 celery stalks, chopped
Herbed Dumplings (recipe follows)

Heat the melted suet in a large Dutch oven until almost smoking, and sear the meat until dark brown. Remove from the heat.

In a large heavy skillet, melt the butter and stir in the onions. Cook over low heat, stirring frequently, until the on-ions are dark brown and almost cara-melized. Add the salt, pepper, cider, and stock. Stir to loosen all the onion bits from the bottom of the pan. Add the onion mixture to the meat and simmer until the meat is almost tender, about 1½ hours. Add the vege-tables and cook just until tender.

Drop dumplings from a tablespoon into the stew, but do not cover the entire surface. Cover tightly and simmer for 12 to 14 minutes longer, or until the dumplings are steamed through.

Makes 8 to 10 servings

Herbed Dumplings
2 cups all-purpose flour
1 cup pastry flour
2 tablespoons baking powder
1 teaspoon salt
¼ cup shortening
1 tablespoon fine-chopped fresh parsley
1 tablespoon fine-chopped mixed fresh
   herbs, such as chives, tarragon,
   thyme, basil, summer savory, or
   chervil
2 large eggs
1 cup milk, approximately

Sift together the flours and the other dry ingredients, and work in the shortening until the mixture is the consistency of flour-coated corn kernels. Toss the parsley and other herbs with the flour mixture, then stir in the eggs and moisten with just enough milk to allow the dough to drop from a spoon.

Makes 8 to 10 servings

Codfish Croquettes and Honeyed Apple Rings with Milk Gravy

Of all the Shaker recipes we use, this dish's successful combination of homely flavors in unexpected juxtaposition makes it the most typically Shaker.

2 cups diced raw potatoes
1 1-pound codfish fillet, skinned
1 tablespoon plus 2 tablespoons unsalted
   butter
2 large eggs, beaten
Dash of ground nutmeg
½ cup fine-diced onion
Salt and pepper to taste
All-purpose flour
1 pound double-smoked bacon, cut into 8
   thick slices
2 green apples, cored and sliced but not
   peeled
2 tablespoons water
2 tablespoons honey

Simmer potatoes in water in a large skillet until tender. Drain and press in a sieve until very dry. In a steamer basket over boiling water, steam the cod until tender. Drain and mash with the potatoes. Beat until smooth.

Add the 1 tablespoon of butter, eggs, seasonings, and onion, and mix well. Taste for seasoning, and add salt if the natural salt in the cod is faint. If the mixture will not drop heavily from a spoon, add flour to thicken. Let stand 10 minutes.

(continued)

Fry the bacon in a heavy cast-iron skillet until almost crisp. Remove and drain the bacon, then reserve.

Drop the fish batter from a tablespoon into the hot bacon fat, then mash down lightly with a spatula to flatten. Cook until brown on one side and turn carefully—the mixture will be fluffy and delicate. When done, place the croquettes on a large platter in a warm oven.

Milk Gravy
Bacon grease
2 tablespoons all-purpose flour
1½ cups hot milk
1 cup heavy cream
Salt and pepper to taste

Garnish
Watercress

To the drippings in the croquette pan, add enough additional bacon grease to make 2 tablespoons. Warm over medium heat, then whisk in 2 tablespoons flour. Cook until the flour is

Melt the 2 tablespoons of butter in a large skillet and sauté the apples. When the apples begin to soften, add the water and honey, and simmer until the water is almost evaporated and the apple slices are glazed. Set the skillet in a warm oven while you make Milk Gravy (recipe follows).

well blended and on the verge of coloring, about 5 minutes. Add the hot milk and cook, stirring, until very smooth. Remove from the heat and add the cream and salt and pepper to taste.

Serve the croquettes on the reserved bacon slices and topped with gravy; garnish each plate with 2 or 3 apple slices. Watercress tastes wonderful as a garnish.

Makes 8 servings

DESSERTS

Sautéed Apples with Honey and Cream

Honey for summer and apples for fall: This dessert is dead simple and simply good, typical of Shaker design.

½ cup (1 stick) unsalted butter
4 tart apples, peeled, cored, and sliced
¼ teaspoon salt
½ teaspoon ground nutmeg or cinnamon
½ cup honey, plus additional
¼ cup fresh apple cider
½ cup heavy cream, warmed

Melt the butter in a large sauté pan over medium heat, and very gently sauté the apples. Cover the pan in the last few minutes of cooking to ensure that they are soft. Uncover the pan and allow any excess moisture to evaporate. Turn up the heat and sauté until browned. Add the salt, nutmeg or cinnamon, and honey, and stir well as the apples simmer. When the honey turns viscous and threatens to brown, add the cider and reduce until the apples are almost sauce. Remove the mixture from the heat and add the cream. Serve at once with an extra drizzle of honey.

Makes 4 servings

Ohio Lemon Pie

The sharpness of lemon curd pales in comparison with this intense lemon dessert. The Shakers were celibate, but unabating in their intensity.

Pastry with Vegetable Shortening (see page 80)
2 lemons
2 cups sugar
½ cup water
4 large eggs, beaten

Preheat the oven to 450° F. Line an 8-inch pie plate with ½ the pastry.

Quarter the lemons and slice them *paper thin*. Toss the lemons with the sugar. Add the water and simmer in an enamel or stainless steel pot until the rind is just tender, about 20 minutes. Cool.

Pour the lemons and syrup into the prepared pie shell, then pour the eggs over the lemons and top with the second layer of pastry. Cut vents in the top of the crust to release steam.

Bake 15 minutes, then reduce the heat to 375° F and continue baking until a knife inserted in the center of the custard comes out clean, about 30 minutes longer. Allow to cool before slicing.

Makes 8 servings

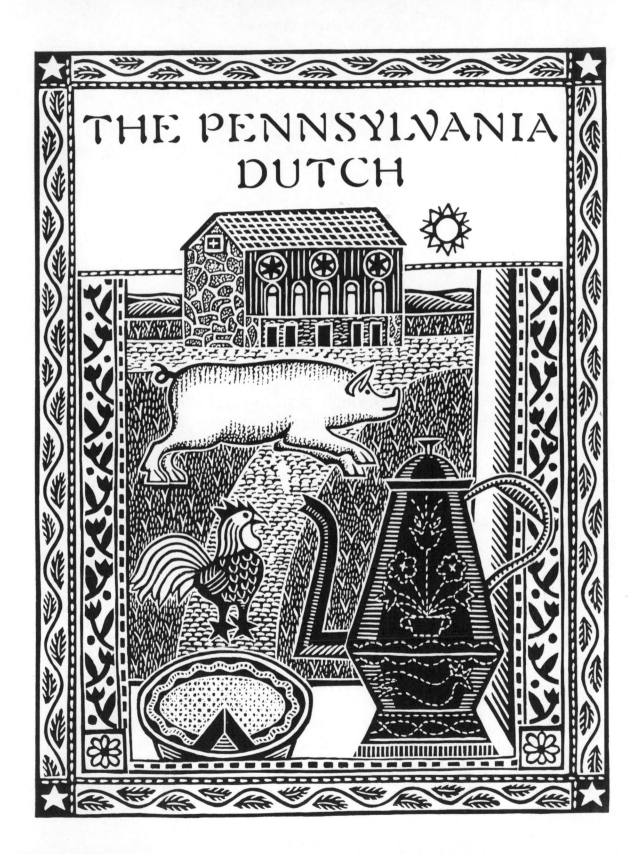

Because so much of the best traditional American cooking is to be found in people's homes, rather than in restaurants, most of my research is done with spiral-bound cookbooks and through correspondence with cooks—most of them home cooks—all over the country. But every now and then it pays to actually visit the source, and my trip to Amish country was one of those times.

In Lancaster County, I found out that Monday is still washday—lines and lines of fresh clean clothes were strung across every farmyard—and that the Amish still dress plainly. It was spring plowing time, and teams of eight horses crossed and recrossed the great wide fields under a perfectly blue sky. Jams and jellies and pickles and bread were for sale under lean-tos at every crossing, and closed buggies rattled along the sides of the roads all afternoon. There are a few too many signs, and a few too many restaurants with hex signs painted all over them. Life still seems to be going on largely undisturbed on the back roads and on the farms, and that continuing lively tradition makes possible a menu like this.

The old outsiders' name for the sectarian cooking of central Pennsylvania, Pennsylvania Dutch, is the one I use because it covers the widest possible range, even the secular cooks not in the Mennonite and the Old Order Amish communities that produced the cuisine. *Dutch,* an anglicization of *Deutsch,* refers not to

Hollanders but to the area's many settlers of German origin. Many of the Amish were Swiss, however, and a lot of Mennonites came from farther north as well. What gives Pennsylvania Dutch cooking its special qualities is not the national origins of the cooks but their closeness in community. Its simple, fresh, hearty approach to fresh ingredients, the enlivening presence of the Seven Sweets and Seven Sours so often found on Amish tables, and an unabashed appetite for good food not at all diminished by a consciously plain life are all part of that community.

About the Seven Sweets and Seven Sours: In traditional French and Italian cooking, the combination of basic food with sauces provides variety and interest at the table; in Pennsylvania Dutch cooking, and in much American cooking, it is the pickle dish, the relish tray, the applesauce bowl that add spark to simple foods. Chowchow; piccalilli; relishes; chutneys; apple and pear butters; cottage cheese in dozens of combinations with fruits and vegetables and sour cream; pickles made from countless vegetables; and preserves and conserves and jams and jellies and every imaginable sort of side dish have found their way onto the American table to enliven simple American food. Try some: They may change your ideas about the dullness of middle-American food.

SMALL PLATES

Onion Squares

These are seductive, addictive, and old-fashioned to the point of producing nostalgia in people who've never heard of them before. As a first course, they should probably be followed by plain fish and an undressed salad; as lunch, they're swooningly good with a tart-dressed salad and fruit for dessert.

3 cups all-purpose flour
2 tablespoons baking powder
1 teaspoon salt
⅔ cup shortening
2 cups milk
3 tablespoons unsalted butter
3 cups coarse-diced onions
Salt and pepper to taste
2 cups grated sharp cheddar cheese
1 cup sour cream

Preheat the oven to 400° F.

Sift together the dry ingredients and cut in the shortening with 2 knives or a pastry knife. Add the milk and stir to create a soft dough. Turn the dough out into a heavily floured sheet cake pan or cookie sheet with sides and pat out the dough until about ½ inch thick.

In a heavy frying pan, melt the butter until frothy, then sauté the onions until lightly golden. Add salt and pepper, then spread the mixture over the surface of the dough. Sprinkle the cheese over the top and bake 12 to 14 minutes, until the dough is done and the cheese melted.

Cut into squares and serve at once with sour cream.

Makes 6 servings

Scrapple

This classic dish is available all over the countryside around Lancaster. But it is not always as good as this, largely because, like so much of our best cooking, it wants to be eaten straight from the pan, hot and soft and very, very good.

2 pounds pork shoulder
Bouquet garni of bay leaf, sage, thyme branch, cracked whole pepper, and 2 whole cloves
1 large onion, diced
2 quarts Chicken Stock (see page 28)
1 cup cornmeal
Salt and pepper to taste
2 tablespoons (¼ stick) unsalted butter

Place the pork, bouquet garni, and onion in a large Dutch oven with the stock, and simmer 2 hours, or until the pork is falling apart. Remove the pork from stock, discard bouquet garni, and chop the pork and onion fine, discarding any gristle and the excess fat.

Skim the pork stock of all fat. Stir the chopped pork and onion into the stock, bring to a simmer again, then add the cornmeal, stirring constantly. When the mixture thickens, add salt and pepper, and pour into a buttered cookie sheet with 1-inch sides. Cool, then slice into 4-inch squares.

Melt the butter in a large skillet and briefly sauté the squares until lightly browned. Serve at once with eggs or tomato sauce, or, if you have no shame, with pork sausage.

Makes 8 servings

Green Bean, Pear, and Ham Soup

This soup feels familiar to southerners, until they detect the odd sweetness of pear under the ham and bean, which lightens the whole effect. The combination is wonderful in late fall, melding flavors that feel like all the pleasures of the declining year.

1 meaty ham bone, or 4 ham hocks
2 quarts Chicken Stock (see page 28)
1 large sprig of fresh savory
1 bay leaf
2 quarts cut Italian green beans
3 large Bosc pears, peeled and cut into
   1-inch chunks
Salt and pepper to taste

Boil the ham bone or hocks in the stock with the herbs until the meat is tender, about 1 hour. Add the beans and pears and simmer until the beans are tender, about 40 minutes longer. Remove the savory sprig, bay leaf, and ham hocks or bone. Pick the meat from the bones and return it to the pot. Add salt and pepper, and serve with boiled peeled or unpeeled red po-tatoes.

Makes 8 servings

Summer Borscht

This hearty refreshing soup can make a meal on a summer's day. Because the meat is boiled without being seared, it has a simple flavor that makes it oddly charming.

2 pounds meaty beef soup bones
8 small red potatoes, quartered
1 cup beets, peeled and cut into 1-inch cubes
2 teaspoons chopped fresh dill
1 medium head cabbage, shredded
6 scallions, green and white parts, cut into ¼-inch long pieces
1 cup beet greens, cut up
1 cup ripe fresh tomatoes, peeled and chopped
1 tablespoon red wine vinegar
Salt and pepper
1 cup sour cream

Place the soup bones in a large Dutch oven and cover with cold water. Bring to a boil, and simmer until the meat almost falls from the bones about 45 minutes. Add the potatoes, beets, and dill, and cook until tender. Add the cabbage, scallions, beet greens, tomatoes, vinegar, salt and pepper, and cook just until the cabbage is tender and the flavors marry. Lift the bones from the soup and cool briefly. Remove the meat from the bones and return it to the soup. Serve hot or cold, with dollops of sour cream.

Makes 10 servings

SALADS

Lamb's-Quarters with Egg Yolk Dressing

2 hard-boiled egg yolks
1 teaspoon sugar
1 teaspoon salt
½ teaspoon pepper
½ cup light olive oil
2 tablespoons cider vinegar
4 cups freshly picked, washed and dried
    lamb's-quarters (or arugula or
    dandelion greens)

Mash the egg yolks, and stir in all
other ingredients except the greens.
Toss with the lamb's-quarters.

Makes 4 servings

Tomato-Mint Salad

4 cups ripe fresh tomatoes, cut into large
    dice
6 large sprigs fresh mint, chopped
Salt and pepper to taste
¼ cup light olive oil
1 tablespoon cider vinegar
Lettuce leaves

Toss the first 6 ingredients together,
using the salt and pepper very lightly.
Serve the salad on lettuce leaves, or as
a relish with a dinner plate.

Makes 4 servings

MAIN COURSES

Schnitz and Knepp

Just about everything the "Dutch" of Lancaster County are known for is in this recipe—smoked meat, dried apples, dumplings. All of it is cooked together in a great one-pot dish designed to be surrounded by the lively Seven Sweets and Seven Sours.

2 pounds dried apples, chopped coarse
6 8-ounce ham steaks
2 quarts Chicken Stock (see page 28)

Soak the apples in water overnight.

Poach the ham steaks in the chicken stock in a large Dutch oven until tender, about 30 minutes. Drain and add the softened apples and simmer until the apples are tender, about 20 minutes. Apples should not dissolve, but should remain in tender pieces.

Dumplings
2 cups all-purpose flour
1 tablespoon baking powder
½ teaspoon salt
1 large egg, beaten
2 tablespoons (¼ stick) unsalted butter, melted
Milk

Sift the dry ingredients together into a large mixing bowl. Form a well in the dry ingredients, then stir in the egg and the butter. Add enough milk to make a batter just stiff enough to drop from a spoon, and stir, until thoroughly moistened.

Drop the batter by tablespoonfuls into the boiling ham and apples. Cover the Dutch oven tightly, and cook 12 minutes, or until the dumplings are done.

Serve portions of dumplings, ham, apples, and juices in big shallow bowls.

Makes 6 servings

Rabbit with Bacon, Raisins, and Carrots

2 cups all-purpose flour
1 teaspoon each salt and pepper
2 teaspoons grated fresh gingerroot
2 rabbits, cut at each joint
1/4 pound bacon, chopped fine
1 large carrot, chopped fine
1 large onion, chopped fine
1 cup celery root, chopped fine
1/3 cup currant jelly
1/2 cup raisins
1 cup heavy cream

Mix together the flour, salt, pepper, and ginger, and dredge the rabbit in the mixture. Heat the bacon in a large frying pan until all the fat is released. Remove the bacon bits from the pan and reserve. Brown the rabbit pieces in the bacon fat, and remove immediately. Into the remaining fat stir the carrot, onion, and celery root, and stir from the bottom.

Return the rabbit to the pan, and add water to cover. Simmer until the rabbit is tender, about 1 hour.

Lift out the rabbit pieces, then stir in the currant jelly and raisins. Simmer 1/2 hour longer, or until the sauce is reduced and the raisins are plumped. Skim any fat from the sauce, then add the cream, and return the rabbit pieces to the pan. Simmer just long enough to warm the rabbit through. Serve the rabbit and sauce on broad egg noodles.

Makes 4 servings

S W E E T S   A N D   S O U R S

"Sweets and Sours" are traditionally served seven and seven on Pennsylvania tables, along with a gracious plenty of meats and side dishes. These condiments enliven the food they accompany, as they still do in many other areas of the country. The selection here is just a sampling—you'll find dozens of others in traditional cookbooks from all over. The rule for serving them is the same as for chutneys and pickles and other condiments in Indian cooking: Have a sweet with a sour, a creamy with a crunchy, a spicy with a mild—or have all of them on the table at once.

Chowchow

The best version of this relish-salad I've ever had was at the Brownstown Café in Brownstown, Pennsylvania. Even if the food had been terrible, its seven calendars (from different years), its five clocks (possibly one of them telling the correct time), and its collection of Toby jugs would have made it worth a visit.

4 cups dried lima beans, soaked
   overnight
1 cup tiny pearl onions
4 cups string beans, cut into 1-inch
   pieces
2 cups dark brown sugar
2 tablespoons dry mustard
1 quart white vinegar
4 cups diced cucumbers
4 cups freshly cut corn kernels
2 cups diced red bell peppers
2 cups diced green bell peppers
2 cups diced celery

Cook the lima beans gently in water to cover until tender but not broken-skinned, about 1 hour.

Blanch the onions and string beans in boiling water 3 minutes, then plunge them into ice water to stop the cooking. Toss the cucumbers, corn, red and green peppers, and celery with the blanched onions and stringbeans.

Combine the brown sugar, mustard, and vinegar in a glass, enamel, or stainless steel pot and bring to a boil. Add all the vegetables to the liquid, stir gently, and return to the boiling point. Remove at once from the heat.

Put into hot jars and seal (see page 72) or into a stone crock and refrigerate for up to 6 weeks.

Makes 8 quarts

Baked Parched Corn

Parched corn—that is, sweet corn cut from the cob and air dried—is known in other places besides Lancaster County, but it is nowhere used so extensively. It is chewy, sweet, almost a confection—baked this way, a delicacy.

4 cups boiling water
2 cups parched corn*
2 cups heavy cream
1 cup minced onion
Salt and pepper to taste

* Parched corn is available by mail order from Bird-in-Hand Country Bake Shop, R.D. 1, Gibbons Road, Bird-in-Hand, Pennsylvania 17505.

Pour the boiling water over the corn, and let stand at least 2 hours, until the corn is tender and almost all the water is absorbed.

Preheat the oven to 350° F. Butter a 2-quart baking dish.

Bring the heavy cream to a boil in a large saucepan, add the onion, and simmer until the onion is tender. Stir the corn, cream, onion, salt, and pepper together and pour into the prepared baking dish. There should be just a bit more cream than corn; add more cream if necessary.

Bake about 1 hour, or until the corn is meltingly tender. Add additional cream during cooking if necessary to maintain level. Serve hot.

Makes 1½ quarts

Gingered Pear Conserve

8 cups peeled cored Bosc pears, cut into
*   1-inch cubes*
1 cup minced fresh gingerroot
1 whole lemon, minced
2 cups sugar

Toss together all the ingredients in a large heavy saucepan and bring to a very low simmer. Cook about 2 hours, stirring frequently from the bottom, until the pears are tender and beginning to fall apart. Seal in hot jars (see page 72) or store in a crock in the refrigerator for up to 6 weeks.

Makes 2 quarts

Rhubarb and Apricot Preserve

3 cups sugar
2 cups water
1 pound dried apricots, quartered
4 cups diced fresh rhubarb

Dissolve the sugar in the water in a large heavy pot and bring to a boil.

Add the apricots and cook gently 30 minutes. Add the rhubarb and cook until the rhubarb is very tender and the flavors marry, about 1 hour longer. Serve warm.

Makes 1½ quarts

Garlic Dill Pickles

20 4-inch Kirby cucumbers, unpeeled
5 or 6 stalks fresh dill
8 garlic cloves
1 teaspoon powdered alum
1 cup salt
3 quarts water
1 quart white vinegar

Wash the cucumbers and let stand in the refrigerator overnight.

Put the cucumbers into a 1-gallon crock and add the dill, garlic, and alum.

Heat together the salt, water, and vinegar to boiling, and pour over cucumbers. Let cool, then chill before serving.

Will keep in refrigerator up to 6 weeks; wait at least 3 days before serving.

Makes 1 gallon

Cottage Cheese with Sour Cream and Dill

Serve a good-quality fresh unsalted cottage cheese topped with a dollop of sour cream and sprinkle with chopped fresh dill.

Hot-Sweet-Sour Mustard

4 tablespoons dry mustard
¼ cup confectioners' sugar
1 tablespoon cider vinegar
Dash of vegetable oil
1 tablespoon hot water

Combine the mustard and sugar. Add the vinegar and oil, and stir until smooth. Add the water to combine completely. Store in the refrigerator for up to 6 weeks.

Makes ½ cup

DESSERTS

Shoofly Pie

This most famous Pennsylvania Dutch dessert requires careful handling: If it is overcooked, this pie can be dry and unappetizing. Bake briefly and don't allow to cool too long before serving.

Syrup
1½ cups molasses
½ cup dark brown sugar
2 large eggs
1 teaspoon baking soda, dissolved in
    1 cup hot water

Beat the molasses, sugar, and eggs together, then stir in the hot water and soda.

Crumbs
Butter pastry, for single-crust pie (see
    page 7)
2 cups all-purpose flour
¾ cup dark brown sugar
⅔ cup (1⅓ sticks) unsalted butter
Whipped cream

Preheat the oven to 350° F. Line an 8-inch pie tin with the pastry. Toss the flour and brown sugar together. Rub the butter into the flour and sugar mixture with your fingers until the mixture is the consistency of coarse crumbs. Set aside.

Drizzle the pie crust with ½ the syrup. Sprinkle on ½ the crumbs, then repeat.

Bake for 30 minutes. Serve topped with whipped cream.

Makes 8 servings

Plume-Moos

This is such an unlikely and wonderful dessert that I would be remiss not to include it. It is deep, dark, and delicious—and as ugly as sin if you don't cope with it. As the antithesis of the beautiful and useless in modern food, it is, indeed, homely and life sustaining.

1 cup seedless red grapes
1 cup dried prunes
½ cup dried peaches
½ cup dried apricots
2 quarts water
½ cup sugar
6 tablespoons all-purpose flour
½ teaspoon salt
1 teaspoon ground cinnamon
¼ teaspoon ground cloves
1 cup heavy cream, plus additional

Garnish
Dried apricots, slivered
Dried peaches, slivered
Seedless red grapes, halved

Cook the fruit in the water in a large heavy saucepan until almost tender, then add the sugar.

Combine the flour, salt, cinnamon, cloves, and 1 cup cream, and stir until smooth. Slowly add the mixture to the fruit, stirring constantly. Cook until slightly thickened, about 5 minutes. Serve in a bowl decorated with slivers of dried apricots and peaches that have been plumped in water and halved grapes. Flood each serving with cream.

Makes 6 servings

★
INDEX
★